THE
LAST
PASS

Also by Gary M. Pomerantz

Their Life's Work
The Devil's Tickets
WILT, 1962
Nine Minutes, Twenty Seconds
Where Peachtree Meets Sweet Auburn

THE
LAST
PASS

Cousy, Russell, the Celtics, and What Matters in the End

GARY M. POMERANTZ

PENGUIN PRESS · NEW YORK · 2018

PENGUIN PRESS

An imprint of Penguin Random House LLC
375 Hudson Street
New York, New York 10014
penguinrandomhouse.com

ISBN 9780735223615 (hardcover)
ISBN 9780735223622 (e-book)

Printed in the United States of America
1   3   5   7   9   10   8   6   4   2

DESIGNED BY LUCIA BERNARD

For my buddy
Kindred,
aptly named,
always there

In the next life, I'll do email and I'll be able to dunk.

Bob Cousy, Boston Celtics, 1950–1963

CONTENTS

THE
LAST
PASS

PREFACE: APRIL 9, 1957

Study the portrait closely. It captures the moment the greatest American professional sports dynasty of the twentieth century took flight. The dynasty was born of a merger of two men more alike than they ever understood. Both outsiders, they were self-analytical and murderously competitive. They moved through separate worlds off the court, but on the creaky parquet floor of the Boston Garden they were interlocking pieces. They blended passing and shot blocking, dribbling and rebounding, offense and defense. They were white and black. They were Cooz and Russ.

At the moment the camera flashed, Bob Cousy was twenty-eight, Bill Russell twenty-three. Cousy, the captain, had been with the Boston Celtics for seven seasons; Russell, the rookie whose arrival was delayed by his participation in the Melbourne Olympics, for about a hundred days. They played in a time when sportswriters still created nicknames for star athletes as if they were comic-book superheroes. As Babe Ruth once was the Sultan of Swat and Joe Louis the Brown Bomber, Cousy was the Houdini of the Hardwood. Russell would become the winningest player in National Basketball Association history, but he escaped without a nickname. He was just Russ.

Richard Meek was the photographer. He shot forty-five covers for *Sports Illustrated* and *Life*. His camera caught Ali, Nixon, Bette Davis, Arthur Ashe, James Cagney. In the tunnel outside the locker room at the Boston Garden before Game 5 of the 1957 NBA Finals between the Celtics and the St. Louis Hawks, Meek used two portrait lights. As Cousy and Russell stood in front of a cinder-block wall, the brilliant lights gave their eyes a celestial spark. In 1928, the arena's creator, boxing promoter Tex Rickard, settled for the industrial ambience of a cramped workingman's arena perched above the cacophony of North Station across Causeway Street. More than once, Cousy declared that the Garden's "rats were bigger than the customers."

The photographer may have reached for symbolism in his positioning of the Celtics: Cousy up front, bathed in satiny warmth, and Russell in the back, partially concealed and in shadow. Certainly, that was how white sportswriters at the Boston dailies—and they were all white—represented the two players in the sports pages, as if to say, "This is Cooz's team and Cooz's town." Still, Meek's photograph suggested another truth. Even as Cousy won the league's Most Valuable Player award in 1957, the rookie Russell loomed. Already he had begun to take over.

They posed for Meek minutes before tip-off. Their minds were elsewhere, on the battle against the Hawks' Bob Pettit, the Bombardier from Baton Rouge. Their expressions are taut, severe. They might have been Civil War soldiers standing for Mathew Brady. The rookie Russell offers a hint of the menacing glower that, years later, he would describe as "a big batch of smoldering Black Panther, a touch of Lord High Executioner and angry Cyclops mixed together, with just a dash of the old Sonny Liston." On first glance, Cousy seems made of porcelain, smooth and soft. But his eyes are fixed in a hard stare.

A Boston sportswriter, Bill McSweeny, had seen those faces before big games. He had entered the Celtics' locker room worried and left reassured by the sight of Cousy alongside Russell. The Celtics' coach, Red Auerbach, didn't much worry. He once broke an uncommon tension in the locker room by barking out, "Hey, if you guys are worrying about playing them, how do you think they must feel having to play *us*?" The Celtics laughed, knowing he was right.

Meek snapped this portrait four months after the successful conclusion to the Montgomery Bus Boycott started by Rosa Parks. In another five months, the Little Rock school desegregation crisis would prompt President Eisenhower to send federal troops. Cousy and Russell played in Boston, birthplace of the American Revolution, the abolitionists, the Kennedys, and all those colleges and universities, including Boston University, which had awarded Martin Luther King Jr. his doctorate only two years before. But there was another side to Boston. Court-ordered busing in the seventies would peel away the veneer and expose Boston's deep racial fissures for all to see, but they were always there. Still, in these years of growing racial unrest, the two Celtics stars, a white man and a black man, merged their ambitions, skill sets, and sweat for a shared success built on a foundation of mutual respect.

Hours after Meek took this portrait, Cousy, Russell, and the Celtics defeated St. Louis in Game 5. Four days later, they won their first title. If anyone called it the NBA championship, Auerbach would wag his finger and correct them: It was the *world's championship*.

Then the Celtics won it again, and again, and again, and . . .

It all began with the ball in Houdini's hands.

Sixty years later, as an old man, Cousy studies the same portrait. He says those two guys might have come "from the wake of a dear friend." Then, upon deeper study: "It really looks like we are on a death march." But he knew better. He knew what the camera caught: "the ultimate game face."

Mostly there is solitude now on Salisbury Street in Worcester,

Massachusetts, near Boston, where Cousy, just months from his nine-tieth birthday, walks with a cane, reads voraciously, and lives alone with echoes and memories in the sprawling 6,300-square-foot house that he and his wife, Missie, bought in the final months of the Kennedy administration. Missie died in 2013—they were married nearly sixty-three years—but her spirit fills the house. The painting of her wearing her good-luck green dress, a gift from the New York Knicks on Bob Cousy Day in 1963, hangs in the dining room. As part of his daily protocol, Cousy begins each morning by walking to his bedroom bureau and addressing Missie's funeral Mass card. "G'mornin', sweetheart," he says. "I love you!"

The men who were the Celtics were more prolific over a thirteen-year span than the New York Yankees, Green Bay Packers, and Montreal Canadiens ever were, winning eleven NBA championships from 1957 to 1969, including eight consecutively. That dynasty began with Cousy. He played thirteen pro seasons for the Celtics, made thirteen all-star teams, won six NBA championships, captured that 1957 Most Valuable Player award, led the league in assists eight times, and averaged 18.4 points per game. It wasn't only what he did but *how* he did it. On the court he was dynamic, every part of his body in motion. His teammate Don Barksdale once marveled at a Cousy maneuver and muttered under his breath to guard Togo Palazzi as they sat on the Celtics' bench, "That sonovabitch." Palazzi knew that he meant it as the highest compliment.

If we draw a line from Dr. James Naismith and the creation of basketball in 1891 in Springfield, Massachusetts, to today's NBA, the midpoint falls on Cousy, in the early 1950s, wearing Celtics jersey No. 14 and black Converse high-tops. Sportswriters still often spelled *basket ball* as two words and spelled the *N.B.A.* using periods so that readers understood it was an acronym. Teams sometimes played doubleheaders, which meant that half the league (four teams) occupied one arena. When the players met afterward at a bar, you knew a fight was about to break out when someone took off his watch.

As Cousy honed his game, he became a revelation to pro basketball, a stylistic revolution, a reimagining of possibilities. Before Cousy, pro basketball had been a highly regimented game dominated by pivot men of questionable athletic skills and unquestioned brute force. Cousy made the pro game come alive by dribbling around his back fancifully, dribbling out the clock evasively, driving to the basket and wrapping the ball around his body in a transfer from right hand to left and back to right while hanging in the air, through sleight of hand and no-look passing, and by leading the fast break with such creativity and daring that if you could stop time and ask the player guarding him as Cousy approached the free throw line, "What do you think he will do next?" the honest answer would have been, "How the hell do I know?" He did this even before the introduction of the twenty-four-second shot clock in the 1954–55 season and before the league moved west of St. Louis to become a truly national association. That fall, he told *Parade* magazine basketball had replaced baseball as the national pastime. He said the game was safe—"I've never heard of a fatality," Cousy deadpanned—and then put on a blindfold, paced off the required steps, drove hard to the basket, dribbled behind his back, and made a layup.

This was how Houdini became Houdini: He slung the ball sidearm sixty feet downcourt, and to the streaking teammate who received it, the ball seemed to have wings and a homing device. On the fast break, he cupped the ball and faked a shot as he dropped it to a teammate behind him. He stared at a teammate when he passed him the ball, or sometimes he looked the other way. His passes had zip, curve, careful measure, and purpose. "Passing," Cousy says proudly, a half century later, "was my raison d'être."

These Celtics have all gone their separate ways in the fifty years since. There are occasional phone calls and reunions, and they will always be connected by those shining moments they shared as teammates. For Cousy, though, the warmth of such triumphs has its limits. All these years later, he wants to share more with Russell than just basketball stories. He wants Russ to know that he cared for him, that he has spent decades asking himself hard questions: *Did I support Russ enough? Did I understand the intense bigotry he faced? Did I show him the empathy he deserved or share his pain?* The captain's answers always come back the same: *No, no,* and *no.* "Russ is a very proud man. His feelings are very intense," Cousy says, perhaps describing himself as well as Russell. The few times he has been with Russell through the years, Cousy was uneasy, never sure if Russell would glare at him or embrace him. He knows only that they are not close.

In his widower's solitude, Cousy has admitted to an old man's regrets. He wants to make things right and close circles. He is introspective and intellectually engaged. He has a wide circle of friends in Worcester, though he is, more often than not, alone. His two daughters, both retired educators, live far away and serve by telephone as his devoted support team. He has always been emotional, and now more than ever. "When you are younger, you say, 'Men don't cry,'" Cousy says. "More important is that you are who you are and don't try to hide it."

He keeps an important list in his mind. "My end-of-life to-do list," he calls it. He answers to his own conscience and to the people who have mattered most to him: Missie, his daughters, and his two grandchildren. And, more important each year it seems, William Felton Russell. Cousy spent seven years of his life with Russell—seven of nearly ninety, all of it around basketball—so why does Russell matter so much? The answer is obvious to Cousy. Those weren't just any seven years, and Russell wasn't just any man. As Babe Ruth and Lou Gehrig defined the early years of the Yankees dynasty, Cousy and Russell defined the beginnings of the Celtics' reign. The Celtics' hallmark fast break belonged more to them than to others because of their shared harmony in its execution—Russ's rebounding and outlet passes, Cooz's dribbling and distribution. Their teammates, grand as they were, seem almost ancillary.

Ruth and Gehrig provide an interesting counterpoint. As anchors of the Yankees' Murderers' Row in the 1920s, they were teammates for twelve years; though occasional fishing buddies for a time, in the end they were not close. Their basic natures and biographies all but assured as much. They never had a chance to share memories as old men: Gehrig died at thirty-seven, Ruth at fifty-three. Cousy and Russell, who is now eighty-four, were two of a kind in important ways; in 2015, sociologist Richard Lapchick, director of the Institute for Diversity and Ethics in Sport at the University of Central Florida, created an all-time NBA team of five great players with a social conscience and placed both Cousy and Russell on it (with Oscar Robertson, Wayne Embry, and Kareem Abdul-Jabbar). Despite this common ground, Cousy and Russell have different basic natures. So why would Cousy expect that a relationship, even a friendship, would grow from his seven years with Russell? That question has no short answer. This book, the product of more than fifty interviews with Cousy over two and a half years, is, in a way, a long answer.

Cousy sometimes speaks of death and "the Big Basketball Court in the Sky." He says, "If I talked to a shrink, I'd say, 'Am I trying to make light of it because I'm afraid of what's coming?' It is my way of handling it. I guess at this point in life, you get more introspective: *What's it all about? What am I doing here? Is there a God out there?* My time is limited."

In that limited time, he wants to make peace with questions of race, particularly as those questions touch him and Russell. He had other black teammates during his Celtics years whom he views as friends, including Chuck Cooper, his roommate as a rookie and the first African American ever drafted by an NBA team. But Russell always stood apart. He was never an approachable teammate, not to Cousy. Through the decades, Cousy hasn't understood why Russell has been friendly with other Celtics but not with him. What created their separation?

Even now he asks, *Is it Russ? Is it me?* To Cousy, time is long and time is short. Thinking of Russell, he has one more pass to throw. The narrative of the Celtics dynasty plays on, not on the parquet floor of the Boston Garden but in the conscience of the old captain.

SECTION I

Becoming Cooz

"SALE BOCHE"

Even as an old man wearing a sweat suit and sitting in his favorite chair at home in Worcester, Cousy engages in conversation with intensity. He wouldn't be Bob Cousy otherwise. He laughs. He cries. He is alternately introspective, wry, philosophical, eloquent, at times snarky, and, on days when he feels an old man's aches and burdens, crotchety. He likes the attention, the intellectual stimulation. He talks about politics, the past, Kennedy and Trump, George Mikan and Kevin Durant, the latest book he's reading. One conversation ends for a sensible reason: "It's time," Cousy says, brows arched, "for my one o'clock fruit." His old stories roll like the mighty waters, and to him those waters are mighty familiar. He's been telling some of these stories for fifty years. He's refined his lines and pauses. He's played the part of Bob Cousy for so long that he has mastered it. Now, though, it seems he has an additional, higher purpose: He is piecing together his life and assigning a sense of order and context. He's earnestly attempting to understand how the world given to him helped shape the world he made. But when the topic shifts to his parents, and the tension that roiled their marriage when he was only a boy, it's as if the mighty waters evaporate and suddenly he is bound for a darker, more somber place. Conversationally, he's in unfamiliar territory. No stories come by rote. The pauses are longer and more numerous. He explains haltingly how his mother sometimes lashed out at his father and struck him. Suddenly his face draws tight. It's as if he is seeing her strike his father again, the scene running through his mind on grainy celluloid. Another pause: lengthy, uncomfortable. Finally, thinking of his father, he says, "He just sat there and took it." Cousy stares across his living room, across time.

In the glory of his time with the Boston Celtics, you saw his big hands, his supple, sloping shoulders and long arms. Those were the optics of Cousy. He wore a thirty-five-inch sleeve; his fingertips reached nearly to his knees. Small wonder he so easily transferred the ball behind his back. He looked like he weighed only about 150 pounds (actually, thanks to his thighs, he weighed 185), and at six-foot-one, if he jumped as high as he could he might reach only halfway up the net.

But physiology didn't make him Cooz. Biography defined him. He lived and played with blast-furnace intensity. He sought to break free of his tenement-house origins and the dysfunction in his parents' marriage by winning basketball games and by defeating enemies of all kinds, including a sense of being an outsider in his own world.

At the center of this inner tumult was his mother, Juliette Corlet Cousy, a native of France, once tall and attractive. When she cooked her husband's favorite meal, pot-au-feu—beef stew with vegetables, including sliced potatoes with butter, fried to a crisp—it was as if she had transported the French countryside to a dinner table in Queens. From France she also brought a prejudice so strong it scarred her personality: She despised Germans. She trembled with rage at the mention of anything, or anyone, Germanic. If misfortune came, Juliette Cousy knew its source. *It was the Germans!* She had witnessed the Germans' wrath during World War I. They trampled French farms, trampled the French way of life, and she never forgot that, even after migrating to America.

As a boy, Cousy saw her scars. During World War II, he walked with his mother to see a neighborhood storekeeper in St. Albans, Queens. In the Old World she would expect a smile or warm embrace, as in Dijon or Paris. But this storekeeper drew back and said stiffly, "What can I do for you?" It didn't take much to stir her anger. Offended by his tone, Juliette jerked her young son's hand, and they left the store at once. Outside, she muttered to him, "That *sale Boche!*"

When her mood turned black, as it often did, she spat out those words, "*Sale Boche.*" *Dirty German.* She was at war with Germany, with her husband, with herself, and with the hard times in which they lived. Anyone she disliked or who had slighted her, whether of German descent or not, she dismissed as a *sale Boche.* Too often to forget, the young Cousy heard his mother's voice explode from the cellar of their house: "*SALE BOCHE!*" On those occasions, her wrath was more personal: She had taken aim, again, at her husband, the boy's father.

Juliette's husband, little Joe Cousy, bore the brunt of her rants. He had made the mistake of being born of French parents in a German-dominated region. He came from Alsace-Lorraine, on the northeastern edge of France up against Germany's western border. The region had been claimed by Germany in 1871 after the Franco-Prussian War. He had been conscripted by the German army during World War I, as so many other Alsatian farm boys had. Public records show Joe Cousy's place of birth as Welschensteinbach, its German name, but Joe always used the village's French name, Eteimbes. For Juliette, that was a distinction without a difference. If in her anger she needed Joe to be a dirty German, his parentage didn't matter.

A quiet, peaceful man, five-foot-six and stout, Joe was raised on the Cousy farm. There his family struggled to raise apples, cherries, and pigs. To his way of thinking, he was no more a farmer than he was a German, and breaking away to go to America was the boldest act of his life; Juliette, accustomed to life's finer things, loved him for all of that. With his new wife and her mother, Joe boarded the ocean liner *Mauretania*, pride of the Cunard Line, and set sail from Cherbourg on December 21, 1927.

For Juliette, their arrival in New York City was a homecoming of sorts. She had been born in New York and moved to Boston, where her French father, Clément Corlet, notable for his handsome, thick mustache, was maître d' of the Hotel Touraine. When Juliette was five years old, Corlet and his wife, Marie, brought her to Dijon, in the Burgundy region of eastern France. She later worked as a secretary and taught language to children of affluent French families. As they boarded the *Mauretania*, Juliette was about six weeks pregnant with their son, the only child she would have.

Juliette's contempt for Germans intensified during the late thirties and early forties when she received letters from friends and family in France telling of the Nazis and their atrocities. Joe Cousy had begun work in America driving a taxi, his old Packard, in New York City. On July 5, 1928, he filled out papers for U.S. citizenship. But then came the Depression. Soon, with hardly anyone using taxis, Joe needed a job. Franklin Roosevelt came to his rescue: In his forties, Joe got a job with the Works Progress Administration digging ditches in New York City.

Her dreams deferred, Juliette became so high-strung that kids in the neighborhood knew her as *the crazy French woman*. Hard times aged her quickly, her cheekbones becoming taut and severe. Assimilation wasn't easy. Juliette and Joe did not read the New York newspapers; nor, as best their son knew, did they vote. Juliette never quite understood basketball, or even television. Years later, to watch *The Ed Sullivan Show*, she put on a nice dress at home. When her son asked why she dressed up, she said, "Oh, Mr. Sullivan sees me. I see him and he's looking at me."

Her son saw more than the eccentricities. He knew her softer, loving side, the way she had gently coaxed him out of his boyhood nightmares and sleepwalking expeditions; she found him once sitting on the third-story ledge of their Manhattan tenement, where he had awakened screaming in French. She waved a white handkerchief from their window when it was time for dinner, and his buddies would say, "Hey, Frenchy, the handkerchief is out!" When the young Cousy opened drawers at home, cockroaches scurried for cover, but his mother assured him that one day she would get him out of the noise and stench and poverty of their Manhattan neighborhood. Of course, as a boy, he assumed that everyone was poor. Despite their own ethnic differences and prejudices, Juliette and Joe Cousy quickly had won the privileges of whiteness. They lived in the big-city melting pot or, as their son would later call it, "the mélange." His closest friends during childhood had last names like Gannon, Field, Kennedy, Blake, and Hackford, all of them white. There were no people of color in his neighborhood that he knew of, no blacks or Hispanics or Asian Americans, and only a few Jews. During the Depression, with hard times and soup lines in Fiorello La Guardia's city, Cousy played stoopball and boxball and pilfered bananas from pushcarts. He never felt threatened in his roughneck neighborhood, though once he saw someone shot dead.

During the late thirties, as the Cousys searched in less crowded areas for a new place to live, Juliette said to her son, "Roby, look at all the green grass! Someday you'll live where there is plenty of it." And once, touring St. Albans in Queens, she said, as if in a dream state, "Roby, breathe deep."

Joe and Juliette spoke French at home and German if they didn't want their young son to know what they were saying. As a boy, Cooz spoke French, thought in French, dreamed in French, and talked French in his sleep. But he wanted to be an American. It didn't help that he had a speech impediment: his *R*s sounded like *L*s. His schoolmates began to call him "Flenchy," and a speech teacher made him try to say, over and over, "Around the rugged rock, the ragged rascal ran." His *L*s poured forth: "Alound the lugged lock . . ."

The tension of his parents' marriage traumatized him. Juliette loomed over the household. His grandmother, Marie Corlet, lived with them and became his safety net. She made sure he went to church and didn't stray from Catholicism. She made him promise that one day he would attend a Catholic college.

Joe Cousy put his taxi in hock in 1939 as a down payment for a $4,500 house in St. Albans. He and Juliette proved resourceful. They lived, and cooked, in the bare-walled cellar, and with their son climbed three flights up the back staircase each night to sleep in the attic, leaving the rest of the house for renters, whose payments helped cover their mortgage. They rented out a five-room apartment on the first floor, a two-room apartment on the second, and a single room on the third. Juliette kept the place clean, and Joe fixed anything that broke. They brought a radio into the cellar to lighten their spirits. Their house in St. Albans was better than their Manhattan tenement, but that wasn't saying much. On summer nights, the attic became an oven. At times when Cousy awoke screaming from a nightmare, his mother would turn on the light to see welts on his back, the work of bedbugs.

Joe never said much. With his boy, he shared no profound father-son conversations about his war experience, or in fact any experience. He had been married to another woman who died during the first war, but Juliette decreed the subject of Joe's late wife off-limits. Many years later, when his son was a basketball celebrity, Joe told a sportswriter that he had raced automobiles before the first war and that, in the 1920s, with his family's farm reduced by war to mud, he fixed cars and rented one of his own to drive rich families on tours across Europe.

Joe wasn't home much. He drove his taxi at all hours, no doubt to escape his wife's wrath. They were in the cellar the first time Bob Cousy saw his mother strike his father. Joe was an easy target: one big room, no place to hide. Juliette smacked his head. Joe did not defend himself. He did not react at all.

"Sale Boche!" Juliette screamed.

She would never let him forget that he had once been in the German army even though he thought of himself as French. Cowering in a corner, the young Cousy watched his mother come undone. It happened this way more than once, Juliette calling Joe a dirty German and striking him. Her blows struck with force. Sometimes Joe threw up his hands in defense, other times not.

My poor father, Cousy thought. He wondered how his father could say nothing. He didn't want him to strike back. But sit there and take it? Even as a boy, Cousy understood there was more to it than a wife's anger at her husband.

HOUDINI

He escaped to basketball. The seed was planted and nurtured at the O'Connell Playground in St. Albans, about six blocks from their house on 116th Road. The park, named for a decorated American soldier killed in 1918 in France, featured ball fields and a handball court. In the winter, kids played basketball in an empty swimming pool, a basket set at each end.

Long before Auerbach came Arkin: Morty Arkin, short, big-bellied, friendly. The playground director, he was also the first Jewish man Cousy ever knew. Arkin taught basketball mechanics to the twelve-year-old Cousy: how to place his hands on the ball, how to spread his fingers to control it, how to keep his left hand under it for balance, the value of a smooth follow-through on shots. The boy showed promise. The year before, Cousy had fallen from a tree and broken his right arm. He learned to play handball left-handed. Arkin told him that might've been the best break he ever had. Cousy went to O'Connell at all hours, hurrying on his walk on Saturday mornings to get there by eight-thirty when the older boys chose up sides.

In autumn 1942, Cousy arrived at Andrew Jackson High School, one of several area high schools named for presidents (Lincoln, Adams, Cleveland). Lew Grummond, the basketball coach at Jackson, had won a few championships and a big reputation in Queens. Cousy failed to catch Grummond's eye during tryouts and did not make the team during his first two years. But he played regularly in church leagues, community leagues, and a league sponsored by the *Long Island Daily Press* newspaper, and for the Laureltons, a Jewish team—all while working on his game with Arkin.

"Don't ever be predictable," Arkin said. "Be sure you can do something different every time."

The words became Cousy's mantra. Soon whispers spread about Cousy's hotshot skills. The Bayside High School coach, Tom Mullins, heard them and told Grummond, "My boys tell me that you have a Chinese boy by the name of Couey, who is terrific." After Arkin mentioned a French boy named Cousy, Grummond finally noticed him in a *Press* league game. Noting how well the boy integrated his left hand, he invited Cousy, as a sophomore, to join the school's junior varsity team.

Cousy's self-confidence grew with his success. In basketball, unlike in everyday speech, he could express himself without impediment. In local leagues he demonstrated flair, even brashness. Playing for Grummond, though, proved constraining. The coach had a structured system and demanded that his players submit to it.

By Cousy's junior year, basketball existed at the center of his life, which made what happened in class that fall even more devastating. He had a problem with his eleventh grade homeroom teacher—or, more precisely, she had a problem with him. The school had more students than seats, and so in homeroom they sat two butts to a seat. Cousy's seatmate was a loud and obnoxious boy who frustrated their teacher. Cousy faced the other way, not paying attention as his seatmate prattled on. Grades came out for the first semester, and the teacher flunked Cousy and his seatmate in citizenship. Cousy rushed to Grummond to explain and to defend himself.

"I never did anything! Honest to God, I didn't do *anything*."

An old-school disciplinarian, Grummond took the homeroom teacher's side, meaning Cousy couldn't play for the school's basketball team during the first half of his junior year. It was, he decided, the worst, most unjust and inhumane thing that could ever happen to a guy in 1944.

As he continued to play in local leagues, Cousy created a buzz among coaches and sportswriters. The schoolboy sportswriter for the New York *Sun*, Bill Roeder, heard about the raven-haired boy with startling ball-handling ability. When Cousy was finally cleared by Grummond to play in a nonleague game against Bryant High School early in 1945, Roeder was there.

"The kid's reputation in the church league was so great he sold out the gymnasium. I had difficulty getting into the place," Roeder later said. He stood atop a table in the back of the gym.

Grummond sensed he was watching a special player that day and allowed Cousy to play outside the usual structured Andrew Jackson system—to create and innovate, to attempt shots from multiple angles, including a few long two-handed set shots. Cousy had waited more than two years for this game. Adrenalized, he scored twenty-eight points in the victory, nearly as many points as high school teams typically scored in a game at the time.

He started every game the rest of that season. Jackson captured the Public Schools Athletic League championship in Queens, winning seventeen consecutive games. It qualified for the city championships at Madison Square Garden but lost in the semifinals to Erasmus High.

In the end-of-the-season team photo, Cousy sits in the front row, one of eleven white players, all born a few years too late to be eligible to fight in World War II. Cousy's hands rest on his knees, his physique lean and underdeveloped, his facial features bony, his hair combed neatly, a portrait of fresh-faced innocence. There was at least one side benefit to playing on the team: Cousy relished the opportunity to shower at school after practices. He had never showered before; at home he had only a bathtub. Showers would become a lifelong fetish; he took two a day for most of his life.

The next season, Jackson won the borough championship again, and Cousy engaged in a battle for the scoring title in Queens against a black player from Long Island City High named Vic Hanson, once described in the *Long Island Daily Press* sports pages as "the ebon forward." Hanson played mostly day games, Cousy at night. In the season's final game, Cousy's teammates knew that Hanson led him by twenty points, and so they passed the ball to him at every chance. He scored twenty-eight points and later was named captain of the *New York Journal-American* all-city team. Thanks to a local newspaper sports cartoonist, the schoolboy magician also gained a nickname that he would carry always: the Houdini of the Hardwood.

Once or twice during his senior year at Jackson, he found his way to the front porch of the three Burton sisters, the hot numbers in St. Albans. Cousy noticed another girl there even lovelier than the sisters; her name was Marie Ritterbusch. He liked her smile and the fact that she had a nickname, Missie, that to Cousy, with his speech impediment, was a lot easier to say than Marie.

Their relationship began tentatively. For a time in high school, Missie dated a friend of Cousy's. Finally, Cousy took her out himself; they went to a stage play in the city. His classmates had a clear idea of Cousy's future. His photo in the 1946 Andrew Jackson High School yearbook carries the caption: *"Bob Cousy, who plays a mighty fine game / Will be among those of basketball fame."* Perhaps because he was only six feet tall, college coaches did not rush to Cousy. Only Holy Cross and

Boston College, still largely a commuter school, offered him scholarships; both were Catholic schools, which appeased his grandmother. Cousy chose Holy Cross in part because he preferred to live in a campus dormitory there rather than in a rooming house near BC. As he prepared to leave for Holy Cross in the fall of 1946, Cousy wanted to see more of Missie, who would remain in New York to work in the invoice department of the Gertz department store. He knew his mother would view with distaste any woman he brought home. He was her only child, her cherished son, and to her no woman could be good enough for him. He feared he would hear his mother cry out, for no good reason, "*Sale Boche.*" The dread only increased later as he began to court Missie seriously. He knew the time would come when he would introduce his mother to a young woman named Ritterbusch.

NEW BEGINNINGS

Cousy rode a midnight train north to New England in the fall of 1946, the same season the Boston Celtics stumbled into existence as a member of the Basketball Association of America, one of eleven teams in the Northeast and Midwest. It was Walter Brown's doing. A hockey man and sports promoter, Brown had succeeded his father as president of the Boston Garden-Arena Corporation in 1937. He cofounded the Ice Capades three years later and then, in 1946, joined with other BAA franchise owners seeking to fill dates on winter nights when the hockey teams or ice shows weren't performing and their arenas were dark. Why not give pro basketball a chance? Franchise owners chose as the BAA's new president Maurice Podoloff, a portly Ukrainian-born attorney (Yale Law class of 1915) already serving as the American Hockey League commissioner.

The 1946 Celtics weren't very good, at least at basketball. Some had other skills. Kevin Connors, a six-foot-five forward, couldn't shoot but he gave a great after-dinner speech. Across New England he delivered talks about the Celtics, trying to generate publicity and sell a few tickets. Mostly he apologized for the team. He missed three out of every four shots he took and lasted little more than a season. Connors would change his first name professionally to Chuck and play professional baseball and then become a Hollywood actor, starring in the TV series *The Rifleman*. ("He went from worst shot in the East," Tom Heinsohn says, "to the best shot in the West.")

At the Celtics' first home game in history—November 5, 1946, an election night, when John F. Kennedy first won a seat in Congress—Connors took a set shot during pregame warmups, and the glass backboard at the Arena shattered, broken shards falling to the hardwood floor in a thousand glittering crystals. It took an hour of mad scrambling to find a replacement backboard. The Boston Arena organist played happy tunes to kill time, and the Celtics engaged in intramural shooting contests at the other basket. The Celtics lost that home opener.

It wasn't just that the Celtics lost 147 of 236 games during their initial four seasons, or that Brown, a ruddy-faced Irishman with a warm heart and a big temper, had hemorrhaged $500,000 and mortgaged his house to keep his team alive. Boston sports fans simply weren't interested in pro basketball. In a region of lakes, ponds, and rinks, they were more enamored with hockey and the Bruins; college basketball, particularly with the startling rise of Holy Cross; and baseball and the Red Sox, especially their star, Ted Williams.

The Celtics, on the other hand, seemed to interest hardly anyone. They averaged just 3,600 fans per game during their first two seasons in the BAA, leaving about 10,000 seats empty. While Williams, his gorgeous swing unaffected by three years of military service, hit .342 with thirty-eight home runs in 1946, the first amalgam of Celtics, put together hastily during the thirty-two days preceding the season opener, finished tied with the Toronto Huskies in last place.

The face of pro basketball was Big George Mikan of the Minneapolis Lakers. Slow afoot as he was at six-foot-ten and 245 pounds,

Mikan did what he had to do. No center in the BAA could handle him. His teammate Swede Carlson loved to hear the sound of air escaping from the lungs of opposing players who ran into screens set by Mikan. More than once, Cousy saw his slim teammate Ed Macauley walk down a city street, bump into a lamppost, and say, "Oh, sorry, George!"

Old-time sportswriters turned away from the pro game, some mocking the tall players as pituitary goons and physical freaks. Ned Irish, president of the Knicks, fretted over how to make pro basketball seem major league to New York City fans, especially when arriving teams came from outposts like Rochester, Fort Wayne, or Providence. In a burst of marketing ingenuity, Irish got around the problem on December 13, 1949, when the Madison Square Garden marquee read: GEO MIKAN VS KNICKS.

You did what you had to do. The Washington Capitols' excitable young coach, Arnold (Red) Auerbach, just twenty-nine, built his first BAA team in 1946 in his own resourceful way. Auerbach had been in the navy for three years and knew talented players, who knew other talented players. He worked the phones. To Auerbach, the best ball handlers came from New York, the best rebounders from the West and Midwest, the best shooters from the South. He sought a diversified offense. He first signed Bob Feerick, a navy buddy, a six-foot-three guard with an unorthodox one-handed set shot, who had played at Santa Clara, and named him captain. Feerick suggested guard Fred Scolari, who had failed to make varsity at the University of San Francisco. Scolari walked into the gym, and Auerbach couldn't believe what he saw: "He looked like some fat broad in slacks." Scolari was five-foot-ten, with paper-thin arms. But Fat Freddie, as he was known, had the fastest hands in the league: He could play. The lanky Horace (Bones) McKinney was on a train to Chicago to sign with the Stags, but only until Auerbach intercepted him on a stop in Washington. He fed him steak and ice cream and a lot of promises. They went to the restroom and there Auerbach signed him. He later signed ex-navy man John Norlander, center John Mahnken, who played at George-town on Elmer Ripley's prewar teams, and Irv Torgoff, a guard on Coach Clair Bee's Long Island University team in the thirties. Torgoff was nine months older than Auerbach, but the young coach liked his experience. The Capitols won seventeen games in a row during that season and finished 49-11, the BAA's best record. A half century and more later, Auerbach puffed on a cigar and said, "The Knicks thought that they could just get these New York guys and beat the world, that all of basketball was there. But it wasn't. . . . Like everybody said, 'The smartest ballplayers by far are these Jewish guards in New York.'" Au-erbach clenched the cigar in his teeth. "Bullshit," he said.

Tony Lavelli did what he had to do, too. As the Celtics' first-round draft pick in 1949, Lavelli brought his miraculous hook shot from Yale. He was six-foot-four and gentlemanly, not an ounce of meanness in him. Opponents, less talented and more physical, pushed and el-bowed Lavelli, knocked him around. A man of music who fancied Gershwin and Cole Porter, Lavelli played the accordion. That first season, he landed a $13,000 salary from Walter Brown, plus a separate $125-a-game contract from Podoloff for playing his accordion to en-tertain fans during halftimes at twenty-five games.

At halftimes, Lavelli rested in the locker room for a few minutes, then put on his sweats, grabbed his accordion, and went out to center court. He played "Granada" and "Lady of Spain." He danced a little, sang a little, and sprinkled in some comedy. His Celtics career ended a year later, at which point he played for the Knicks and attended the Juilliard School of Music. Later, Lavelli traveled with the Harlem Globetrotters, playing against them in games and playing his accor-dion at halftimes.

From the moment he set foot in Worcester, Cousy felt more at peace. So much smaller and quieter than New York, Worcester, its population soon peaking at about 200,000, allowed Cousy to think unhurried thoughts. It felt like a refuge. The Holy Cross campus, with its rolling hills, was lovely. Downtown Worcester flourished with businesses along Main Street, and down the road in Shrewsbury young people flocked to the White City amusement park to ride the Zip. Settled in 1673, Worcester had its own place in American revolutionary history. Future president John Adams spent several years there during the mid-1750s as a schoolteacher. And on July 14, 1776, Isaiah Thomas, editor of the radical *Massachusetts Spy*, stood at the steps of the Old South Church in Worcester and made the first public reading of the Declaration of Independence.

At Holy Cross, Cousy's reputation for basketball cunning and derring-do built slowly, much as it had at Andrew Jackson. He remained rail thin, with narrow shoulders. The Crusaders, with Coach Doggie Julian running a two-platoon system, won the NCAA title in 1947, beating Navy, City College of New York, and Oklahoma in a remarkable underdog's run through the tournament. Cousy, just eighteen, manned the second platoon. He wasn't the star: George Kaftan was.

"He arrived with a reputation," Kaftan says, that of a stylish playmaker. But, Kaftan adds, "In college you play the system. Give-and-gos, pick-and-rolls." Kaftan was the smiling Greek golden boy, and Cousy, to one sportswriter at least, was "the taciturn Frenchman, who took basketball with a business-like seriousness."

The future sportswriter Dave Anderson arrived at Holy Cross as a freshman in 1947 and watched Cousy during practices in the old barn on campus. At Thanksgiving, Anderson went home to Brooklyn and told his friends, "I saw the greatest basketball player I've ever seen! Wait till you see this guy."

Even so, Cousy was still finding himself. Back home in Queens, Missie sensed his discomfort. "One night he asked me if I would write to him," she said, "because he was lonely." Noting his serious demeanor, Al Hirshberg, sports columnist of *The Boston Post*, wrote,

"Cousy is not a man to make friends easily. If he's talking basketball, he talks well but he has to be drawn out. Words do not come easily to him. He also has a vague air of independence, a severe indifference to what others think of him, and a suspicion of strangers which is eliminated only after he is certain that their intentions towards him are honorable."

Cousy struggled with Julian, a taskmaster coach. He missed an afternoon practice after attending a dance the previous night at a girls' school two hours away; he didn't return to campus in time. As punishment, Julian benched him at the start of the next game against Loyola of Chicago at Boston Arena. He called for Cousy with only thirty seconds remaining in the first half, but Cousy refused to enter the game, a decision he later regretted. His ego got the best of him. Late in the game, with Holy Cross trailing by seven points, the crowd chanted Cousy's name. Julian called for him, and he led the Crusaders to a stirring comeback victory. His relationship with Julian, though, was irretrievably broken.

In time, a new coach, Buster Sheary, took over, and soon Cousy was dominating games, and headlines. "Our new coach is a very good man," Cousy wrote in a letter to Missie in September 1948, before the start of his junior season. "Comparing him and Julian is like comparing black and white. I'm sure we'll have a very good season under him. He is a very strict disciplinarian but I'm afraid that is what we need."

Holy Cross brought structure to Cousy's life and to his thinking. He rose early for morning Mass, wore jacket and tie to class, practiced with the Crusaders in the afternoon, and studied at night. His classes, taught mostly by priests in robes, reflected the intellectual rigor and humanistic philosophies of a Jesuit education. Most of his courses were required, with little room for electives. Through homilies and Jesuit teachings, Cousy's Holy Cross curriculum emphasized the importance of serving others. Majoring in business, Cousy took classes entitled Logic, The Sacraments and the Mass, General Ethics, Epistemology, God and Redemption, Urban Sociology, and Applied

Economics. He took four semesters of advanced French, a "softie" for him since that was his first language; even so, as a boy he'd learned only to speak French, not to read or write it. He was merely an average student, but became more focused as an upperclassman, and made the dean's list. Thinking about prejudice and racism, Cousy wrote a senior thesis in 1950 on the persecution of minority groups, with a focus on anti-Semitism.

His relationship with Missie deepened over the course of a torrent of late-night letters between St. Albans and Worcester. They had agreed that they could date others, but in the fall of 1947, when Missie saw Cousy with another girl at a favorite haunt back in St. Albans, she was wounded. She wrote him a candid letter:

> It made me feel like I was fourteen again and caught my
> steady out with another girl. To me that's a horrible
> feeling. Since I was fourteen I've done everything not to
> feel like that. That's one of the reasons I don't tie strings
> to anyone. . . . My feelings don't get hurt easily so please
> give it to me straight, O.K. Love, Missie.

Stirred by her words, Cousy wrote back an hour after receiving her letter:

> Honest to goodness Miss I really didn't see you. Gee
> I wish there was something I could do or say to really
> convince you. . . . I tried to make it plain how I felt about
> you even tho you kept your feelings pretty much hidden
> but you seemed to think I was handing you a line.
> Believe me Miss I wasn't. I hope this clears
> everything up.

By the following fall they'd grown closer. In October 1948, Cousy began his letter, "My Darling." He wrote, "It's funny every time I have anything to do with any girls it increases my love for you. When I come back from a date I would give all the money I own to have you close to me. I suppose that's because sub-consciously I compare the girl with you and it makes me realize more and more that you're the most wonderful girl in the world." In another letter that fall, he wrote of missing her deeply. "I suppose it's good in a way but it isn't doing my studying or classwork any good. My mind keeps wandering and some-day the priest is liable to ask me a question and I'll probably blurt out your name. I have to see you soon Missie to hold you, to kiss you. I know I couldn't stand waiting till Christmas."

But their relationship cooled, and they broke up later in his junior year. Only twenty, and suddenly an unattached big man on campus, Cousy became involved with a different woman. A year passed before he would speak with Missie again.

It was a time of conservatism in America and in basketball. Most college coaches insisted on strict regimentation on the court, rigid of-fenses built on structured passing, two-handed set shots, and cuts to the basket. No jump shot for him—Cousy favored a one-handed push shot, refusing to commit to the air and limit his options. Some coaches in the Midwest wouldn't permit a player to shoot a hook shot; if a player tried it, his coach might yank him from the game. A behind-the-back pass might mean expulsion from the team. Cousy figured he received outsized exposure because he was the only one attempting such fancy maneuvers, even during summers in the Catskills, where he served as a waiter and played outdoor games on lighted courts to en-tertain guests at Tamarack Lodge. The Holy Cross Crusaders soon became known in Boston's sports pages as the athletic clubs, Fancy Pants A.C. and Cousy A.C.

Holy Cross drew big crowds at Boston Garden, much bigger than the Celtics, including a few sellouts in doubleheaders. Gerry Ahern of *The Boston Post* wrote in 1949 that Cousy was the main attraction: "To Holy Cross games in Boston, not yet an enthusiastic basketball center, the stylist draws hundreds of non-basketball fans who merely are intrigued by his slick athletic performances. . . . He plays with a deadpan expression that makes him look cold and uninterested, but that appearance is a cover-up for intense emotions."

The date that Cousy became *Cooz* is carved in stone: January 11, 1949. On that day, during his junior season at Holy Cross, more than simply last-second heroics beat Loyola of Chicago at Boston Garden. It was a signature moment for an artist in the making.

A few weeks before the Loyola game, Sheary told Cousy that he needed to further develop the dexterity and coordination of his left hand: "They're overplaying your right side. Everybody knows you're going to shoot with the right hand." Sheary suggested how to improve: "Open doors with your left hand. Shake hands with your left hand. Carry your books with your left hand. And if you can, come up to the gym early and work on your left hand. You need a better left hand." This echoed Arkin's advice from years before. Alone in the gym before team practices, Cousy worked on left-handed dribbling and hook shots.

Against Loyola, the score tied, 57-all, the Crusaders inbounded the ball from midcourt with eighty-seven seconds remaining. They stalled, shuttling the ball out near midcourt as the Loyola defense sagged and waited for the Crusaders to attack the basket. Cousy, wearing a white T-shirt beneath purple jersey No. 17, positioned himself way out on the left perimeter. Sheary wanted one last shot and had ordered no attempt made before ten seconds remained. The red second hand moved inexorably around the face of the big Boston Garden clock. The crowd of more than ten thousand stood as one.

Finally the ball came to Cousy. He dribbled toward the free throw line, overplayed to his right by a Loyola defender. Then, improvising and putting his big hands and long arms to good use, he stopped short and whisked the ball behind his back, gaining a step on the defender. As the ball came smoothly into his left hand, Cousy cut on a diagonal and then, into the air, from about fifteen feet, swept seamlessly into a left-handed hook shot. It banked in with nine seconds to play for what became the game winner.

According to the *Boston Herald*, "The atomic, chain-reaction explosion that ran up to the last row of the top balcony was deafening."

Afterward, Cousy's teammate and best friend, Frank Oftring, said, "He's done something like it in practice—I've seen him dribble in and spin with the ball—but I never saw him make this precise play in practice."

This shot would assume a special place in the Cousy canon. Certainly there was ego in it, the very idea that Cousy sought to create a dribbling move and shot that no one had seen before and to execute it at the game's most critical moment. What if he had missed that shot? What if Holy Cross had lost instead of won? Then who would he have been? Just a failed showman.

Sheary leaped from the bench when he realized Cousy was shooting with his left hand. "I was on my way out to strangle him," Sheary said. "But when it went in I skidded to a stop. He looked right at me and seemed to say: 'How's my left hand now?'"

Sportswriters asked Cousy if he had been practicing this move. "I don't know where that came from," he said. "I have a basketball imagination. That was the thing to do. That's what was called for."

He became the talk of the town. The *Boston Globe* artist Gene Mack drew a cartoon of Cousy spinning a defender into confusion as he dribbled the ball behind his back. The Holy Cross publicity department sent letters to leading college coaches across the nation to solicit testimonials about Cousy. Two years earlier, the Boston Braves had mailed a brochure detailing the exploits of third baseman Bob Elliott, who then won the 1947 National League Most Valuable Player award. It worked to great effect here, too: Adolph Rupp, the noted Kentucky coach, wrote back that Cousy was surely one of the nation's finest players. In early March, *Look* magazine produced a glossy four-page photo spread on a day in the life of Cousy at Holy Cross, featuring images of Cousy leaping for a rebound against Harvard, playing billiards, walking across campus with Oftring, wearing his letterman's sweater in the dining hall, and kneeling beside Oftring in noontime prayer.

The Crusaders finished a disappointing 19-8 that season, but bigger results lay ahead in 1950. For coach Buster Sheary, Cousy's game-winner against Loyola was a portent. "This boy was made for basketball and basketball was made for this boy," Sheary later said.

From the talk of the town, Cousy, in the winter of 1950, became the talk of the nation. The Crusaders won twenty-six consecutive games at the outset of the 1949–50 season and were ranked No. 1 in the Associated Press's NCAA poll for five weeks. Most games weren't even close. Holy Cross led the nation in scoring margin, at more than seventeen points per game. Earle Markey, a freshman on the team, practiced each day against Cousy, a senior. "You want to learn fast?" Markey says rhetorically. Cousy wanted to win in practice as much as in games. "He was intense."

Another national title seemed possible. But Cousy's final college season crashed to earth in an 87–74 defeat to North Carolina State in the opening round of the NCAA Tournament. Still, the Crusaders finished fourth in the final AP poll, and the nation's basketball writers named Cousy, a three-time All-American, as the nation's most outstanding college player.

At the time, Cousy searched for ways to leverage his growing celebrity. He and Oftring paid visits to local bank presidents, seeking business advice. One suggested they open a string of service stations. They trained for two weeks in a program run by Texaco and then put on their service attendant uniforms for three days for a grand opening of the Cousy and Oftring service station at the corner of Main and Piedmont streets, near the heart of downtown Worcester.

"People would bring their car for a tune-up," Cousy says, "and

Frank and I would empty the hydromatic instead of the oil." They soon sold the business.

They turned to the Cousy and Oftring Driving School, with Cooz, in a 1950 Plymouth, giving driving lessons to housewives in Worcester. Women took driving instruction better than men, he learned, though not always with better results. Cousy rehearsed with one woman how to use a clutch and emergency brake while driving up a steep hill he knew was on the route used during formal driving tests. When test day came, the inspector sat in the front seat beside the woman, while Cousy took the backseat with instructions not to say a word. The woman was beyond nervous and, when asked to drive up the same hill, she inadvertently threw the Plymouth in reverse and pressed the accelerator, and the car leaped over the curb and cut a groove in Mrs. Murphy's lawn before coming to a sudden halt. It was all Cousy could do not to scream.

He had more luck with the Bob Cousy All-Stars. He joined with some of his Holy Cross teammates to tour New England. They were celebrities of sorts. They had won an NCAA championship and been in the newspapers for four years. On tour, they played to big crowds, and the players pocketed good money.

Cousy had yet to see a National Basketball Association game. He wondered if the league would last. In spring 1950, the NBA was finishing its first season. Born of a merger between the BAA and the National Basketball League, it encompassed seventeen teams in three divisions, including a few in places Cousy couldn't find on a map, like Sheboygan (Wisconsin), Anderson (Indiana), and Waterloo (Iowa). Kaftan, his former Holy Cross teammate, was playing for the Celtics during that inaugural NBA season, when some teams played games in high school gyms. "You had to be careful what you said, and what you did, in these local towns," Kaftan says. "Everything closed down at ten o'clock."

Cousy had heard more about the Harlem Globetrotters, an all-black team that barnstormed with their clowning bag of tricks. He heard stories about guard Marques Haynes sliding to his knees during his dribbling act, and center Goose Tatum hiding a basketball beneath his jersey and yukking it up with the crowd. Sometimes, Tatum would score on a hook and say to his defender, "How'd you like that, young white boy?" That April, the Globetrotters invited Cousy to join them on an eighteen-city cross-country tour as a member of the opposing College All-Americans, coached by Long Island's Clair Bee, Oklahoma A&M's Hank Iba, and DePaul's Ray Meyer. Abe Saperstein, the Globetrotters' owner, offered Cousy five hundred dollars per game, more than he was paying his Globetrotter players.

With his own tour under way, Cousy was able to squeeze in only three appearances against the Globetrotters, on April 2 in Chicago and April 17–18 in Philadelphia and Buffalo. Cousy didn't think much of the Trotters' basketball skills: "They used to win three hundred sixty-six games in a row. But we all knew that it was a show."

A show indeed: Cousy and his teammates ran through a flaming hoop onto the court, and jugglers from France and Mexico performed at halftime along with a drum major twirling flaming batons while riding a unicycle. The game program touted the Trotters' season record as 153-2 and added, "Approximately one month from tonight they will be putting on their dazzling show at the Palais Des Sports in gay old Paris. After that they will fly to London for a series of games at Wembley Stadium, then on to Belgium, Holland, Switzerland, Spain and Italy. The name—Globetrotters—is, indeed, no misnomer!"

Cousy was fast becoming a basketball showman, but the Globetrotters took showmanship to a different comedic level. He thought they were the only basketball professionals who promoted their games vigorously. The three games he played against the Trotters were competitive; Cousy knew that if the All-Americans fell too far behind, the Trotters would move into their ham-it-up stalling act, which would be humiliating. He and his College All-American teammates played to win, and won two of Cousy's three games, including one by twenty-one points.

Cousy covered Haynes, one stylish dribbler against another, and was impressed by his ball-handling mastery, less so by his shooting. Two of the Globetrotters, Nat (Sweetwater) Clifton and Chuck Cooper, figured prominently in his near future.

A man watching from the crowd in Buffalo, Ben Kerner, also figured prominently in Cousy's future. Seeing Cousy play against the Globetrotters that night, Kerner, owner of the NBA's Tri-Cities Blackhawks, was dazzled. He decided that Cousy was the greatest college player he had ever seen.

THE CELTICS

Around the NBA, opinions varied on Cousy's potential. Tony Lavelli said, "The kid can't miss. He's got everything." But Rochester Royals owner Lester Harrison called Cousy's on-court flourish "bush league stuff, good enough for colleges." He insisted his guard Bob Davies could make the same flashy moves, but the Royals wouldn't let him. "This is professional basketball and you don't make fools of other pros," Harrison said.

Friends assured Cousy that the Celtics would select him with the first pick in the draft. Taking Cousy seemed logical and commercially prudent for the Celtics. As a local Holy Cross star, Cousy would draw big crowds to the Garden, and since he and Missie wanted to live in Worcester, it was perfect.

But when his phone rang on draft day, April 25, 1950, a reporter told him he had been drafted by the Tri-Cities Blackhawks.

"Where the hell is Tri-Cities?" Cousy said.

Answer: Along the banks of the Mississippi River, on the border of

Illinois (Moline, Rock Island) and Iowa (Davenport). Ben Kerner, with images of Cousy's performance against the Globetrotters fresh in his mind, got his man with the third pick in the first round.

Cousy, in a tiff, told the reporter he would not play for Tri-Cities. He said he would play only for Boston or Syracuse. Cousy said he had a driving school, which now had three cars running full time, and soon he would have a wife. He was also thinking about creating another tour for his Bob Cousy All-Stars and maybe playing more regularly against the Globetrotters.

Moline, Illinois?

The Celtics, with the first pick, had turned away from Cousy to select a big man, six-foot-eleven center Charlie Share of Bowling Green State University. What Boston sportswriters didn't know was that Walter Brown had hired Red Auerbach as his new coach only a few days before. As a sports promoter involved with the Boston Marathon and about to purchase the Boston Bruins, Brown knew Boston's sportswriters, and needed them, and occasionally even loaned them money that wasn't paid back. He had gathered at Freddie's Deli months before with a trusted group of radio broadcasters and local sportswriters, including Joe Looney of the *Herald* and Sam Brogna of the *Daily Record*, and laid bare his dilemma.

"You guys are my friends and you've been closer to this team than anyone else," Brown said. "So I want to know—who do you think should coach the Celtics?"

Auerbach, coaching Kerner's Tri-Cities team in Iowa, was one of their suggestions. Soon after, Brown contacted Kerner and received permission to interview Auerbach. During their conversation, Brown told Auerbach the Celtics were losing money and he couldn't offer much security.

"If we are still in business next year, we can talk about raises," Brown said. "What do you say?"

Auerbach accepted.

Though it wouldn't be known for another day or two, Auerbach had made the decision to go for Share over Cousy. He had watched Cousy play a game against the Globetrotters. "I just wasn't too impressed," Auerbach said later.

Kerner heard about Cousy's rejection of Tri-Cities and boldly announced that Cousy would play for Tri-Cities or no one in the NBA.

Cousy went to see Brown at his office. "Boston is my town," Cousy said. "Please do something."

Brown apologized but said the Celtics needed a big man. They needed Charlie Share. Besides, Brown pointed out that other Holy Cross players he had drafted in the past hadn't panned out. In the most polite way, Brown said there was nothing more he could do.

His options limited, Cousy flew to Buffalo to see Kerner. He asked for a $10,000 salary. Kerner blanched and offered $6,000. Cousy flew home without a contract.

A Boston Garden publicist introduced the new coach, Red Auerbach, to Sam Cohen, sports editor of the *Daily Record*. Cohen sized him up quickly: abrasive and full of himself, a bum of a navy man who must have spent too much time rocking on the high seas. But he thought Auerbach's wife, Dorothy, beautiful and classy, and so he got to thinking that maybe he ought to give Auerbach a chance. Maybe there was more to him than met the eye.

Talk of Cousy, and how the Celtics had passed him up in the draft the day before, consumed the press conference announcing Auerbach's hiring. Jerry Nason of the *Globe* wondered aloud in his column, "Is Walter Brown public enemy or public benefactor No. 1 in passing up Bob Cousy, Holy Cross glamor guy, in the pro basket ball draft?" Nason's answer: "Brown was cooking on all cerebral burners when he drafted Giant Chuck Share instead of Cousy."

Sportswriters had told Brown about Auerbach. They said he was smart, full of moxie, and in personality a pugilist. They said he studied the nuances of the game and harassed referees with impunity. Auerbach had produced an impressive 115-53 record in three seasons as coach in Washington; in his one season with Tri-Cities, he made deals involving twenty-eight players over six weeks to transform a last-place team into a contender. "I know what I want in a ball player," Auerbach said. He also knew what he wanted in the league schedule. The Philadelphia Warriors' owner, Eddie Gottlieb, created the schedule on a legal pad that he carried with him at all times. Auerbach didn't like it when his team was forced to travel from Washington or Boston to Chicago and then back to Washington and then to St. Louis. That cost too much money and added unnecessary wear and tear on his players. He protested loudly to Gottlieb. A good listener, Gotty, as he was known, took out his pencil and pad and erased a date or two. "Okay," he told Auerbach, pointing to the changes he had made. "I took care of this. I put you here."

Auerbach, us-against-the-world battler, was convinced of a vast conspiracy in league headquarters that favored the Knicks—a strong New York team was said to be good for the league—and the Philadelphia Warriors. Gottlieb, he knew, kept not only the league schedule in his pocket but also the league's referees. Auerbach believed NBA president Podoloff masterminded this conspiracy and that some sportswriters were in on it. And so were referees, especially his prime antagonist, the volatile Sid Borgia.

This much Auerbach knew: They were all out to screw Red Auerbach.

In conversation Auerbach put people on the defensive instantly.

"What time is practice?" one of his players asked.

"Who wants to know?" Auerbach answered.

He greatly admired Harry Truman and General Douglas MacArthur for their no-nonsense manner. He said he did not want to be stereotyped as a "typical, wise-ass Brooklyn character" from *Thoity-thoid* Street even if the stereotype fit. Soon he would teach his two young daughters two essential life lessons: 1. How to shake hands (firmly while making eye contact), and 2. How to make a fist. When his eight-year-old daughter Nancy slugged another girl, he couldn't have been more proud. He coached the Celtics through rigorous two-a-day practices during training camp with a whistle and an attitude, sometimes turning his chair backward and sitting to watch his players run wind sprints in the gym, taking note of who excelled and who didn't.

His players were about to learn some of Auerbach's aphorisms: "You can't shit an old shitter," and "That's false hustle," and "When a man has the ball watch his hips. He can't go anywhere without them." He also liked to say: "You know what BOSS spelled backwards is? Double S-O-B."

Now, at the press conference, Brown began, "Meet Red Auerbach. He tells me he always wanted to coach basketball in Boston. The opportunity has come. How long he holds the job depends on what he makes of the sport during the coming season."

"I don't give a darn for sentiment or names," Auerbach said, pugnaciously. "That goes for Cousy or anybody else. A local yokel doesn't bring more than a dozen extra fans into your building. But a winning team does, and that's what I aim to have." He might have mentioned that Baltimore, selecting after Boston, passed on Cousy, too, in favor of Wisconsin forward Don Rehfeldt.

Instead he said, "I'm going to build Boston basketball to the level of Syracuse and Rochester"—big talk for a young coach.

Sitting beside Auerbach, Brown tried his best. Wearing a suit, his hair slicked back, Brown put it like this: "I'd love to have Cousy, but we've had that hole in the middle for four years and I had to have Share. I laid awake all night before draft meetings, trying to get up enough courage to pass up Cousy for the big man."

Then Auerbach barked, "If there was an open draft in the professional league, I'd wager that at least eleven of the [twelve] clubs would take Share as their first choice." He also seemed ecstatic about acquiring center Ed Macauley, the leading scorer from the just-folded St. Louis Bombers. "Macauley is the second best center in the league to Mikan now," Auerbach said, "and as time goes on I feel he'll be the best. He is unselfish as a team player."

As for Cousy, Auerbach insisted, "He still has to learn what to do when he doesn't have the ball."

Auerbach's comments in the Boston sports pages disappointed Cousy. The *Boston Traveler* had a more prescient spin on the press conference, though, suggesting that, given Cousy's wish not to play for Tri-Cities, "[Walter] Brown also stands a good chance of getting the Worcester Wizard." "Owning a player who won't sign," the *Traveler*'s Tom Monahan wrote, "is like owning a hole in the head. So the possibilities are very good indeed that Brown will be able to wangle Cousy back home."

The NBA was in turmoil. Five of the seventeen franchises had dropped out a year earlier, after that first season. The old National Basketball League was attempting a revival, and so NBA owners moved to sign top players. Kerner wanted guard Frankie Brian, a big scorer for the defunct Anderson club, but the Chicago Stags owned Brian's NBA rights. No one told Cousy, but Kerner traded him to Chicago for Brian. Then Chicago folded.

Utter chaos. Podoloff oversaw a dispersal draft for Chicago's players on October 5, 1950, at New York's Park Sheraton Hotel. It all went smoothly, each player assigned team by team, until only three Stags guards remained—Max Zaslofsky, a four-time all-star, veteran Andy Phillip, and Cousy. Brown wanted Zaslofsky, but so did the Knicks' Ned Irish and Philadelphia's Gottlieb. Irish insisted Zaslofsky would appeal to New York's large base of Jewish fans. Gottlieb wouldn't give in, and neither would Brown. Voices grew loud, tensions rose.

Podoloff decided to put the three players' names in a fedora handed over by Syracuse Nationals owner Danny Biasone.

"Whoever you draw," Podoloff said to Brown, Irish, and Gottlieb, "that's who you got."

Brown had the first pick from the hat, but offered it to Irish, saying, "Ned, I had the first draw in the other two drafts, you can draw first now." Brown regretted that gentlemanly act when Irish drew Zaslofsky's name.

Now it was Brown's turn, and he wanted Phillip, a fine playmaker. He drew Cousy's name instead. "I figured I'd got the dirty end of the stick all around," Brown said.

On a visit home, Cousy waited in St. Albans at his parents' house, expecting Kerner to call and tell him when to report to Tri-Cities. Cousy didn't know that he had been traded to a team that had folded, or that his name had been pulled from a fedora in a New York City hotel room.

The phone finally rang, postmidnight, not Ben Kerner on the line but Walter Brown, saying to Cousy, "Get in your car and drive back to Boston. You're with us."

Cousy was ecstatic, Auerbach considerably less so. But the coach harbored no hard feelings. He didn't like Cousy's fancy passes— "monkey business," he called them—but he would take care of that. Auerbach quickly came to respect Cousy's determination and devotion to basketball as a craft. After Cousy's first practice with the Celtics at the Fargo Building in South Boston, Auerbach whispered to the team's publicist, Howie McHugh, "He's going to be one of the great ones." That fall, Auerbach named Cousy his team captain, a rare honor for a rookie and a role he would retain for thirteen seasons.

By design, Auerbach kept at a remove from his players. To him this was a business; he might need to trade or release a player and he wouldn't be compromised by friendship. Over time, his relationship with Cousy would challenge that. To the rest of the world he was "Red," but Cousy, who struggled to pronounce his *R*s (especially when it was the first letter of a word or name), called him Arnold, and only Auerbach's wife, Dorothy, did that.

The two men couldn't have been more different in personality. To Cousy, Arnold Auerbach could be contentious and rude, hardly lovable, but he began to feel a deeper connection with his coach. "Arnold and I came rolling out of those ghettos ready to fight, fight, kill, kill!" Cousy says. Once the two men realized they shared an intense desire to win, Cousy says, "Christ, we bonded."

Tony Lavelli was still on the team during that 1950 exhibition season. Early in one game, an animated Lavelli returned to the Celtics huddle during a time-out, and Cousy heard him say, "Fellows, let's get mad! Let's get REALLY mad!" To Cousy, this was odd in the extreme. Did he just say . . . *fellows?* Cousy read his teammates' expressions: *Is Lavelli out of his mind?* At halftime, while Auerbach was laying out the game plan for the second half, Cousy saw Lavelli leave the locker room, accordion in hand. He wondered what Auerbach thought of that.

He got his answer: In a flash, Lavelli was released, a member of the Celtics no more. Arnold Auerbach could handle a little monkey business, but not an accordion player.

It was after Cousy's graduation that Missie, working as a waitress for the summer, had sent a card for his August 9 birthday. They talked, they met, and the old sparks caught. In the fall, they became engaged.

They married on a Saturday morning in early December 1950. Both were twenty-two. They squeezed the ceremony onto their schedule, knowing the Celtics were playing that night. One of his ushers forgot to pick up Missie and bring her to the church in Worcester. In his pin-striped suit, a boutonniere pinned to his lapel, Cousy paced nervously as he waited at the church. When Missie finally arrived in her elegant white, Chantilly lace–over-satin gown, she fought tears, and her mother glared at Cousy. "I could feel her eyes piercing me from behind," he says. The ceremony at St. Peter's church started twenty-five minutes late as mourners gathered outside, waiting for a funeral to start. "I think I cried all the way down the aisle," Missie would say. By the time Father John Tiernan of Holy Cross blessed them, and they walked outside for the first time as husband and wife, celebrants tossed rice from one side of the church steps, while on the other mourners gathered behind a casket, waiting for them to pass.

At their wedding reception at the nearby Syrian-American Club, Cousy discovered the champagne breakfast he had arranged wasn't available because an oven blew up in the club's kitchen the night before, hospitalizing the caterer. Guests ate cold food and toasted Bob and Missie with tomato juice.

Juliette Cousy wasn't much in the mood for celebrating. She wore black to the wedding. Privately, Cooz had told Missie, "Sweetheart, I love you dearly, but if you and I end up like my mother and father, I can't live in a relationship like that." Missie's late father was of German descent, her mother of the Irish O'Hanlons. When Cooz came home with Missie Ritterbusch, Juliette glared at her from the moment she walked in. Missie, meanwhile, thought, *Oh my God, his mother is the crazy French woman!* The relationship between his mother and wife just wasn't going to work, Cooz knew.

There was still a game to play that night against Syracuse at Boston Garden. Brown had given Cousy twenty-five tickets, so the wedding party drove to Boston. After Cousy carried Missie over the threshold of their suite at the Hotel Kenmore that afternoon, Father Tiernan held hands with them. It wasn't as if he kept Cooz from his amorous intentions.

"You never had sex the day of the game," Cousy says. "That was one of Auerbach's Ten Commandments."

Missie wore a corsage as she sat at Boston Garden that night with other Celtics wives, and when her husband ran onto the court during pregame introductions, the organist struck up "Here Comes the Bride." Cousy scored nineteen points, but the Nationals beat the Celtics, 86–85. Some of his teammates came up to their hotel suite after the game.

Cousy's celebrity at this early hour was such that Ed Sullivan, in his gossipy theater column in the New York *Daily News*, wrote, "Garbo dating George Schlee . . . Ex-Holy Cross cage star, Bob Cousy, and lovely Marie Ritterbusch honeymooning . . . Howard Hughes personally supervising the most minute details of Faith Domergue's trip to N.Y. . . ."

It wasn't much of a honeymoon for the Cousys. The next day, a Sunday, they attended a play, their tickets a wedding gift from Brown. They saw *Death of a Salesman*—"not the most exhilarating play," Cousy says, "to see on your honeymoon."

ROUGH AND TUMBLE

Auerbach opined, Cousy listened: "Every time a pass is dropped, it's your fault." From the start, Auerbach laid down the law. "I don't care if you throw it behind your back, between your legs, off your ear, or how," he said, "just as long as the guy it's meant for catches it. The criterion of a great passer is the completion of the pass."

Auerbach told one writer about Cousy, "His receivers are highly-coordinated, well-conditioned men, so it stands to reason that ninety per cent of the time a pass is dropped it's Cousy's fault."

Cousy viewed it differently, though not until 1960, when his career was a decade old, would he publicly state his view. "After a man has played with me for a few weeks," Cousy said, "there is no excuse for his being fooled."

Auerbach admitted Cousy's dribbling was an effective weapon. In Cousy's four seasons before the adoption of the twenty-four-second clock in the 1954–55 NBA season, Auerbach, with a six- or eight-point lead with a few minutes to play, instructed him to dribble out the clock. His posture low to the floor, Cousy dribbled this way and that way, his right hand dominant, opponents lunging but unable to take the ball from him, cursing at him and threatening to knock him into the second balcony. His fancy dribbling maddened and sometimes embarrassed opponents, entertained home crowds, and infuriated gamblers worried about the point spread. At Madison Square Garden, Cousy saw irate gamblers appear from out of the thick cigarette haze. Cousy was costing them money. They ran almost onto the court and screamed obscenities at him for his dribbling antics.

Cousy wasn't the only target. On other occasions on the road, inflamed by nothing in particular, matronly women rushed onto the court between halves to swing their handbags at Celtics players or jab them with the points of umbrellas. As the Celtics passed under the stands en route to their dressing rooms, some fans spat down at them.

The early NBA seemed an odd hybrid of pro wrestling and vaudeville. In November 1950, the Fort Wayne Pistons stalled to keep the Minneapolis Lakers' Mikan from scoring. The Pistons took just thirteen shots in the game, one every four minutes. Minneapolis fans booed as the Pistons held the ball for minutes at a time. Fans threw pennies, oranges, and a shoe onto the court. But the stall worked: Fort Wayne won, 19–18.

Every night, NBA referees, with veins popping, blew their whistles, and coaches screamed and heaved rolled-up game programs into the crowd. Fistfights broke out on the court among players and coaches and fans, and then along came Cousy, stealing the moment in a more artful way. The NBA game slowly evolved. Soon, a player needed more than a set shot. He needed a hook (left and right), a one-handed push shot, and maybe a jumper.

Early on, Auerbach understood the promise and raw power of Cousy's skills. Cousy was "like atomic energy that hasn't been controlled," he said. Cousy produced scintillating moments during the 1950–51 season but played inconsistently. He surprised teammates with his passes and unwisely tried to force his way into tight spaces. Auerbach told him that when he led the fast break, Cousy needed to decide before he reached the opposing free throw line whether he would shoot or pass. Still, Cousy finished ninth in the league in scoring in his first season and fourth in assists. In 1951, at the first NBA All-Star Game in Boston (the brainchild of Walter Brown), Indianapolis's fleet guard, Ralph Beard, tried to steal the ball from Cousy on a fast break. As Beard reached for the ball, Cousy took it behind his back and raced by him, electrifying the crowd as Beard's momentum forced him to leap over the press table. Auerbach admitted, "The only kick I have with Cousy is that he makes practice sessions hard on a coach. All the other players just want to stand still and watch him."

The Celtics finished 39-30, in second place behind the Philadelphia Warriors, and then lost to the Knicks in the first round of the playoffs. With Cousy as a box-office magnet, the Celtics drew six thousand fans per home game, an increase of more than 30 percent over the previous season.

They drew bigger crowds when paired in a doubleheader with the Globetrotters. In the Celtics' locker room, Cousy heard the sellout crowd's roar as the Trotters performed their comic ruses. When the Celtics came out for the nightcap, Cousy noticed that the lion's share of fans had left and only several thousand remained. The Celtics still had a long way to go.

Cousy's roommate on the road during that rookie season, assigned by Auerbach, was Chuck Cooper. The day the Celtics selected the forward from Duquesne University in the draft's second round, a sportswriter asked Brown, "Do you realize that Cooper is a Negro?" Brown replied, "If he can play basketball, he can be polka-dotted or plaid for all I care." This prompted Dave Egan of the *Daily Record* to write,

"Thus another invisible barrier crumbled under the steadfast words of an honorable man, and thus was a colored boy given an opportunity to play in the big league of basketball for the first time."

Cooper was the first black player drafted in the NBA. He was joined in the league that season by three other African Americans—Earl Lloyd with Washington, Sweetwater Clifton with the Knicks, and, later in the year, Hank DeZonie with Tri-Cities. Abe Saperstein had lost his monopoly on black players. In a tiff after the NBA draft, he threatened that his Globetrotters wouldn't play in lucrative double-headers in Boston or Washington ever again; Brown, though cash-strapped, held his ground. Cousy and Cooper became friends. They drank beer together and hung out at nightclubs favoring jazz or the blues. Once they heard Errol Garner on the piano at Storyville in Boston. The Brooklyn Dodgers' Jackie Robinson had created international headlines when he desegregated Major League Baseball in 1947. Seven months earlier, in autumn 1946, two black players, William (Dolly) King and William (Pop) Gates, had joined the premerger National Basketball League, whose rosters during the war years had included other black players. When integration came to the NBA in 1950, it happened quietly, beneath the newspapermen's radar.

"Complete silence," Cousy says.

The NBA circuit proved challenging for the league's first black players. Indianapolis fans jeered Lloyd: "Go back to Africa!" In letters to his future wife, Cooper described segregation in hotels and restaurants as well as his frustrations with Auerbach, who thought he was a hypochondriac feigning injuries. Cooper told her about discrimination in Boston. He also told her that Cousy was his best friend on the team, trusted without question.

"He's a different kind of person, a good person," Cooper wrote.

Jackie Robinson once thanked a white teammate, pitcher Carl Erskine, for talking to Robinson's wife and children in front of white fans. Cousy and Cooper socialized in public more freely, and their wives would become friends, sitting together at games.

In his second season in Boston, Auerbach emphasized the fast break. He wanted Cousy to push the ball upcourt, hard, fast, and often. He understood this was Cousy's great gift—his court vision and passing. Cousy received the outlet pass (often from Macauley) and four or five strides later stormed into the front court, on the attack. Guard Bill Sharman joined the Celtics in 1951–52, and in their first game together, Cousy threw him a pass he wasn't expecting, and the ball ricocheted off Sharman's head.

"You know he looks one way, feints a second, and passes a third," Sharman said. Every game, Sharman added, brought "a continual adjustment—and a continual amazement—that he could hit me with a perfect pass when I didn't think any pass was possible."

The fast break wasn't new to basketball. It had been around for decades, used by West Coast colleges during the thirties. But as Herbert Warren Wind wrote in *Sports Illustrated*, "Cousy made it work with a speed and fluency no one had ever dreamed were possible." Cousy added stylistic flourishes such as behind-the-back passes and no-look passes over his shoulder. He drove to the basket and, as his right hand went up into the air, he slyly dropped a pass behind him to an oncoming teammate. He heard the crowd's gasps; he knew some fans showed up to see him work his tricks. Sometimes, late in games in which the outcome was already determined, Cousy executed one of his newest innovations purely for the sake of entertainment.

He also pushed the limits of his relationship with Auerbach through good-natured fun. At training camp in Ellsworth, Maine, in autumn 1951, Cousy and Macauley stole Auerbach's prized red fedora. When Auerbach stepped from the shower, he noticed it was missing. He looked at Cousy. "If you did anything to that hat, so help me, I'll murder you," he said. "Where is it?"

"Right there," Cousy said, and he pointed to Macauley, in the shower, wearing the red fedora as water cascaded down on it. Auerbach exploded with rage as Macauley tossed the hat to Cousy, who began cutting it with scissors. Auerbach's howls lasted only until he found a new red fedora, purchased by his players, in the front seat of his car.

Cousy tried to draw attention to the league. In Fort Wayne, Indianapolis, and Rochester, sometimes with Macauley or Sharman in tow, he taxied to local radio stations to promote that night's game. Deejays spun records by Patti Page, Eddie Fisher, and Tony Bennett and asked him a few questions about a sport they didn't understand.

That fall, following the birth of their daughter Marie, he and Missie purchased a home in Worcester but couldn't move in until year's end. For three months, Cousy shared an apartment with Cooper, while Missie, at Walter Brown's invitation, took their infant daughter to Brown's second home on Cape Cod, a nice place near the water. Cousy paid visits whenever he could. At that time of year, the Cape was isolated, and Cousy invariably drove back to Boston thinking, "Geez, it could be spooky for a young pretty girl with a baby all by herself here." Missie, he decided, was a strong, independent spirit.

The Celtics again finished second that season, this time with a 39-27 record, a game behind Syracuse in the Eastern Division, and the Knicks eliminated them again in the playoffs. Cousy made first-team all-league in 1951–52 for the first of ten consecutive seasons and averaged nearly twenty-two points per game, third best in the league. His star continued to rise.

On February 17, 1952, Chuck Cooper, typically self-contained, snapped during a game against the Milwaukee Hawks in Moline. With 1:21 to play, Milwaukee leading 96–95, a Hawks player called Cooper a "black bastard." Cooper dared him to repeat it. When he did, Cooper pushed him as hard as he could. His opponent didn't fight back, but both benches cleared, and opposing players paired off and started swinging. Cooper and the Hawks' Dick Mehen exchanged punches.

Milwaukee coach Doxie Moore charged Auerbach, hit him, and jumped on his back. Bob Brannum, the Celtics' brawny forward who counted protecting Auerbach among his chief assignments, pulled Moore from his coach; just then, Milwaukee's Mel Hutchins punched Brannum. As twelve hundred fans jeered, police rushed onto the floor to restore order; a squad car was paged. Both coaches were ejected, as were Cooper and the Hawks' Don Boven. After the game, won by the Hawks, 97–95, fights between opposing players broke out in the dressing rooms; police ushered the teams from the field house.

In another game in Boston, Warriors center Neil Johnston threw a hard block at Cousy, and Cooper grabbed Johnston and threw him over the scorer's table. Benches cleared. Cooper punched Johnston and put another opponent, forward Bob Zawoluk, in a choke hold. It wasn't until Cooper saw the photos in the next morning's newspapers that he realized that Cousy hadn't participated in this free-for-all. He stood to the side and casually watched it. That was Cousy's way. He wasn't a fighter.

Though much less publicized, the Cousy-Cooper cross-race friendship was akin to the relationship between Dodgers shortstop Pee Wee Reese, a white Kentuckian, and Jackie Robinson. In sensationalized retellings of a Dodgers-Reds game at Crosley Field in Cincinnati in 1947, fans in the box seats targeted Robinson with racist harangues, and Reese walked over, stood by his teammate's side, and put his arm around his shoulder. That gesture is even commemorated in a bronze statue of the two men in front of Brooklyn's minor league ballpark, except Reese never did that; contemporary news accounts made no mention of it.

Cousy and Cooper shared their own moments of solidarity. On February 28, 1952, two weeks after the fight in Moline, the Celtics traveled to Raleigh, North Carolina, where they beat Rochester, 91–72, in a neutral-site regular-season game. Cooper wasn't permitted to stay with his white teammates that night at their segregated hotel. The Celtics were scheduled to catch a flight to New York the following morning. Cooper told Auerbach he would take a postmidnight sleeper train to New York by himself.

Hearing this, Cousy told Auerbach he wanted to travel with Cooper, and he did.

In the late-night darkness, the Raleigh train station was quiet and mostly empty as the two Celtics drank a few beers and waited for their train. Together, they walked to the men's restroom, only to discover there were two, "White" and "Colored." Cousy had read about such signs but had never seen one. He fumbled for words to ease Cooper's discomfort, at one point saying, "Hitler persecuted the Jews and so did a lot of others. And I was just reading in the papers where they threw bombs at Catholic churches somewhere in Louisiana not long ago." Cooper spoke softly: "But you can't always tell a Jew or a Catholic by looking at him." Cousy felt embarrassed in a way he never had before: He felt embarrassed to be white.

Cousy and Cooper walked away from the restrooms toward the far end of the platform. They shared a mischievous grin and looked around to see if anyone was watching. Then, in an act of brotherhood, they unzipped their flies and, side by side, peed off the platform. To Cousy, this defiance of segregation felt good and right.

"It was our Rosa Parks moment that we couldn't talk about," Cousy says now.

Cooper later would say of Cousy, "I had great respect for his attitudes and approach to life. There was a certain bond between us that went beyond being teammates; we were *friends*." Cousy, he said, was "the highest kind of individual. . . . Bob is as free of racism as any white person I've ever known. He's just a beautiful person."

Such moments pushed Cousy to begin to think more deeply about racial prejudice. He sat next to Jackie Robinson on a plane flight from Boston to Montreal, the two athletes bound for the same dinner banquet. Robinson might have played in Boston, too. In April 1945, the Red Sox had given a secret tryout at Fenway Park to him and two other Negro Leagues players; nothing came of it, though, and the Red

Sox wouldn't have a black player for another fourteen years. Robinson viewed the experience as a humiliating charade and signed with the Dodgers eighteen months later. Cousy attempted to make small talk during the flight, but Robinson seemed to withdraw. Cousy did not push it and let the rest of the flight pass in silence. Later he reflected on this missed opportunity: "I didn't say anything to him that gave him reassurance about which side I was on. If I were black, I would put all white people in the same category—until proven otherwise."

During this time, Cousy learned that Catholic churches in the South were segregated, and he sought an explanation from Father Tiernan at Holy Cross. Cousy told the man who had officiated at his wedding that he was confused. The Catholic Church had been teaching him about the equality of the human animal since he had reached the age of reason, Cousy explained. Yet in the South it practiced segregation. He asked Tiernan, "How do you reconcile that?" Only two years out of Holy Cross, Cousy was not looking to make waves. He believed deeply in the church. Still, he heard nothing from the priest that convinced him the church's segregation was acceptable. He just didn't know what to do about it.

It was no secret that gamblers lurked in the shadows of the NBA. The Celtics sometimes played on Saturday nights in the Northeast and caught a train back to Boston, arriving in the wee hours on Sunday morning. The team rented some rooms at the Hotel Buckminster so players could sleep a few hours before playing at Boston Garden on Sunday afternoon at two o'clock. Cousy and Macauley typically got up and lumbered off to eight o'clock Mass on Sunday morning, and as they passed through the hotel lobby they saw the "unsavory types sitting around and waiting to see how you would come in with a game that afternoon," Cousy says. These, they knew, were gamblers, seeking information and insight to gain a competitive advantage. Cousy wouldn't make eye contact with them. If they called out to him, as they sometimes did, asking, "How ya' feelin' today, Cooz?" he wouldn't answer. Sometimes, as they passed through the lobby, Cousy, Macauley, or Sharman faked a limp as if they were hurt, or hid an arm inside their winter coat, letting a sleeve hang loose as if they'd injured their shoulder, Cousy says, "just to piss off or throw off anybody who was watching us."

A point-shaving scandal erupted in 1951 and devastated the college game. The district attorney in New York, Frank Hogan, made dozens of arrests after discovering that gamblers had fixed college games in seventeen states, spreading outward from the City College of New York to the University of Kentucky and other schools. The scandal decimated the NBA's Indianapolis Olympians when two of its stars, Alex Groza and Ralph Beard, admitted to their involvement in a point-shaving scandal while in college at Kentucky. After the 1951 season, Podoloff banned both players from the NBA for having consorted with gamblers; not long after, the Olympians folded.

Where others saw destruction, the shrewd Auerbach saw opportunity: Kentucky's 1952–53 season was canceled, but its stars, Frank Ramsey, Cliff Hagan, and Lou Tsioropoulos, planned to return the following year as graduate students to play one more intercollegiate season. In the 1953 NBA draft, Auerbach drafted Ramsey in the first round, Hagan in the third, and Tsioropoulos in the seventh. Their class had graduated, Auerbach reminded executives from other teams; Auerbach was willing to wait a year for them to join the Celtics. "You can't do that," the Knicks' Ned Irish said after Auerbach selected Ramsey, to which Auerbach replied, "Read the minutes of the meeting." All three Kentuckians suddenly belonged to the Celtics.

Rumors spread that Cousy was involved in the college fixes; point guards were especially vulnerable to such charges since they controlled the ball near game's end, when point spreads often hung in the balance. On January 31, 1953, two detectives approached Cousy outside Madison Square Garden. They asked him to come to the DA's office to answer questions. With the Celtics about to board a train, Cousy arranged to see the district attorney when the Celtics returned to New York on February 17.

Walter Brown heard the rumors. The thought of Cousy being involved with gamblers haunted him. He pulled aside sportswriter Clif Keane of the *Globe* and asked a favor: "Will you go to Cousy and ask him if he is involved in any stuff with gamblers? If he is, I'm ruined."

Keane had three distinguishing qualities: He seldom stopped blinking, constantly fiddled with his tie, and wrote some of the most acerbic prose in town. For thirteen years, he had been a low-level worker in editorial and advertising. When a spot in the sports department came open in 1939, Keane took it. In locker rooms, he needled and provoked players, all but daring them to retaliate. Players called him Poison Pen.

Keane approached Cousy to report Brown's concern about the gambling rumors. Keane said, "Are you involved in any way? If you are will you talk to Brown fast? He's getting sick about it." Cousy assured Keane that he wasn't involved with gamblers, never had been, and never would be. He went to Brown's office and told him as much and said he was bound for the DA's office in New York.

"Mr. Brown, I've never in my life done a dishonest thing either on or off the court," Cousy said. Brown accepted him at his word.

Cousy read the newspapers. He saw the boldface headlines about the bust of Beard and Groza. They had been approached by investigators after leaving an NBA game at Chicago Stadium in October 1951, and that night, under intense questioning, admitted they had accepted money from gamblers to shave points in order to affect the final point spread in college games. Beard, just twenty-two and an all-NBA selection as a rookie, spent fifteen hours locked up in Cook County jail with prisoners he later described as psychos and winos. He told investigators that he took a total of $1,300 from gamblers for five games. "I wish I knew why I did it," Beard said a few days after his arrest. "I've been asking myself and it doesn't make sense. The money was nothing." Suspended from the NBA for life, Beard later tried to form a minor league team, but the judge sent him a telegram, according to Beard, saying, "If I so much as touched a basketball in a YMCA, he'd put my ass in jail."

Walter Brown wasn't the only one with big stakes in the outcome. For Cousy, still just twenty-four, with a wife and now two daughters in diapers, the personal stakes—his reputation, his NBA career—were immense.

On February 17, a handful of detectives grilled him with questions. Vincent O'Connor, the assistant DA, told him that a bookmaker, who had since died, had implicated Cousy among the college players with whom he had done business. Even as Cousy insisted he didn't know the bookie, the grilling continued, his guilt seemingly assumed. He suddenly wished he had brought an attorney. After several hours, the detectives took a break. Cousy went to dinner and, when he returned, stewed in an anteroom for several hours. The detectives finally called for him. They told him two gamblers had just confessed that they had double-crossed the bookie and used Cousy, without his knowledge, to do it. The detectives cleared Cousy. Though he knew he had never accepted a dime from gamblers, his relief was enormous. There was so much to lose, he knew. Ralph Beard was a tenacious little player, Cousy thought. He might have become a Hall of Famer, but he had lost everything: his basketball career, his marriage, and his good name. Soon, Beard was in Louisville, bouncing from job to job, laying pipe and selling cars. At O'Connor's request, Cousy later testified before a grand jury, restating what he had told the New York detectives. O'Connor thanked him and said if he ever needed proof of his innocence, he would provide it, gladly.

Juliette Cousy liked to say, "Everybody loves Bob Cousy!" She didn't know whether a basketball was inflated or stuffed. She took pleasure in her son's success in the game anyway.

She attended a game at Madison Square Garden and saw her son collide with another player and fall heavily to the floor.

Groggy, he looked up with blurred vision a few moments later to see three figures kneeling over him—Auerbach, trainer Buddy Le-Roux, and . . . his mother.

"Roby," Juliette said, with a look of fright, *"comment ça va?"*

Her presence worked faster than smelling salts. Bob Cousy's head cleared at once; his eyes grew wide. *Jesus, Mary, and Joseph!*

His mother was on the court in front of his teammates, in front of Arnold Auerbach, in front of the fans at Madison Square Garden, hub of the basketball universe. It was the most embarrassing moment of his career.

He stood and directed his mother off the court.

For all future games, he decided, Juliette Cousy was persona non grata. No more free tickets for Mom.

6

COURTING FAME

By the middle of his third NBA season, Cousy and his style of play had become the subject of three magazine covers and nine feature articles in seven weeks. "Now Cousy is Target for Tonight every night in the NBA," wrote the *Globe*'s Jerry Nason in February 1953. "Bumped, elbowed, pushed, held—Cousy's scoring average is shrinking, as his publicity expands, but his assists are piling up like the Alps."

The pro game needed Cousy's infusion of élan. NBA games tended to be slow, grinding affairs with too many fouls and too many free throws. Once a team opened up a lead, it put the ball in a deep freeze— stalling, stalling, stalling—until finally time expired. It certainly did not make for good television.

Cousy worked hard to diversify his game. The sports editor of the Worcester newspaper spotted him practicing alone in a local high school gym on an off day, dribbling hard up the court and putting up at the free throw line a one-handed runner. Cousy explained that NBA teams were reacting as if they knew he would pass on the fast break once he reached the opposing foul line. He would remake his game, keep opponents guessing.

The Celtics won a playoff series in 1953 for the first time in their seven-year history largely because of Cousy. It required four overtimes and Cousy's career-high fifty points to eliminate Syracuse, 111–105, in the Eastern Division semifinals, a performance one Boston writer called "the greatest one-man show ever seen in Boston Garden or any other place in this town." The game was a long, tedious, brawling affair with 130 free throws, twelve players fouling out, two ejected for fighting, and Cousy, playing all but two of the game's sixty-eight minutes, converting thirty of thirty-two free throws, including his final seventeen in a row. He was the only player to make more than five field goals. In the second quarter, players exchanged blows, and Boston police and Garden ushers needed five minutes to restore order and clear the floor. Cousy delivered one big play after another. As time expired in regulation, Cousy was fouled and made his free throw, tying the game at 77. In the first overtime, he scored six of Boston's nine points. Too tense to watch, Brown walked out before the start of the second overtime to have coffee in his office. The Celtics' publicity man, McHugh, overcome by headaches, stretched out on the floor near the scorer's table. In the third overtime, Cousy scored eight of the Celtics' nine points, including a twenty-five-foot set shot at the buzzer to tie the score at 99. The Nationals took a five-point lead in the fourth overtime, but Cousy scored the next five points to tie it, and then four more to win it. Cousy broke Mikan's playoff-game scoring record of forty-seven points. A *Globe* writer suggested that Cousy could have brought back baseball's Boston Braves, who had just moved to Milwaukee, because on this day "he could have done anything." Normally Missie would have been cheering from Wives Row, but two couples were visiting, and so she listened by radio from home, though not until the Red Sox exhibition baseball from Florida finished. Only then, with two minutes left in regulation, could she hear the Celtics-Nationals radio broadcast in Worcester. After the game, Cooz called her from the Garden and told her to "get right over to church and thank God for what He did for us."

Only that morning, Cousy was writ large in Dave Egan's column in Boston's racy afternoon tabloid, the *Daily Record*. "The Celtics have won their way to a high place in our affections. They won it on raw ability alone. Nobody helped them to the highest stature that any team in the history of our town has known. They are humble men, as they play their second fiddle," Egan wrote, "but believe me when I say that they created the greatest sport ever known to the race of man in the history of civilization. These basketball players are our greatest athletes, and of all of them, the greatest is Bob Cousy."

As Boston's most widely read sports columnist, Egan helped the Celtics gain a foothold in Boston. A Harvard man (he played on its freshman basketball team) with a fondness for the horse track and controversy, Egan didn't attend many games, though occasionally he was seen sitting in his sports editor Sammy Cohen's Box No. 1 at the Garden (center court, best seat in the house) or at Fenway Park with Red Sox owner Tom Yawkey. Egan had a fondness for alcohol, and Cohen tried to keep him from bars. His column, known as "The Colonel" (though no one knew why) was eminently readable and often inflammatory.

Egan gushed over Cousy. "He used to write [glowing] columns about me," Cousy would say, "that would embarrass my mother." Bill McSweeny, a colleague on the *Daily Record*, says of Egan, "He'd call up at ten o'clock in the morning, or ten thirty, and he'd say [dictating], 'The Colonel by Dave Egan. Finish the rest of it for me, will you?'" In such instances, a colleague would write Egan's column for him. The *Daily Record*'s managing editor once read Egan's column in the office and marveled to sportswriter Alex Maclean, "Wouldn't you like to be able to write like that?" Maclean suppressed a laugh since he had written Egan's column that day. After Cousy's fifty points, Egan (presumably) turned up the hyperbole a few notches in his column: "They tore the rafters from the Garden roof, and they went crazy for Bob Cousy as they never went crazy for any athlete in the history of New England sports."

Though the Knicks subsequently eliminated the Celtics in the division finals, Brown would say that Cousy's fifty-point game brought a new level of acceptance for the Celtics. Attendance climbed by 11 percent the next season, to nearly 7,500, a nice bounce, though that still meant that about half of the Garden's seats remained empty.

Not until Cousy's fourth NBA season did Auerbach publicly call him the greatest backcourt man he had ever seen. Even so, some opponents didn't take well to Cousy's dribbling act. In Baltimore in December 1953, the Celtics led in overtime as he attempted to dribble out the clock. A brutish guard for the Bullets named Paul (The Bear) Hoffman, frustrated by his inability to take the ball from Cousy, body-blocked him to the floor, twisting Cousy's knee. Auerbach was aghast. Earlier he had been thrown out of the game by referee Arnie Heft. "Get out or I'll call the cops," Heft had warned, and when Auerbach wouldn't leave, he called for the cops. Baltimore's public address announcer celebrated Auerbach's removal. When Auerbach got tossed, the announcer leaned into his microphone and said, "There goes Auerbach out of the place! He's kicked out of the building!" Auerbach took a seat in the crowd but rushed back to the court when Hoffman leveled Cousy. Heft pushed the coach away, saying, "Rules is rules. You're out of the game. Stay away from Cousy." "There's the greatest basketball player in the world," Auerbach replied, "and you won't let me help him?" Heft waved Auerbach away. Auerbach shouted at Hoffman, "I'll get you for this!"

The Celtics' strongman, forward Bob Brannum, would have his vengeance. The two teams met again in Boston six days later, and fans from Greensboro in the South to Omaha in the West would see the game on television, the first of fourteen NBA Game of the Week telecasts that season. Many of those viewers would be watching an NBA game for the first time. Podoloff warned coaches and players on both teams to be on their best behavior. The league, he said, couldn't afford a hooligan spirit to turn away fans.

Clif Keane, writing in the *Globe*, expected to see a Celtics payback—and blood. "There may be some spilled," Keane advised readers who planned to watch on television. "Keep a sponge handy so it won't sprinkle on your rug."

Brannum, as Cousy's protector, had fully scripted Hoffman's payback. When the Bear penetrated from the top of the key, with Cousy backtracking and guarding him closely, Brannum shouted from the low post to Cousy, "LET HIM THROUGH! LET HIM THROUGH!"

Cousy stepped aside and Brannum moved in front of the onrushing Hoffman and assumed the posture of a football blocker, fists nearly touching in front of his chest, elbows out at his sides. He caught Hoffman under his throat and dropped him. "The damn building shook," Cousy says. Brannum stood over the fallen Hoffman, payback exacted. Hoffman rose, sprinted toward the Celtics' bench, and screamed at Auerbach, "You did it, you sonovabitch." And Auerbach, smirking, answered, "You're damn right I did it."

A year later, the league instituted a new rule: A team must shoot within twenty-four seconds of taking control of the ball or lose possession. Its impact was immediate. The twenty-four-second clock not only increased scoring, it kept teams from stalling for minutes at a time and reduced late-game fouls and fights. With the shot clock, the Celtics, in 1954–55, became the first team in league history to average more than a hundred points per game; NBA teams averaged ninety-three points per game that season, an increase of thirteen points a game from the previous year. Three seasons later, every NBA team averaged more than a hundred points per game. The shot clock liberated players and brought new energy to the game.

Cousy would lead the league in assists for eight straight seasons between 1952 and 1959, and his scoring average, among the league leaders, never deviated from between eighteen and twenty-one points per game. Perhaps more than anyone, Cousy was grateful for the twenty-four-second clock. It fed his playing style: More offensive motion and fast breaks meant more opportunities for Cooz to perform as the stylist. It also saved him from physical hardship near game's end and likely added a few seasons to his career.

Cousy pushed the limits of basketball style and etiquette. Other American showmen of the time—actor James Dean and singer Elvis Presley, renegades of a different nature—creatively pushed boundaries in their own ways and flourished. By his own estimation, 90 percent of Cousy's game was orthodox—"straightforward, conservative, bread-and-butter," he says. But it was the fancy stuff—the remaining 10 percent—that made him famous. "It's kind of a misnomer," he says now, "that I am associated to the degree that I am with that. Anytime I could do it the orthodox way, that's what I would choose."

His bravado grew. If a player on the court or a fan from the crowd got under Cousy's skin, he would get even in his own way. Once, Sweetwater Clifton of the Knicks pulled one of his old Globetrotter maneuvers, holding the ball out wide from his body, toying with the Celtics—not shooting or passing, just palming it in his massive right hand—and the crowd roared with laughter. Cousy responded on the next possession by dribbling up to Clifton and pretending to throw an overhand pass directly at Sweetwater's face. But as he wound up, Cousy let the ball roll across his back and caught it in his left palm. Then, completing his windmill delivery, he stuck out his empty right hand as if to shake with Clifton. The fans loved it. Later, Cousy decided that he'd let his competitiveness get the best of him and apologized to Clifton.

To Cousy, the most rabid and malicious fans tended to be in smaller cities such as Rochester, Fort Wayne, or Syracuse, where one woman stuck opposing players with a hairpin. At Convention Hall in Philadelphia, one fan habitually abused the Celtics without mercy. Loud, obese, and a friend of Eddie Gottlieb's, he sat in the first row beneath the basket at nearly every game. Cousy dreaded seeing and hearing him.

One day, the fan cursed the Celtics with a steady stream of four-letter words. Hearing this during halftime warmups, Cousy stood at the free throw line, called for teammate Jack Nichols, and choreographed a plan to silence the fan once and for all. "Jack, station yourself with your back to the guy," Cousy instructed. "Try to line yourself up with him. I'll throw you the ball and you step out of the way." The fan was only about six or seven feet beyond the baseline. Nichols took his place; Cousy nodded to him and threw his fastball. Nichols stepped back as the ball whistled past.

It caught the fan by surprise and struck him on the nose. He yelped. Blood spurted. He fell to the floor. Cousy wasn't sure if he had broken the man's nose, but he saw a lot of blood.

Auerbach loved it.

Cousy thought it might have been the most accurate pass he threw in thirteen NBA seasons.

Cousy knew that Walter Brown was one in a million, but not a millionaire. In a 1960 interview, Brown would say that Cousy, Macauley, and Sharman weren't overpaid for their skills and energy during the team's early years, "but they were overpaid for what it brought in at the box office." Brown approached him and Macauley with a look of sadness to ask if the players might give him a few extra months to deliver their playoff shares.

Cousy, as captain, made the pitch to his teammates: "This guy is the best owner in the league," Cousy said. "Let's face it, we'll all have to go out and sell insurance and, God forbid, we don't want to do that. So let's go along with it." They agreed to wait.

Every NBA team was losing money. Cousy understood that, but increasingly he believed that players had no voice and that team owners took advantage of them. This violated his sense of fairness. If players were fined unfairly, or forced to play in an unreasonable number of exhibition games, or given only a five-dollar per diem, they had no outlet to express their dissatisfaction, no established method through which to negotiate. They needed representation. Though never a union member, Cousy grew up with an allegiance to the working class.

He decided in 1952 that it was time for pro basketball to have a players union, and that he would be the one to create it. He rated among the league's best and highest-paid players, and, like Mikan, his unique playing style sold tickets in every arena in the league. That made Cousy less vulnerable to retribution by owners.

He went to see Brown first. "I sugared him off," Cousy said. Careful not use the word *union*, he told Brown, "We need some sort of interaction between players, coaches and owners. We are going to start a group. I feel that I'm the one to do it." Brown gave Cousy his blessing.

"We need class," Cousy said at the time. "We've got to stabilize so we can command respect. . . . We can't go around apologizing because we're professional basketball players. We've got to have pride—pride in ourselves and in our teams and in our league. What's good for the NBA is good for us all—and what's bad is bad for us all. We need a players association so we can fight for these things." Podoloff had bigger problems as league president and little patience for a burgeoning players union.

It took time. In summer 1954, Cousy contacted a top player from each of the other eight NBA teams, including Dolph Schayes of Syracuse, Philadelphia's Paul Arizin, the Knicks' Carl Braun, and Andy Phillip of Fort Wayne, seeking their support for a new players union. They were all in except Baltimore, which soon folded, and Fort Wayne.

"Why?" Cousy asked.

Fort Wayne's Phillip said, "Why do you think?" The answer was that Pistons owner Fred Zollner, an industrialist, never had a union in his company, and he sure as hell wasn't having one meddling with his basketball team.

For two years and more, Cousy and his loosely organized association pushed on without the participation of Fort Wayne's players. Cousy listened to players around the league and heard their gripes. He took careful notes. In January 1955, he delivered five demands to Podoloff: 1. Pay the back salaries of the defunct Baltimore team's players; 2. Establish a twenty-game limit on exhibition games (players didn't get paid extra for playing in these games); 3. Abolish the so-called whispering fine referees could unilaterally dole out to players during games ("That will cost you fifteen bucks!"); 4. Pay twenty-five dollars to players for public appearances other than media interviews or charity functions; and 5. Establish an impartial arbitration board to settle player-owner disputes.

Owners, struggling for every nickel, refused to recognize the union and agreed only to award two weeks' back pay to Baltimore players. Even this seemed a colossal victory for the players given the stinginess of owners across the league. Eddie Gottlieb often paid his Philadelphia players in cash; once, in 1954, rookie Gene Shue stepped from practice at Convention Hall and watched Gottlieb count out the money Shue was owed—$550 paid in five-, ten-, and one-dollar bills. Shue grew up poor and couldn't believe that his pockets were filled with so much cash, but when he threw the bills on his bed, he counted only $540. He told Gottlieb he was ten dollars short. "You sure?" Gottlieb asked. He handed over the ten bucks and, a few weeks later, traded Shue to the Knicks.

Bit by bit the union took shape. Cousy sought help from Connie Hurley, a lawyer at the white-shoe Boston firm Hale and Dorr. "We'll have to do it pro bono," Cousy told him, "because we don't have any money." Hurley was a former minor league baseball player; Casey

Stengel was once his manager, and he served as Ted Williams's personal attorney. He agreed to help NBA players. Cousy thought his presence legitimized the cause. Soon Cousy and Hurley were sitting outside Podoloff's office at the end of each season with their list of grievances and demands, and they were usually made to wait at least forty-five minutes. "I never felt any love for Podoloff," Cousy says. "I never had any respect for him."

They made union representatives out of the NBA's all-star players, a pragmatic decision. Cousy wanted to meet with the player representatives once a year, and they could do that at the annual All-Star Game and have their trips paid by owners. Some players around the league weren't interested in participating in a union; others took too long before paying their ten dollars in annual dues. As his frustrations deepened, Cousy considered stepping aside.

Finally, in spring 1957, nearly five years after he had conceived of the idea, the NBA Board of Governors formally recognized the players union and agreed to nearly all of its demands. The Celtics center Gene Conley deadpanned decades later that owners agreed to give players "more soap in the shower room, and two towels instead of one." But the gains were, for the time, significant. Owners agreed to: 1. Abolish the whispering fine; 2. Raise the per diem to seven dollars per day; 3. Free regular players from reporting to training camp earlier than four weeks prior to the season; 4. Eliminate exhibition games within three days of the season opener; 5. Pay reasonable moving expenses for players traded during the off-season; and 6. Refer player-owner disputes to the NBA president or a committee of three NBA governors chosen by the players.

The effects would ripple across the decades. Sixty years later, the average NBA player salary exceeded $6 million, more than the average salaries in professional baseball and football. In 1957, Cousy wrote a note from the road to Missie after the union achieved formal recognition: "I don't think I've ever received a greater thrill or felt more personal satisfaction than I do at this moment."

AUERBACH'S SECRET

Cousy had spent five seasons with Auerbach. He knew him inside out. Auerbach was the most exasperating, maddening, and uncouth man he had ever met, but a great basketball coach. Auerbach was worth at least six victories a season, Cousy believed, just from his bench tactics. Auerbach knew basketball. By game's end, Arnold Auerbach, through intimidation and manipulation, had worked his way inside the heads of his own men, the opposing coach and his men, the referees, and even the shot-clock operator, and when he lit his cigar from the bench to signify a Celtics victory was in hand, he got inside the heads of every fan rooting for the opposing team. By the end of his coaching career, fans across the league had thrown at Auerbach a beer can, a lighted cigar, rotten tomatoes, eggs, paper hatchets, snowballs, women's handbags, and peanuts still in their shells. They booed him, naturally, but that didn't upset him. He expected boos. "What are you going to do?" he would say. "A boo is a boo. Generally, you don't take the time to figure out what kind of boo it is, whether it's a good-natured boo, for instance. It's a boo and the hell with it."

Both Auerbach and Cousy knew the Celtics had hit a wall. The Knicks had eliminated them in the playoffs during Cousy's first three seasons, and Syracuse the next two. One season ended in the playoffs with Cousy sprawled on the court, drained and bawling. The Celtics needed to make some personnel changes; that much they both knew.

Even without an NBA championship, Cousy's celebrity grew. He was pulling down a $20,000 salary and endorsing toothpaste, chewing gum, sneakers, and a Seamless rubber basketball. At a testimonial dinner, his teammates had presented him with a small sterling silver box on which they engraved "Houdini, 1954." When a writer from *Sports Illustrated* arrived at a practice in 1955 and told Auerbach he was working on a Cousy profile, Auerbach, hoping to spread publicity among his players, suggested he write about Brannum instead. Auerbach didn't like the way sportswriters godded up Cousy. It wasn't helpful to the inner workings of his team.

Auerbach was not turning away from his point guard. In fact, they were about to draw closer. He asked Cousy to join him, in summer 1955, on a month-long tour of France, Belgium, Greece, and Germany sponsored by the U.S. State Department. When Cousy agreed, they met with Secretary of State John Foster Dulles, heady stuff. The trip, under the auspices of the U.S. Information Service, was designed to spread American culture to foreign lands—in this case, teaching the American game of basketball through lectures, demonstrations, and clinics. Auerbach and Cousy would be joined by Adolph Rupp, the Kentucky coach, and two referees, Sid Borgia and John Nucatola.

The trip proved memorable. Auerbach wore a beret, and Cousy needled, "Hey, I'm the Frenchman. . . ." In restaurants and hotels, Auerbach acted like the rude American, and Cousy pleaded, "Arnold, you are embarrassing me!" Auerbach shopped aggressively along the way, buying clothes, furniture, and knickknacks and adding to his growing collection of letter openers, always bargaining for the best deals.

Escorted by State Department officials, the group spent a few days sightseeing in Paris, visiting the Louvre, the Folies Bergère, and, more discreetly, a Parisian sex house. There, they sat downstairs in a living room, and a madam brought out beautiful young women. These women approached the Americans, sat on their laps, and twirled their hair. Cousy says, "Arnold was kind of shy—not that I was any James Bond about it." To these young women, the Americans politely said no thank you. They were escorted into a room to see a live performance—a threesome having sex on a bed. Cousy knew that Rupp had a heart condition and saw him throw a heart pill into his mouth. Nucatola looked as if he couldn't wait to get out of the room. On the way out, Cousy saw Rupp sit on the stairs, ashen-faced.

In Germany they gave a clinic for U.S. military stationed in Europe as well as delegates from seven European nations. Cousy lectured in English and impressed Auerbach by answering questions in English and French. In Wiesbaden, Cousy happened onto some old Holy Cross friends and, after a night with them drinking too much beer, awoke early, hungover and thinking, *Oh my God, I've got to lecture at nine!* His lecture topic: physical conditioning. Cousy worked long hours to prepare for his talks. Auerbach didn't. In his lectures Auerbach did not use notes or a blackboard. He just stood up and started talking, and when he finished he would say to the State Department man, "Come on! Where are we going shopping today?" In lectures Auerbach often cited his book *Basketball for the Player, the Fan and the Coach*, a handy primer published by Pocket Books in 1953 that would later be published in Russian, Italian, Polish, and Romanian. Auerbach said he wrote the book to improve the image of professional coaches. "People had a tendency to rate us as ruffians," he said. Auerbach's fighting spirit infused the book, particularly in the strategies he recommended: "Grabbing or pulling the pants or shirt of the opponent can be very aggravating. . . . Study the official's personality.

Decide your attitude on that basis. . . . Wait until the other team has started warming up and then request their basket. This request must be honored away from home."

Basketball was still a curiosity to most Europeans. The audiences at these lectures and demonstrations weren't large, but those who came usually stayed until the end. It was the first of several foreign trips for Cousy and Auerbach. Together they would see the world. Their relationship deepened.

There was a talented big man out on the West Coast who could transform the Celtics, and Auerbach was determined to get him. He was a dominant rebounder and extraordinary shot blocker. His name was Bill Russell, and he played for the University of San Francisco, a team that had just won the NCAA championship. Russell was about six-foot-ten and a lean 215 pounds, a track-and-field athlete, wiry strong, and if the Celtics could obtain him, everything would change. Auerbach's college coach at George Washington, Bill Reinhart, saw Russell play and told Auerbach, "This kid is as smart as hell and he can really get you the ball."

Auerbach had people out west keeping close tabs on Russell. Pete Newell, the Cal-Berkeley coach, reported that Russell blocked shots from all angles. Newell said Russell moved laterally in a wide arc and used his quick leap to block shots from the shooter's back or side. He put a trauma on Newell's shooters that lasted several games. Auerbach's former players Scolari and Barksdale liked what they saw in Russell, too. "This kid can't shoot to save his ass," Scolari said. But then he added, "He's only the greatest basketball player I ever saw." Sammy Cohen, the sports editor of the Hearst papers in Boston, heard Auerbach making phone calls to the West Coast from Cohen's house at three o'clock in the morning (midnight out west). Auerbach reminded his friends in the West to say nice things to Russell about the Celtics.

Perhaps it was an omen of big things to come that Cousy first laid eyes on Russell at the White House. President Dwight Eisenhower, concerned about the lack of fitness of America's youth, hosted a luncheon on the topic in July 1955 and invited amateur and professional athletes of the past and present, in what *Sports Illustrated* called "the greatest array of U.S. sports stars ever gathered together in one place." Sitting with Eisenhower were baseball's Willie Mays, Hank Greenberg, and Commissioner Ford Frick, boxers Gene Tunney and Archie Moore, rower John Kelly, tennis star Tony Trabert, Cousy, and, representing college basketball, Russell.

It was a big year for Cousy, first a trip to Europe and now to the White House. As he stood with the other sports celebrities, a presidential aide said, "The president will be down in two-and-a-half minutes. Would you kindly form a semicircle because the president would like to greet you individually?" Eisenhower arrived exactly on schedule. He greeted each athlete and said a few words to the group ("You all look bigger on television," he said, "all but Mr. Russell"). Then he asked the group to follow him outside for a photo op.

A voice called out: "Wait a minute. I've got something to say." Eisenhower turned. It was the boxer Archie Moore, who took out a few notes and talked for several minutes. Moore said he wanted to help raise money for the president's initiative by holding amateur fights across the nation and he assured that he would show up at each one. After an awkward silence, Eisenhower cleared his throat, and said, "Well, Archie, you probably should have been a politician." That broke the tension; the group laughed and followed Eisenhower out to the waiting press cameras.

Russell had driven across the country for this event with his father and his future wife, Rose. Cousy shook Russell's hand that day and, in passing, they politely agreed it would be wonderful to play one day as teammates.

Sammy Cohen sat with Auerbach at the weekly basketball luncheon at the Hotel Lenox and heard Harvard's basketball coach give a report on a tournament, won by USF, that he had just attended out west. No one in the Boston sports press knew at the time that Auerbach coveted Russell.

When the Harvard coach said that Russell had no chance of making it in the NBA, Auerbach leaned toward Cohen and said, loud enough for everyone in New England to hear, "He's full of shit."

SECTION II

Dynasty

RUSSELL'S ARRIVAL

The old captain has time on his hands. He closely follows current events in the nation and around the world, more than he ever did as a player. He's affected by what he reads and by what he sees on TV day after day, the terrorism and mean-spirited politics and young black men shot dead by police. He immerses himself in history. He's just read two books about the Founding Fathers and wonders about Thomas Jefferson. Now he's on the phone ("It's old number fourteen," he says in a playful greeting) and he's calling from his enclosed back patio. About Jefferson, he says, "An intellectual, a great, curious mind interested in everything from gardening to the state of the world, all of that is in his favor." He's troubled, though, by Jefferson's intimate relationship with his slave Sally Hemings. "But he was still bonking Sally every time he was home, produced kids, never introduced them or took responsibility for them other than they lived on his plantation." He reconciles it this way: "In theory, intellectually he was against slavery. Well, I know it's different times that we have lived through, but I am sorry, slavery is forever. I'd like to think that if I'd lived two hundred years ago, I would've felt as strongly about 'How the hell do you enslave a group of people?' as I do about it now." In such moments, when a topic stirs his intellect, his voice quickens, and he attacks that topic, as he once did opposing defenses, from different angles, his summation often beginning with the phrase, "And so at the end of the day . . ." As part of an old man's ruminations, he's also trying to map his own history, and the Celtics' evolution during his career, and Auerbach's genius, and Russell's arrival, which, over time, redefined, or perhaps diminished, his own stardom. Perceptions change, and so does the way history is told. What he once believed as a young man, as all driven, self-certain young men do—that in the heat of competition it was about him, even when Russell was there—he's not so sure about as an old man. What once seemed sharply defined, etched in black and white, now seems more nuanced, etched in gray. His thinking about the past deepens, it evolves. An old man long removed from making history remembers what he did with the Boston Celtics and reckons how and where he fits in, and what it all means.

As coach, Red Auerbach had no time to read history. He had no assistant coach, no general manager, no full-time scout. When a Boston sports columnist told him, "I'll write you a basketball column if you tell me something funny," it was clear that Auerbach had no time for lazy writers, either.

He replied, "How's about 'Fuck you.' How does that hit you?"

A moment passed, and Auerbach said, "That's funny." He raised a brow. "Write *that*."

Thirty-six years before, in January 1920, Boston Red Sox owner Harry Frazee sold Babe Ruth to the Yankees. Frazee produced

Broadway plays, and though his Red Sox were winning, show business squeezed his finances. He began to sell off his players, more than a few—Joe Dugan, Waite Hoyt, Carl Mays, Herb Pennock, George Pipgras—to the Yankees. All told, the Yankees reportedly put up more than $400,000 in cash and credit to acquire Ruth, who through the cult of his personality and home run power would lead baseball away from the 1919 Black Sox gambling scandal and into the live ball era. Even before the sale, there was ample evidence that Ruth was headed for slugging stardom. In 1919, his final Red Sox season, Ruth not only won nine games as a starting pitcher but, as an outfielder, hit a record twenty-nine home runs, more than the combined totals of ten other teams. In his first two seasons with the Yankees, Ruth hit fifty-four and fifty-nine home runs. It's no wonder that when Frazee hung posters at Fenway Park in 1920 advertising his farcical play, *My Lady Friends*, one Red Sox fan sniffed, "Those are the only friends that son of a bitch has." The Curse of the Bambino darkened the skies over Fenway for generations.

Auerbach didn't yet sense in Russell a Ruthian power to transform a sport, but if Russell was everything he seemed to be, he could remake the Celtics, in particular the team's fast break. Long, lean, and springy, Russell on defense became like a Venus flytrap, thwarting shots that flew toward him. In college, Russell's defense and shot blocking proved game altering. His University of San Francisco coach, Phil Woolpert, said that in one game against Cal-Berkeley, Russell blocked twenty-five shots. By the second half of many games, opposing shooters weren't the same; Russell's psychological warfare reduced them to dupes, their shooting confidence gone. Auerbach understood this, just as he understood that he needed a center to battle the Knicks' Harry Gallatin and Sweetwater Clifton and Syracuse's Johnny Kerr and Dolph Schayes. Ed Macauley couldn't win those battles. He was too thin. The Celtics had lost in the playoffs for six straight seasons to those two teams in large part because Auerbach didn't have a rugged big man. He also needed someone to get Cousy the ball on the fast break.

Auerbach had friends watching Russell, and he strafed them with a thousand questions. As a rebounder, he heard, Russell had long arms, inside quickness. A master of positioning, Russell always seemed in the right spot for a rebound. Auerbach listened to the criticisms as well: Russell was not a good shooter or ball handler, and he seemed moody, though a year earlier, the *New York Times* sports columnist Arthur Daley interviewed Russell and thought him "a well-spoken young man of twenty-one with a sly wit and philosophical turn of mind." It was widely known that Abe Saperstein wanted Russell for the Globetrotters, reportedly offering as much as $50,000, but Russell wasn't interested.

Russell was not a conventional center; he wasn't a primary scorer. Not everyone was convinced he would become an NBA star. Auerbach brushed aside such thinking. Russell, he believed, was a winner: He had just won consecutive NCAA championships and, at the moment, was riding a fifty-six-game winning streak at USF. All eight NBA teams knew Russell was available in the draft. Even though he played beyond the media spotlight, in the Far West, he would not slip through any cracks, not at nearly six-foot-ten. Auerbach told Brown the Celtics had to have him. The trouble was, Boston had the sixth pick in the draft, much too low to get Russell. Besides, the Celtics intended to give up that first-round pick to select Tom Heinsohn of Holy Cross, the NCAA's fourth leading scorer, as a territorial selection; in this way, the NBA allowed teams to select a popular college player in their region, within a radius of fifty miles, figuring that would help at the gate.

Sportswriters applied their adjectives to Auerbach—*arrogant, tempestuous, mercurial, irritating, vain*—but pejoratives never stuck to him.

Here's what he thought: *Fuck 'em.*

Auerbach was who he was and he would not deviate from that. He had coached a full decade in the NBA for three different teams, won many more games than he'd lost, but still had not won a championship. His basketball legend would be built as a game-day coach, but his greater contribution to the Celtics dynasty might have been, the Cousy draft-day botch aside, as a judge of talent during these early years (he would make plenty of drafting mistakes in years to come) and as a draft-day operator. Auerbach could never undo what Harry Frazee had done to Boston sports by selling Babe Ruth in 1920, but by acquiring Russell in the 1956 NBA draft he would bring to the Hub a luminous new star whose effect on his sport would be nearly as dramatic as the Babe's on his. What Ruth did for baseball with his offense, Russell would do for basketball with his defense. Both became the foundational piece of a dynasty.

No one knew for certain what was to come on draft day, April 30, 1956. Rochester had the first pick. Auerbach knew that Royals owner Lester Harrison was bleeding money, and that his team already had an excellent big man, Maurice Stokes, an African-American all-star who as a rookie had averaged nearly seventeen points per game. Russell was said to be seeking $25,000 per season, probably too rich for Harrison's blood, Auerbach thought. Besides, Harrison needed a guard and privately told Brown that he wanted Duquesne's Sihugo Green with the draft's first pick.

St. Louis picked second. Here, Auerbach thought, was his opportunity. He knew that Russell didn't want to play for the Hawks, an all-white team in the league's southernmost city. Auerbach negotiated a deal with his old boss, Ben Kerner, who had moved his Hawks from Tri-Cities to Milwaukee to St. Louis: Auerbach would trade Macauley, a seven-time all-star, popular with Boston fans and with Brown, in return for Russell, who would be selected with the draft's second pick. Much as he enjoyed playing for the Celtics, Macauley, a St. Louis native, wanted to play for the Hawks because his young son had been diagnosed with spinal meningitis and Macauley needed to be closer to home.

Kerner pondered the offer. He wanted more. He wanted Macauley and Cliff Hagan, an all-American from Kentucky who had been fulfilling his military obligation and had yet to play for the Celtics but now was ready to go. Auerbach nearly choked on his cigar. *Macauley and Hagan? That's a kick in the head!* He desperately wanted Russell, and Kerner knew that, so Auerbach and Brown agreed to it. Preparing for all possibilities, a few weeks before the draft Auerbach and Brown secretly met at Boston Garden with Kerner and his coach, Red Holzman, and agreed that if Rochester changed its mind and took Russell with the first pick, then St. Louis would choose another big man and send him to the Celtics.

On draft day, Auerbach's insides churned. But when Rochester took Green, the Celtics' coach reveled in his great fortune: Russell was his. Then, in the second round, with the thirteenth pick overall, the Celtics chose Russell's USF teammate guard K.C. Jones. In one draft, Auerbach obtained three future Hall of Famers, a feat that hasn't been equaled by an NBA team in the more than sixty years since. Of course, in so doing, he traded away two future Hall of Famers in Macauley and Hagan.

"A shrewd maneuver," the *Globe*'s Herb Ralby wrote of the Russell acquisition. In the *Boston Evening American*, Larry Claflin went a step further, praising the Celtics for "shocking the basketball world."

Preparing that fall with the U.S. Olympic team for the Melbourne Games, Russell played an exhibition at the University of Maryland. Auerbach and Brown showed up to see their new game changer for the first time. Russell played terribly. Auerbach thought, *What did I do?* If this was the real Russell, he decided, *I'm a dead pigeon.* That night, after the game, Russell apologized to Brown and Auerbach, saying he had never played so poorly. "I am much better than that. It will never happen again," Russell promised. Auerbach pulled aside Brown and told him that he'd never heard a young player apologize in this way. A classy kid, Auerbach thought. He recalibrated his thinking, telling Brown, "Maybe there is something here."

Russell returned home from Melbourne a conquering hero. At the San Francisco airport, reporters saw him kiss his fiancée and hand her his gold medal. They married days later, and Brown was among those in attendance. When Bill and Rose Russell arrived in Boston in mid-December at two o'clock in the morning after a long, lousy flight, the Celtics were on the road, but Brown and Sharman, who was injured, were there waiting, and presented the Russells with a ceremonial key to the city. On December 18, Russell joined the Celtics at Madison Square Garden, though only as a spectator. He nervously approached the team captain he had met at the White House a year earlier, saying, "How do you do, Mr. Cousy?" Wanting to make a strong first impression, Cousy scored thirty-five points against the Knicks.

The veterans watched Russell closely in his first practices. Sharman was impressed, saying, "I'm sold."

No trumpets had blared when Cousy, emerging like a rabbit from Danny Biasone's fedora, arrived on the team six years earlier. But now hyperbole filled the Boston sports pages. The *Boston Traveler* featured a photo of Russell in a Celtics uniform as "The Photo Boston Waited to See." In the *Evening American*, an artist sketched Russell in a swirl of adjectives—"Sensational! Gigantic! Can't Miss! Astounding!"—and with the catchall line, "A victim of the greatest build-up in Hoop History." The *Herald*'s Sam Brogna wrote, "The Celtics have acquired their dream big player to match with the little wizard of them all, Bob Cousy." The *Herald*'s gentlemanly beat writer, Joe Looney, played along with the hype, writing that Russell "has had the biggest buildup since one stone was laid on top of another and the result became the Bunker Hill Monument in 1843."

At a press conference, Boston sportswriters got their first look at Russell. He had been born in rural Louisiana in strict segregation. His mother, Katie, tried to keep him from white people because, as she told him, "You don't know what they'll do." Russell's father, Charlie, moved the family out of the South, to a housing project in Oakland, California, and went to work in the shipyards. Soon after, Katie Russell died of kidney failure. Charlie Russell had promised her that he would raise their two boys himself and get them an education. A close-knit family, the Russells would pass down a motto from grandfather to father to Bill Russell: "A man has to draw a line inside himself that he won't allow any man to cross." Later Bill Russell would modify that: "If you disrespect that line, you disrespect me."

His father, known as Mister Charlie, had told him that black men needed to understand white men, not vice versa. That's just the way it was, he said. Bill Russell carried that belief, and other racial lessons, into the world beyond his own. "Some people call it instinct. It's not instinct—it's learned," he said. He also said, "It is far more important to understand than to be understood."

By Russell's own reckoning, his mother had taught him to be a tough fighter, and his father taught him to be philosophical. After he had delivered the first of two NCAA championships to USF and won the MVP award at the Final Four, sportswriters inexplicably gave the 1954–55 Player of the Year award in the West Coast Conference to Santa Clara's Ken Sears: white sportswriters voting for a white player. Maybe what his mother said about white people was true: "You don't know what they'll do." Years later Russell admitted he was "enraged" by this snub, and from that point forward he decided to count his championships, not honors as voted by others. "I found out that in order to get any recognition," he would say decades later, "I would have to change my complexion."

In Boston, where he would become the only black player on the Celtics during the 1956–57 season, Russell revealed none of these deeper thoughts as he met the most segregated segment in American sports—the men of press row. Russell didn't know what to make of these Boston sportswriters, and they didn't know what to make of him. In the *Globe*, Keane quoted Brown saying that Russell's one-year contract, prorated for missing the season's first twenty-four games, was less than Cousy's, which Keane said was $22,000.

"You don't think I'd give anybody as much as I'm giving Cousy, do you?" Brown said. "I'd be crazy to do such a thing after the way Cousy has killed himself around here for seven years playing the style of ball he has."

Already Brown was managing his stars carefully, letting everyone know the locker room hierarchy was unchanged and that his captain was still his captain.

The *Daily Record* sportswriter Bill McSweeny struck up a conversation with Bill and Rose Russell after the press conference. "You want to have lunch?" Bill Russell asked. They sat together at a little café at North Station. McSweeny, just twenty-seven and raised in working-class Dorchester, viewed himself as a typical Irish kid. He had been a newsboy, hawking newspapers at Filene's Corner. Then, in 1943, with everyone away fighting in the war, McSweeny got hired as a police reporter by the *Daily Record*. He was only fourteen. He sat at a desk in Station Two, near Faneuil Hall. To McSweeny, the old brick police station, with its jail cells and big wooden desks and cops moving in and out, seemed drawn by Dickens. Most of the policemen were Irish or Italian, and they watched out for young Billy. At the station, he had a padlocked telephone from which he dictated his news to a rewrite man on the city desk. McSweeny later commanded an army rifle company in the Korean War, 180 men, including more than two dozen African Americans. He heard the black soldiers' personal stories and came to know and respect them as men. When he returned to Boston, he covered boxing and wrote about the life struggles of black fighters. McSweeny began to think deeply about race and, in 1956, for fifty dollars, became a member of the NAACP.

Now, over lunch, Russell ordered a martini, took a sip, and passed it to McSweeny, offering him a drink. McSweeny put the glass to his lips and sipped from it. Only much later, when they became close friends, did McSweeny realize that Russell had put him to a litmus test; if McSweeny drank from Russell's glass, he was likely a good, fair-minded man on matters of race.

The Celtics were in first place with a 16-8 record at the time Russell arrived. They played veterans Arnie Risen and Jack Nichols at center, and sometimes the rookie Heinsohn. Russell finally debuted on December 22, in a nationally televised game against St. Louis at Boston Garden.

"He must learn to fit in with the fast breaking style of the Celtics and this, I am sure, he will do with little trouble because he is extremely fast for his size," Dave Egan wrote in the *Daily Record*. "He must also adjust himself to the fantastic playmaking and passing of Bob Cousy, the likes of which he has never seen."

Russell entered with five and a half minutes left in the first quarter. He would play twenty-one minutes and make just three of eleven shots, including two left-handed hooks, and only one of five free throw attempts. One young fan sitting courtside wondered, *They dumped Ed Macauley to get this guy?* Russell was nervous, and admitted it to sportswriters after the game.

His debut featured a thrilling finish, with Cousy at the center of the excitement. With the Celtics trailing 93–91 with fifteen seconds to play, Cousy prepared to inbound the ball from midcourt. Macauley, an opponent now, guarded Heinsohn in the left corner and shouted to his teammates, "They are going to give the ball to Sharman!" Slater Martin, covering Cousy, shouted, "Ed, be careful!" Just then, Heinsohn saw Cousy nod at him. Heinsohn brought Macauley up and then suddenly broke to the basket, backdooring him. Cousy unleashed an overhand bullet that neatly sliced through a crowd of players and, more than forty feet later, into Heinsohn's hands near the basket. "A one-in-a-thousand pass," Hawks coach Red Holzman called it. Heinsohn laid it in for a 93-all tie.

Then Macauley committed another blunder by misjudging the clock and heaving an eighty-foot shot that missed badly. (Holzman fined Macauley fifty dollars after the game for "two plays you couldn't condone if a rookie had made them.") Three seconds still remained, and Auerbach called a time-out. By design, Cousy then inbounded to Sharman, who leveraged a Jim Loscutoff screen near the Hawks' free throw line to sink a game-winner at the buzzer. Cousy rushed to hug Sharman, and so did Russell and Auerbach. Fans emptied onto the court and carried Sharman and others to the locker room, a wonderful sight for Brown's sore eyes.

"Never saw the Boston fans so steamed up," Auerbach said happily.

Podoloff attended the game and liked what he saw in Russell. "They'll love him everywhere in the league," Podoloff said, and he was right; Russell's presence would produce sellouts across the NBA that season.

There were other silver linings in Russell's opener: He pulled down sixteen rebounds and at one point blocked three consecutive shots by Bob Pettit, the league's top scorer. Auerbach protested a goaltending call against Russell, and in the postgame locker room Russell thanked him for it. "It made me feel like he really cared," Russell said later. "I don't think the referee had ever seen anybody make a stop like that before so he called goaltending."

As Cousy drove home to Worcester after the game, he thought about the team's new center. *He's going to be everything we need rebounding-wise*, a pleasant thought. *And he might have some defensive possibilities.*

ACK-ACK

The rookie Heinsohn liked to shoot. "But in his defense," Cousy would say, "he only shoots when he has the ball."

A big personality, garrulous, and gung ho, Heinsohn was a formidable player, a six-foot-seven power forward with a low line-drive shot and a hook he sometimes took from way out near the corner. Auerbach rode him hard. He made Heinsohn his whipping boy, blaming him for things that went wrong on the court, knowing that he would respond.

Heinsohn figured Auerbach wouldn't scream at Cousy because he was captain or at Frank Ramsey because it would send him into a funk or at Sharman because "Sharman would've cold-cocked him" or at Russell, whom he handled privately. Occasionally on the road, Auerbach took Heinsohn to see a war movie; Heinsohn, of German descent, kidded his coach that they were cheering for opposite armies. Not that it mattered: Auerbach usually fell asleep ten minutes after the show started. Other times Heinsohn went on business calls with Auerbach, who in his side job worked as a salesman in the cellophane business.

Heinsohn became the playful butt of locker room jokes. Team-mates called him "Ack-Ack" because that was the sound of a tommy gun, and on the court Heinsohn was a gunner. Cousy noticed how quickly Heinsohn ran into the locker room at halftime to smoke a few cigarettes. "If only you'd run that fast in games," Cousy said. Veterans made the rookie carry the team's ball bag and retrieve soft drinks, the usual rituals. Russell, also a rookie, never had to do that because the white veterans had a hard time getting a true read on him and didn't want to overstep.

Heinsohn adjusted to a pro basketball player's itinerant life. The Celtics took a late-night sleeper out of Rochester to Fort Wayne and, at about five o'clock the next morning, stopped and got out in Waterloo, Indiana, by Heinsohn's description "in the middle of this cornfield." At the end of the train line, though still more than twenty-five miles from Fort Wayne, the players carried their bags some distance to the Green Parrot café, a local greasy spoon, where, Heinsohn said, they had to "bribe some high school kids to drive us the rest of the way."

At twenty-two, Heinsohn was six years younger than Cousy and viewed him much like a big brother. Most of the Celtics lived in Boston or close to it, but Heinsohn followed Cousy's lead by moving from the Holy Cross campus across town in Worcester to Pleasant Street, not far from Cousy's white stucco home at 12 Chamberlain Parkway.

Together, they drove each day to practice or games, a drive they would share for seven seasons. On their commute, they talked about sports, the Celtics, the next game, or Auerbach. The team held practices at the unglamorous YMCA in Kendall Square in Cambridge, a run-down gym with a dilapidated locker room, sometimes following a junior high school team onto the court.

As Cousy and Heinsohn grew closer, their wives became friendly. For a time Missie and Diane Heinsohn were inseparable, Missie showing her around Boston Garden and introducing her to other Celtics wives. Once, Missie and Diane walked into a Celtics practice, thinking it was done, and Auerbach bellowed, "Who the hell let the broads in here?" The women couldn't get out fast enough. The Cousy daughters, Marie and Ticia, soon called Tom and Diane Heinsohn Uncle Tommy and Aunt Diane. When Diane gave birth to their first son, the Celtics were on the road, and Missie was at the hospital with her.

Diane admired Missie for her love for children; the Cousys would have had more, but Missie suffered several miscarriages, including one on Father's Day at the Heinsohns' house. She also admired her strength. Once, Missie introduced Diane to her mother-in-law, Juliette Cousy. Missie knew Juliette wasn't fond of Germans. Now, hearing the name "Heinsohn," Juliette raised her chin slightly and asked, judgmentally, "One of *your* friends?" Missie shook her head and said, "No, actually one of Bob's friends," and walked off.

Any prejudice or perceived unfairness drew Missie's attention, Diane noted. An inveterate letter writer, Missie wrote regularly to Congressman Harold Donohue, a Democrat from Worcester, about local and international politics. She wrote to Harold Stassen, director of the U.S. Foreign Operations Administration, to express concern about where the United States stood on the overthrow of President Juan Perón in Argentina. She wrote a letter to the pope, and it was sent, through church back channels, to the local parish priest, Father Casey, who appeared at the Cousys' front door to state the view that it was much better to express her personal concerns about the church to the parish priest than to the pope. Later, Missie brought her young daughters to a civil rights march in Worcester. "Funny, kind-hearted, religious" is how Diane Heinsohn would describe her.

It was Cousy's team; that much Tom Heinsohn knew. Cousy was the star, and in his seventh year, he had seen more and done more in the NBA than any of his teammates. He got the headlines and the endorsements. His Peter Pan style of play stirred fans' imaginations. He was the captain, his intensity and competitiveness surging. At Graylag, his boys' summer camp in Pittsfield, New Hampshire, Cousy challenged Heinsohn in Labyrinth, a table game of manual dexterity, and at horseshoes. Heinsohn beat him in horseshoes, and the next time he showed up to direct a rebounding clinic, he discovered Cousy waiting for him at the camp entrance for a horseshoes rematch. "He'd been practicing," Heinsohn says. "He kicked my ass." Heinsohn knew about Cousy's nightmares, another expression of his intensity. At his camp, Cousy, in the throes of a nightmare, once tore out of bed in his cabin and terrified Missie with his cursing and screaming. He bolted outside into the darkness and ran face-first into a tree. Stunned, he crouched there, alone in the woods. Later a doctor told him that he suffered from an anxiety complex. He suggested that Cousy at summer camp was too sedentary. He needed movement in his life, and excitement and pressure. He prescribed tranquilizers, and the nightmares soon faded.

Auerbach considered Cousy's competitiveness exemplary. During a preseason game at Fort Devens, Cousy's man got a step on him at midcourt. He might have let him go but instead turned and ran him down, catching him going in. Auerbach turned to Heinsohn on the bench. "See that, rookie?" Auerbach shook his head in amazement. *There are one hundred fifty people in this joint*, Auerbach thought. *Ninety-nine out of a hundred pros would've let their man go.* "When you can play like that," Auerbach said to Heinsohn, "you're a pro."

Cousy thought Heinsohn lacked discipline: He needed more running, fewer cigarettes. He saw Heinsohn sitting with radio man Johnny Most in hotel coffee shops postmidnight, swapping stories about NBA games and Most's days during World War II as an aerial gunner. They smoked cigarettes and drank coffee into the wee hours.

"Why do you have to be the social butterfly all the time?" Cousy asked Heinsohn.

For his part, Heinsohn wondered about Cousy's intensity and how the game meant everything to him. Heinsohn had broader interests, including art. On the road, he sat in his hotel room, staring out a window at a spire or building, and painted the scene with watercolors.

In the dingy Boston Garden dressing room, each player got a single hook for his shirt and trousers; players handed their wallets and watches to trainer Buddy LeRoux, and during games he kept them in a black satchel beneath the bench. In the dressing room, Heinsohn sat between Cousy and Russell. He watched the two men closely and noted a common trait. "They took so much out of themselves," Heinsohn says. "I didn't have this drive to be the world's greatest like they did." To win an NBA title, Heinsohn thought, *They'd kill their mothers.*

Nothing made Auerbach happier than seeing his Celtics in transition, running the fast break, their opponents in a furious, futile retreat. The Celtics used only seven offensive plays, with three or four options for each. In mid-January 1957, after about a dozen games with the team, Russell mapped out his thinking for Cousy.

If Cousy's man slipped past him on defense, Russell said he would slide over, block the shot, and outlet the ball to Cousy, starting the Celtics in the other direction on a fast break.

Cousy told Russell, "After they take a shot and you rebound it, I'll go to that spot over there. Look for me there first."

They would merge their skill sets and, as Russell saw it, "The other team would shoot and, four seconds later, we'd be making a layup at the other end." On most teams, when a guard got beaten by his opponent he'd yell, "Help!" The Celtics would yell, "Russ!" Russell later estimated that about one third of the shots he blocked were taken by the player Cousy was covering, but he sent the same signal to other Celtics. He would back them up, too, and never complain about it. Russell would transform defensive lapses into an offensive scoring protocol.

Still, at twenty-three, Russell remained a work in progress. The NBA's best-scoring centers waged war against him. On December 26, Russell held Philadelphia's Neil Johnston, a two-time league scoring champion, scoreless for the game's first forty-two minutes. But on

January 8 at Madison Square Garden, the Knicks' Harry Gallatin, a wily vet, turned Russell inside out, threw elbows, and outmuscled him, scoring twenty-six points in the Knicks' 113–102 victory. Knicks guard Willie Naulls, the former UCLA star who once had four shots blocked by Russell in a college game, warned his teammates, "Don't talk too soon. This guy will be twice as tough next time. I know." Auerbach described Russell's first performance against Gallatin as "timid." He told Russell that he needed to strike back, and hard. Auerbach told sportwriters, "He didn't seem to want to hit anyone." Russell had just gotten married, and Auerbach thought, *That doesn't do a guy any good, at least on a basketball court.*

Naulls proved prescient. Twelve days later at Boston Garden, Russell, lessons learned, threw elbows and limited Gallatin to two baskets and nine points, and the Celtics won by thirty-six. Afterward, Russell said, "I'm not afraid of any man in this league. Nobody."

Auerbach was giddy: "He destroyed him," he said. He liked that word—*destroy*. "That's a word you can use about him—he 'destroyed' players." Of course, Clif Keane, in the next morning's *Globe*, led with Cousy rather than Russell's startling defensive transformation: "It's come to a point where you sit down and want to write something about the game Bob Cousy played again yesterday against the Knicks. But what's left unsaid? Sure, Cousy was wonderful, scoring thirty-two points in twenty-eight minutes. He did everything—but doesn't he always? He passed blindly behind his back, and the 11,082 in the Garden blew fuses all over the place. And he stole the ball several times, blocked shots." Auerbach often struggled with Keane, once threatening him in the postgame dressing room, "Take that finger off me or I'll tear it off your goddamned hand!" But there was a larger issue at play, Auerbach believed: "The writers began forming their own fan clubs: You'd see pro-Cousy stories, pro-Heinsohn stories, pro-Ramsey stories. Forget the game—they were too busy writing about their heroes! But they didn't know what was happening out there." Russell didn't get the attention he deserved, Auerbach believed. He often joked with his players at practice about how little sportswriters knew: "Did you fellows see the papers today? Was that guy *really* at our game?" "It hurt Bill Russell," Auerbach said later. "He played his guts out and couldn't get his name in big type. He did so much to bring the Celtics all those titles only to find, more often than not, that Cooz alone was the Man. It was wrong."

The Celtics won eight in a row in late January to move to 31-14 and finished a league-best 44-28, winning their first Eastern Division title, six games better than Syracuse. Thanks to Russell, attendance at the Garden surged by more than 20 percent, to more than ten thousand per game, an all-time high for the Celtics. Ramsey rejoined the team in January from his military service and noticed immediately how much it had improved since he had last played two years earlier. The scoring sheet was well balanced: Sharman with 21.1 points per game, Cousy 20.6 (he also led the NBA in assists for the fifth consecutive year), Heinsohn 16.2, and Russell 14.7.

When Charles Russell came to see his son Bill play for the Celtics for the first time, in March 1957, he stopped by the basketball writers luncheon at the Hotel Lenox and told sportswriters the captain impressed him. "That Cousy!" he said. "I naturally had been reading about him in the Oakland and San Francisco papers, but I kept saying to myself . . . 'What they write can't be true.' Now I've seen him and I still can't believe the things I've watched him do with a basket ball, and what's more he looks as though he can go on playing for seven more years with the speed he shows."

The Celtics swept Syracuse in three games and faced St. Louis in the 1957 NBA Finals. The series extended to the full seven games, with four games decided by two points and two stretching to double overtime.

Prior to Game 3 at Kiel Auditorium, Sharman, going through his scrupulous warm-up shooting regimen, sensed the basket wasn't the appropriate height. To him, it seemed too low; Cousy, Russell, and Ramsey agreed. Auerbach demanded a measurement; the referees brought out a measuring stick. Seeing this, Kerner exploded. He rushed onto the court and called Auerbach a "bush-leaguer." Even before Kerner finished saying it, Auerbach punched him in the mouth. Kerner fell to the floor, his mouth bloody, a tooth dislodged. "You can coach that team of yours from a hotel room!" Kerner howled. "And on top of that you can't even punch." The basket's height measured the required ten feet.

The Celtics led 91–87 with 4:46 to play, Sharman with twenty-eight points. But then Sharman fouled out, and the Hawks stormed back. In the final moment, Pettit made a twenty-five-foot jumper to win it, 100–98, giving the Hawks a two-games-to-one lead in the series. Podoloff fined Auerbach $300 for punching Kerner, calling it "unbecoming conduct," an understatement. Cousy's thirty-one points led the Celtics to a 123–118 victory in Game 4 at Kiel to even the series, and then the Celtics won Game 5. The Hawks' Pettit, sensational throughout the Finals, scored thirty-two points in Game 6 at Kiel to force a decisive seventh game.

With 13,909 filling Boston Garden, Auerbach apologized to Kerner before the game. Cousy had played seven years for this moment. Even so, with the Celtics in their eleventh season and on the cusp of their first NBA championship, he and Sharman lost their shooting touch. Cousy made just two of twenty shots, and Sharman only three of twenty. Heinsohn took over. He converted seventeen of thirty-three field goal attempts, Ack-Ack scoring on jump shots, drives, hooks, and off the fast break. He scored thirty-seven points in all, and, in a show of ferocious determination, pulled down twenty-three rebounds.

With less than fifty seconds to play, Cousy fed Russell to give the Celtics a 102–101 lead. The Hawks inbounded immediately to forward Jack Coleman, already moving toward halfcourt. Here came the dividends of Auerbach's steadfast belief in Russell. *Maybe there is something here*, Auerbach once thought. With his track-and-field bona fides, Russell turned from the backcourt and gave chase, his strides elongated. Among the Celtics, Cousy was closest to Coleman and trailed him by about ten feet.

"All I know," Cousy says, "is that Russ whizzed by me."

Heinsohn was giving chase, too. "Russell went by me like I was standing still," Heinsohn says. "It was like the state trooper going after someone."

Sixty years later, as Heinsohn remembered the play, it grew all out of proportion, Russell starting his chase from behind the Golden Gate Bridge and sprinting across the Rockies and then swimming the Great Lakes before finally catching Coleman at the basket. Coleman, the Hawks' six-foot-seven power forward, slowed slightly as he rose for a layup. Just then, he saw Russell coming at him from the middle. Russell blocked Coleman's layup, a stunning athletic achievement that saved the day, at least for the moment. "I don't know how he could've stopped it," Coleman said after the game. "I took the ball and curled it along the boards. I'd say it was goaltending. But the referees didn't say it." Up in the balcony, along press row, Bill McSweeny turned to colleague Murray Kramer of the *Daily Record* and said with disbelief, "Did that just happen?"

Tied at the end of regulation, Game 7 moved into overtime. When Heinsohn fouled out with two minutes left in overtime, the game still in doubt, he sat on the bench and hung a towel over his head, overcome with emotion.

The game extended to a second overtime. The Celtics led 125–123 with one second remaining. The Hawks' Alex Hannum inbounded the ball the length of the court. Per design, the ball ricocheted off the backboard into the lane to Pettit, who, with his game-high thirty-nine points, nearly scored again to tie it, but the ball spun off the rim.

Boston fans stormed the floor. Cousy wept and received another ride to the locker room on fans' shoulders. Celebrating players threw Auerbach into the shower for a victory soak. Russell shouted, "Who has got a razor?" He had promised teammates he would shave his goatee if the Celtics won the NBA championship. He allowed a drenched, shirtless Auerbach to do some of the shaving. Russell rubbed his smooth chin. He said, "Well, there it is, boys. Or, I mean there it isn't. No more goatee. It's gone down the drain."

Sportswriters clamored for Heinsohn: Ack-Ack on radio, Ack-Ack mugging for press photos, Ack-Ack asking everyone in the room, "Want to be my agent? Sign me up quick. I'm goin' for a big price." Sharman, typically understated, said, "Tommy, that was a wonderful basketball game." Cousy shook his head. "Kid's the greatest," he said of Heinsohn. "What pressure. And how he played under it all." It was rare for Cousy and Sharman to fail in such a big moment. For years they had carried the Celtics, but this time the rookies carried them. Cousy admitted to fatigue. "Me? Guess I was tired, awful tired. But that St. Louis team really fought us."

McSweeny had the distinct feeling "that this was the moment that basketball was made in Boston. You could feel it in the Garden." He saw Walter Brown's joy. "That afternoon you could feel that he had finally made it. . . . You could see that Russell and Cousy—and this was one of Ramsey's big games [with sixteen points]—you could suddenly see this team had crystallized into something very special," he says.

The series was too good to be ignored, and some of it appeared on television. These Finals had showcased several of the game's biggest stars—Cousy, Russell, Pettit—and overlapped with the first week of the Major League Baseball season, which meant the leading sports columnists and sportswriters had returned from spring training in Florida. They watched. They noticed.

For Cousy, winning an NBA title was "a huge weight lifted." He was at the midpoint, and apex, of his playing career, and in his innovative prime as a point guard. The league's players voted him the NBA's Most Valuable Player in 1957, outpolling Pettit and Philadelphia's Paul Arizin.

Heinsohn found a letter from the NBA office at his locker.

"What's that?" asked Russell, standing nearby.

"I don't know," Heinsohn said. "Probably a fine."

Inside the envelope Heinsohn found a check for a few hundred dollars and a letter saying he'd been voted the NBA's Rookie of the Year.

"You ought to give me half of that," Russell said.

"Why?" Heinsohn asked.

Russell replied that if he had played the entire season, Heinsohn wouldn't have won the award. Only later did Heinsohn learn that Russell had once lost out to Ken Sears for a college player of the year award. He thought, *So I was another white guy.*

A day after Boston won Game 7, a headline in the *Daily Record* set the expectations high: CELTS CINCH TO REPEAT.

BEING COUSY

The Celtics announced their intentions early the next season. They won their first fourteen games of the 1957–58 season, and it was five weeks before they lost, 97–80, to the Knicks at Convention Hall in Philadelphia, a game the injured Cousy sat out. They generated an up-tempo style, with Cousy leading the break and opponents struggling to keep up. He added some new moves, including blind passes hooked over his shoulder, and burnished some old ones. No NBA team had an antidote for Russell. He broke the NBA's single-season rebounding record by mid-February, and his peers voted him the league's Most Valuable Player at season's end, though sportswriters mysteriously placed him on their all-NBA second team behind three white players up front, Schayes, Pettit, and Detroit's George Yardley.

The Celtics finished 49-23, five games better than the year before, a dynasty taking flight. In the first three games of the playoffs against Philadelphia, Russell grabbed twenty-five, twenty-eight, and forty rebounds. Several times Warriors coach George Senesky benched Neil

Johnston in favor of a more physical player, Joe Grabowski. It didn't work.

The Celtics moved on to St. Louis for the NBA Finals and split the first two games with the Hawks. In the third minute of the third quarter in Game 3, Russell blocked a shot by Pettit, landed on Pettit's foot, and turned his right ankle. The game was lost, and Russell was diagnosed with severely sprained tendons. He spent the next three days on crutches, receiving whirlpool and diathermy treatment.

In Game 4, with Russell unable to play, Auerbach ordered Cousy to slow down the fast break and lead a more patient halfcourt attack. At times Cousy slid into the pivot, where he annihilated little Slater Martin, a rugged defender, with a series of hooks and spin moves, scoring eighteen points in the first half. Cousy finished with a triple-double: twenty-four points, thirteen rebounds, and thirteen assists in a 109–98 Boston victory.

After St. Louis took Game 5, and a three-games-to-two series advantage, Russell, wearing a cast over his ankle, returned for Game 6. He played twenty-four minutes but couldn't move freely and produced just eight points and eight rebounds. When Auerbach pulled him from the game for the last time, he said, "There will be other seasons, Russ."

Pettit owned the day, scoring fifty points, including nineteen of his team's final twenty-one points. The Celtics played gamely, missing two shots in the final minute with a chance to pull ahead, but lost 110–109 at Kiel.

Afterward, Ben Kerner, an NBA champion for the first time, said that this title validated his decision to trade Russell two years before. His St. Louis Hawks would be the last all-white team to win an NBA crown.

In the postgame locker room, Cousy lost his stoic façade. He wept. He had scored fifteen points, not enough. From the moment he had broken into the NBA, Cousy had led the league in a department he practically invented, that of self-analysis. In the months that followed the 1958 NBA Finals, he decided why his team had lost. Most NBA observers cited Russell's ankle injury. But not Cousy. He had driven himself hard. He had contrived mind games to demonize his opponents and fire up his determination. His analysis: Before Game 6, he didn't feel the inner rage that had always driven him, and he had failed to lead. As Cousy saw it, it was at once that deep and that simple. The Celtics' failure was his failure.

Let us see Cousy as he was on Boston Garden's parquet floor, in his white home jersey set off by CELTICS 14 in Kelly green. He looked quintessentially French with his long, thin face, dark features, and deep-set eyes. For much of any game, his face was impassive. But seldom was it impassive for an entire game. In moments that mattered most, the mask came off, replaced by a game face, drawn tight for battle. He often moved with a captain's strut and an artist's impatience. Maybe he saw a referee miss a call. A teammate might have fumbled a pass. At those moments, Cousy could be a demanding master. He wanted the ball when he wanted it, not when a teammate might finally get it to him, and in a time-out huddle he might scream, "Give me the fuckin' ball!" They gave it to him. With a game already in hand, he sometimes became a mischief maker: He brought the ball upcourt and called a nonexistent play: "Twenty-two!" He passed the ball to Sharman and turned his back, leaving Sharman unsure what the hell was going on.

Cousy's body seemed designed by two architects with competing visions. Taken as a whole, his physique seemed incongruous and unsymmetrical, though what it lacked in aesthetics, it made up for in basketball function. Leanness defined his upper half. Basketball players of this era did not lift weights because of a time-worn belief that enhanced upper-body musculature adversely affected shooting accuracy. Cousy had small, rounded shoulders, no chest to speak of, and long, childlike arms, thin as pipes, that allowed him to whip overhand passes seventy feet downcourt on a fast break; his arms were nearly three inches longer than Sharman's, and the two men were roughly the same height. Cousy had big hands with long fingers, excellent tools for gripping and controlling a basketball. Fans frequently asked him to hold up his hand; when he did, they put their palm against his, and their fingers came up short, making them feel like children. From the waist down, Cousy's architecture changed dramatically: everything thickened, his buttocks, his thighs more like the physique of a wrestler; his lower half carried the lion's share of his 185 pounds. Cousy had a low center of gravity, splendid for protecting the ball as he dribbled. His lower half provided him with sturdiness and an ability to absorb the physical pounding of long seasons that, with exhibitions and the playoffs, extended to more than one hundred games. He wore size thirteen black high-tops; every other team in the league wore white sneakers, but Auerbach believed that black shoes hid dirt better and lasted longer and thus saved Brown money, and no one could tell him otherwise.

Cousy viewed himself as a creator. In this, there was an inner conceit and truth. As point guard, his role was to divine scoring possibilities: The ball was usually in his possession, after all. He created plays on the fly, through intuition and improvisation. He played by sound and sight and catalogued his teammates' tendencies and running speeds, as if flipping through the pages in his mind while running the break, turning to page 23, "Ramsey, Frank: Dependable, great effort, always the same, though runs, oddly, on his heels. He'll dribble high and right over a defender. A good closer on the break," and then sliding the ball to Ramsey—and there he was, running the right lane, two steps ahead of his defender, right on schedule—for an easy layup. Or turning in his mind to page 24 about Sam Jones, the six-foot-four guard drafted in 1957 from North Carolina Central: "Jones, Sam: Like Sharman, automatic as a shooter, only with better breakaway speed. A penetrator and finisher." Each of the Celtics had a modus operandi, and Cousy, an altruist, did his best to put them in a favorable scoring position; he sought to put them in the spotlight, make them heroes.

To Cousy, a fast break was a work of art, the point guard with brush in hand. Each time down the floor, he painted a different canvas based on what he saw, heard, and felt. "You don't know going in what you are going to paint because your reactions are going to be predicated on what the other nine people are doing," he says. Every action prompted a reaction. To him, this was a *beautiful scenario*, all things possible: "You are the guy in this game that is painting this picture, and it's a revelation. Every time down it changes. It's never the same." With Auerbach, he had visited the Louvre in Paris, and together they saw the *Venus de Milo*, and da Vinci's *Mona Lisa*, and the *Winged Victory of Samothrace* from ancient Greece—all of it impressive, but to Cousy none of it carried the creative majesty of a fast break. "It is in the eyes of the beholder," he says. "I see ten big freaks running up and down the floor and I think that's beautiful."

As he received an outlet pass from Russell, just before turning upcourt, in his mind's eye Cousy took *the photograph*. In that instant, he deciphered his four teammates' locations on the court—detecting them instantly by size or swatch of uniform color—essential information to process as he dribbled toward the opposing free throw line as the Celtics mounted their attack, ideally before opponents could assume their strongest defensive positions. It was important to know the defenders, but to Cousy more important to know his teammates. If Heinsohn and Russell trailed on the break, and if Russell started from beneath the opposing basket and needed to run all ninety-four feet, Cousy knew that by the time he reached the opposing top of the key, "Russ will be ahead of Tommy, if Tommy is running the lane. Russ will be right on my ass." Given this, Cousy often simulated a pass to the wing, drawing out the defender from the middle, which left only the opposing guards to face the onrushing Russell. Then he timed his pass just right and let his big man devour those poor guards.

Across New England, Cousy noticed baskets appearing on garages. Basketball was taking off. In 1953, the *Boston Globe* had sponsored a basketball clinic at Boston Garden that drew 2,500 participants; four years later, more than 6,000 attended the event. In March 1957, all 244 public high schools in Massachusetts featured boys' basketball teams, and 189 schools had girls' teams.

The *Globe*'s Harold Kaese gave five reasons for this surge in basketball's popularity: 1. The Celtics; 2. Bob Cousy; 3. Holy Cross; 4. Television; and 5. Boston Garden tournaments. Cousy was connected to all of that. "The player boys most wanted to emulate, of course, was Bob Cousy," Kaese wrote. "He probably is the most remarkable average-sized player in the history of basket ball. Every youngster is enthralled by a magician; every boy who saw him play basket ball was enthralled."

Cousy established his brand on the court and off. Most NBA players worked a second job during the off-season—Heinsohn in insurance, Ramsey construction, the Knicks' Richie Guerin as a Pinkerton detective at the Yonkers racetrack. Cousy's year-round schedule in 1957 was full and hectic:

Mid–September through April (NBA season);
May through July (State Department trip to Europe with Auerbach,
*   plus local speaking engagements and basketball clinics);*
July through late August (Camp Graylag for boys);
Early September (Home in Worcester for two weeks of family time
*   and golf).*

At a time when *Lassie, Gunsmoke,* and *I Love Lucy* were television hits and Elvis Presley and Pat Boone topped the *Billboard* music charts, Cousy segued fluidly into his life as an American sports celebrity. He became the face of professional basketball. As he sold the game, the game sold him. Men admired him, boys wanted to be like him. There he was on *The Ed Sullivan Show* (with Otto Graham and Cab Calloway) and on *Captain Kangaroo*, looking into the camera and waving hello to Marie and Ticia in Worcester. National magazine writers flocked to his doorstep, the glossies featuring images of Cousy as a basketball magician in midair and as a family man at home with Missie and the girls. Sportswriter Al Hirshberg helped him produce an as-told-to memoir, *Basketball Is My Life*, in 1957, and later profiled him in *The Saturday Evening Post*. "Cousy has a hard time generating a feud with anyone," Hirshberg wrote, "because he is probably the most popular man in the league."

As conformist as a tie tack, Cousy was careful in public about what he said and did. Missie might speak her mind in letters to politicians, but he was more guarded.

As Boston became a league power, Brown said at the weekly press luncheon, "I'll tell you how smart we were. We didn't want *that* guy!" and he jerked his thumb toward Cousy. This embarrassed Cousy and infuriated Auerbach, his judgment of talent seemingly called into question. Sitting nearby, Auerbach stewed in silence. *I'm going to have to be nice to Arnold for the next two weeks*, Cousy reminded himself.

Privately Cousy told Brown that being billed as the NBA's highest-paid player mattered deeply to him—whether it was true or not—primarily to help him land endorsements. "I was told that to ad agencies—the people on Madison Avenue—basketball was not that big a deal," Cousy says. "They don't know a basketball player from a bocce player. When they need a basketball player [for an endorsement], they ask, 'Who is the highest-paid player in the league?' . . . I simply wanted to be billed in the boardrooms of Madison Avenue as the highest-paid player in the league." Brown went along with this request. He added to Cousy's contract a bonus clause based on home attendance, knowing full well that Cooz wouldn't receive any extra money.

In time Cousy endorsed Ovaltine, Wheaties, a Florida orange juice, a gasoline additive called Cristy Drygas, and Kent cigarettes. There was a "Bob Cousy" sneaker, and he earned a royalty on each pair sold. He also endorsed Roman Meal bread, though with his speech impediment he struggled in one take after another, *Roman* becoming *Loman*. ("I had a bitch of a time," Cousy says. "I thought I'd blow the thing. We rehearsed and rehearsed that sucker. I thought they were going to say, 'Cooz, we love you but you don't speak English very well.'") He delivered speeches to companies, civic groups, and fraternal lodges. He worked hard to improve as a public speaker. He studied a dictionary and tried to learn five new words each week. He incorporated those words into his conversations, expensive words like *innocuous*. His public speeches focused on fitness, the fast break, and being Houdini. He attached himself to a cause, cystic fibrosis, serving for six years as chairman of its statewide fund-raising drive. In a steady stream of stories, the Boston newspapers admired and glamorized him: a touching front-page story about Cooz meeting in the locker room with a blind teen who idolized him, a variety of soft features about Missie, including one in the *Globe* in March 1958 ("Mrs. Cousy Talks of Her Bob") in which she provided such insights as, "He isn't an overly talkative person," and "You can't lead the league in assists for eight years and not be a team man."

Cousy was now part of a rarefied sports galaxy. At banquets and airports, he befriended Ted Williams, Dom DiMaggio, Rocky Marciano. Williams admired Cousy's athleticism and said that when he led the fast break it was "as beautiful as any ballet movement," and when Ted Williams praised you that meant plenty in the Hub. Others might prefer Elgin Baylor or Bill Russell, Williams said, but "I'll still take the Cooz." Soon, on photo shoots for Jantzen swimwear, Cousy palled around on beaches and in hotel bars with Paul Hornung, Don Meredith, Bobby Hull, Dave Marr, Ken Venturi, and Frank Gifford.

His fame grew outward: When a Boston track promoter and Olympic hammer thrower returned from meets behind the Iron Curtain, they told stories of Russian coaches asking to see movies of Cousy in action. It wasn't just Cousy's reputation that reached Europe; Cousy made his second trip there with Auerbach in May 1957, sponsored again by the U.S. State Department. Four hundred people watched their basketball demonstration outdoors in Porto, Portugal, in a driving rainstorm. On this trip, Auerbach and Cousy also spread the gospel about basketball in Turkey, Austria, Belgium, and Denmark, countries where the game was still relatively unknown.

On the one hand, Cousy says, "Arnold had the image of being rough, burp-when-he-wanted-to, and expel gas . . . but he was kind of chameleon-like in his personality. You could take him into almost any company and he could hold his own conversationally." He saw Auerbach converse effortlessly in Tehran with the shah of Iran. But then in Turkey, after Auerbach spoke for about five minutes to make a point in a basketball lecture, his interpreter spoke only about three words in translation, at which point Auerbach, nearly offended, threw up his hands and said, "Is that all I said?"

During the NBA season, alone late at night in his suite at the Hotel Lenox, Auerbach ate Chinese food and, the next morning, using a hot plate, warmed up the leftovers for breakfast and washed them down with a Coke.

"Arnold," Cousy warned, "you are going to explode one of these days." In Europe, Auerbach proved a finicky eater, telling Cousy he refused to eat "anything strange."

By January 1959, Boston was sprinting toward a third consecutive Eastern Division title, and Minneapolis coach John Kundla was saying that Cousy, at thirty-one, was "greater now than he ever was." Auerbach agreed. "Cousy is having his finest year in pro ball. . . . His reactions are as quick as they have ever been; second, he is shooting better than he ever has before. The guy is a perfectionist," Auerbach said, "a player with tremendous pride. He may make a mistake, but never the second time."

Cousy developed a running one-handed shot from about twenty-five feet and experimented shooting off his right foot, an unorthodox move that surprised defenders. He battled leg injuries and developed elbow chips that made his long overhand pass too painful, so he began to throw sidearm windmill passes downcourt.

In a 119–114 loss to St. Louis at Kiel Auditorium in late January, fans turned on the Celtics. One threw a towel at Auerbach and another a paper cup at Cousy after he had fallen to the floor, his breath momentarily knocked from him. Fans booed Cousy. "The worst fans in the league," Auerbach seethed afterward. The teams met again eight days later in Boston, and Auerbach, still miffed, said, "I hope Boston fans give them a taste of their own medicine." Boston fans heard their coach's call to action and responded. Some threw eggs and oranges at the Hawks, but only until Brown, via loudspeaker, asked them to refrain and publicly apologized to the Hawks.

On February 27 at Boston Garden, the Celtics offense, with Russell nursing an injury, erupted in a 173–139 victory over the Lakers. Howie McHugh told Auerbach at the end of the third quarter, when the Celtics held a twenty-six-point lead, that they were in line to break some NBA scoring records. Only that morning Auerbach had given a clinic to four thousand boys and coaches and emphasized defense. He left his starters in the game, and records fell. Cousy finished with thirty-one points and a league-record twenty-eight assists—thereby accounting for eighty-seven points—as the Celtics scored 173 points, another league record. The game provided an exclamation point to a season in which Auerbach drove his players as hard as he drove his car. (Sometimes Auerbach drove Brown and backup center Gene Conley, who lived at the Lenox that season, to practice at the YMCA in Cambridge. Conley sat in the backseat and held on for dear life, and heard Brown pleading, "Red, you are driving too fast! Slow down, Red!")

In an otherwise meaningless season finale against the Knicks, Cousy was told he needed to score thirty-seven points to reach a twenty-points-per-game average for the season. "We'll see what we can do," he said. With teammates feeding him the ball, he scored exactly thirty-seven points. He also averaged nearly nine assists per game in 1959, once again tops in the league. Knicks veteran guard Dick McGuire, a fancy dribbler and passer in his own right, said, "Covering Cousy's dribble for nine years . . . is like trying to catch a yo-yo."

The Celtics finished with a 52-20 record, a dozen games better than the second-place Knicks, and Auerbach puffed out his chest and called his men "the greatest team ever assembled." But he said no NBA team would emerge as powerful as baseball's Yankees. "They could lose Mickey Mantle and still keep going," Auerbach said. "But a key injury can wipe out a basket ball team. If we were to lose Cousy or Russell we'd be in real deep trouble."

Trouble came in different forms. Before one playoff game, Cousy sat in Heinsohn's kitchen, waiting to make the drive together into Boston. The phone rang and no one answered, so Cousy picked up.

"You fucking son of a bitch," a man on the line said, "if you step on the court tonight I'm going to shoot you."

"Thank you very much," Cousy replied, and hung up.

Heinsohn appeared. "A friend of yours just called," Cousy told him. "He said if you show up on the court tonight, he'll shoot you." They put the threat aside and drove to Boston.

With the Celtics extended to Game 7 by the Syracuse Nationals in the 1959 Eastern Division Finals at Boston Garden, and Auerbach's *greatest team ever assembled* on the brink of elimination, Cousy produced a moment that pushed sportswriters to a hyperbolic frenzy. It wasn't that he scored twenty-five points and dealt ten assists, but how he did it. As McSweeny of the *Daily Record* saw it, with the Celtics trailing by seventeen points in the third quarter, "professional basketball in Boston was on trial" with the home crowd "half hostile." McSweeny would reflect on this game four years later, hyperbolic about it still, writing, "Cousy on his knees . . . the Garden in tumult . . . a

basket needed for the victory . . . [trainer Buddy] LeRoux going over
him with an ice pack and applying smelling salts in a time out. 'Point
me in the right direction, will you Buddy? I'm awful tired.' A couple of
grown men I know cried that night."

In this Game 7, Cousy played in the second half with a season-
saving flourish, leading the Celtics' comeback. He fought exhaustion
and cramping muscles and by one count went to his knees five times
in the game's final two minutes. Auerbach called time-out with
twenty-three seconds left, Boston, led by Cousy's scoring and passing,
ahead by five. Cousy dribbled out the clock in a 130–125 victory and
at the buzzer threw the ball toward the rafters and fell to the parquet
floor as the crowd rushed to him. Nearly rhapsodic, McSweeny would
write:

> There he was playing with almost blind eyes. Pausing every
> now and again with the dry heaves of exhaustion. Stum-
> bling, agonized. It was a moment out of the history of sport
> which can never be recaptured by mere words. It was a mo-
> ment when a whole area was stock still. Not a word . . . not
> a sound . . . not a match flickering to a cigarette. But some-
> where he found the last ounce of sheer courage. He took the
> ball up, worked it in, fed a man, got it back for the clutch
> shot, broke from [Syracuse guard Larry] Costello, drove
> through and made it. The bell and the crowd went off si-
> multaneously as the Celtics won. Cousy fell to his knees,
> then to all fours, then on his side. They lugged him off.
> Forty-five minutes later he still lay on the table in the
> dressing-room, unable to move. It was the most startling
> tableau in the history of basketball.

Facing the Minneapolis Lakers in the Finals, Cousy had few worries. The Lakers finished a middling 33-39 during the regular season
but eliminated Detroit and St. Louis in the playoffs. Cousy looked

forward to a brief beach vacation after the Finals with Missie and the girls in Delray Beach, Florida; they were scheduled to leave on Sunday. After Boston won the first two games, and with Games 3 and 4 scheduled for Tuesday and Thursday in Minnesota, Cousy told Missie he expected a four-game sweep, and instructed her to move up their flight reservations to Friday.

Coming off the bench as Boston's sixth man, Ramsey tore apart the Lakers, averaging twenty-two points per game in the series. "He is, by any odds," *Sports Illustrated* decided, "the best substitute this game has ever seen." The Celtics swept the Lakers in four games, Russell won his second league Most Valuable Player award, and the Cousys flew to Delray Beach on Friday.

Soon after, Cousy and Auerbach were off on their third State Department trip, this time taking their basketball lectures and demonstrations to Morocco, the United Arab Republic, and French West Africa, where they gave one clinic on a dirt floor with broken-down hoops and a shredded ball. Auerbach couldn't help but notice that when Cousy played for one local team, his new teammates began to make the right plays and move to the appropriate spots on the court; then Cousy changed teams, and a similar transformation occurred. "His moves," Auerbach said, "are contagious. Same identical thing wherever we went." In restaurants Auerbach loudly hailed waiters who didn't speak English. Embarrassed by his coach's antics, Cousy told him, "Arnold, you are the poster boy for the ugly American. You are so crude." Once, an exasperated Cousy moved to a different table and Auerbach, unable to speak French or translate the menu, called out to him: "You little Frog sonovabitch, get over here!" Cousy wanted to crawl under the table.

WIVES ROW

Missie Cousy would be heard. Her voice carried the sound and bravado of New York. She sat on Wives Row, several rows behind the Celtics' bench at Boston Garden, in front of the railing, and gave an earful to the referee: "SID BORGIA, YOU ARE BLIND!!!"

Missie spoke her mind, always. She did that at a restaurant once, prompting her more subdued husband to caution, "Missie, duck, people are looking." Missie had seniority now among Celtics wives, knew the game better than most, and oozed pride in "My Bob." She took the star seat on the aisle. To Sunday afternoon games, she sometimes brought the girls in their matching plaid dresses, and they waved to their father on the court, but as focused as he was he never waved back. Getting one of the limited seats on Wives Row wasn't easy. Decisions had to be made: Should an unmarried player's girlfriend be allowed? Kids? Friends? Somehow, it all worked out.

Even so, the wives became territorial. They had to dress and act the part. As Lynn Loscutoff saw it, "We were appendages of the players. We were on display." If Bob Cousy was Mister Basketball, Missie embraced the role of Missus Basketball. She became the mother hen of Wives Row. She took new arrivals, such as Rose Russell, on a tour of Boston Garden. It was dark, yes, and there were shady characters to avoid in the alleys on the way in, and thick smoke from Lucky Strike, Camel, Kent, and Salem cigarettes clung to every fiber in your dress for days, but it was, for better or worse, *home*.

Auerbach viewed Celtics wives as a necessary evil. He thought they gossiped and took their husbands' private comments about the team ("That guy won't pass me the ball!") and spread them with a corrosive effect. Auerbach did not allow the wives to travel with the team. His brusqueness offended them. No wonder, the wives whispered, his wife, Dorothy, stayed with their daughters in Washington, D.C., all season long. Once, Auerbach spotted Diane Heinsohn and said, "Jesus Christ, is that a new hat you got on?" It got worse. On another occasion he snapped, "Are you pregnant again?" On this subject she took him on: "Listen, Red, if you planned your schedule with my schedule, these things wouldn't happen." Too late: Auerbach had already turned and walked away. To Lynn Loscutoff, Auerbach was "dictator, patriarch, godfather, puppeteer," and to Celtics wives he was "especially unkind and unsociable."

Not to worry, Missie told the other wives: If Red flicks cigar ashes on your jacket shoulder, that means he likes you.

The wives became a unit unto themselves. With their husbands on road trips, they got together for dinners and baby showers. They shared diets and snow shoveling chores, and when they heard Johnny Most say on radio broadcasts, "He is down! He is on the floor!" they all hoped that he didn't mean their man. Frank Ramsey and his wife, Jean, rented a rambling house in Wellesley Hills, and during one lengthy road trip some of the wives who didn't have school-aged children spent a couple nights there, just gabbing. Once, Celtics wives were featured in a fashion show at the Garden. "Bill Russell refused to let Rose be in it," Diane Heinsohn says. "We never knew why." But she noticed how when Jean Ramsey, in a great outfit, passed in review, Frank looked at her with glowing pride.

Typical for the times, Celtics wives were expected to manage the home front—handling not only the kids but house chores. Ileana Sharman, a chatty Californian, had four children and made sure that at three o'clock in the afternoon before home games she served her husband, Bill, his dinner, exactly so: a small steak, small salad, and baked potato. He then took a half-mile walk through his neighborhood and returned home for a nap of one hour, not a minute longer. Ileana made certain the children didn't make a peep.

Before some games the wives met at the Iron Horse, a bar-restaurant on the street level of the Garden. Once, they shopped at a nearby department store and paraded back to Wives Row, each holding a shopping bag. The joke was on Frank Ramsey, known among wives to be a little tight with money: He looked up at them from the bench, and the wives pointed to their bags, laughed, and hollered, "These are all Jean's!"

Some of the wives, Missie included, smoked cigarettes during games. Frank Ramsey suggested they use cigarette holders; that way, he said, they would consume less nicotine. The wives tried it, but found the cigarettes burned faster and created more ash. Missie accidently burned the man sitting in front of her when ash fell from the tip of her cigarette holder onto his bald head. She apologized, even as the other wives couldn't stop laughing, and that was the end of cigarette holders.

There weren't many perks to Wives Row, though once the lady in charge of the nearby women's restroom got to know the wives, she would open the stall door for them, saving them from paying a dime.

Bill Russell confounded Diane Heinsohn. He always called her "Heinsohn," which she hated, until finally she mentioned that her name was Diane. "Bill wasn't the most gregarious person around the wives," she says. Around the Celtics kids, though, Russell revealed a common touch. He called young Jerry Sharman "Bullseye Junior," adapting the nickname he had given the boy's father. And once he lifted little Marie Cousy high above his head—so high, she felt she could almost touch the sky—and said with giddiness, "Hey, lil' Cooz!"

BUSH-LEAGUE IMPRESSION

The NBA faced growing pains and seismic challenges. In 1959, anemic attendance in Cincinnati (2,445 per game average) and Detroit (3,978) transformed arenas into echo chambers. In relocating the Pistons from Fort Wayne to Detroit in 1957, franchise owner Fred Zollner had lost $100,000 and more. It seemed that many big-city sports columnists—the most influential voices of the sports pages—didn't like pro basketball. Dave Egan was a rarity in that regard, though he died suddenly from a heart attack in 1958 (Cousy was among his honorary pallbearers). Some sports columnists thought pro basketball was still infested with gamblers, an enduring legacy from the college betting scandals earlier in the decade. In New York, traditionalists such as Red Smith of the *Herald-Tribune*, Jimmy Powers of the *Daily News*, and Arthur Daley of the *Times* preferred more masculine sports like baseball, football, or boxing. Columnist Shirley Povich of *The Washington Post* was of a similar mindset. He had been a sportswriter since 1924 and had covered the Dempsey-Tunney fight in 1927 and Babe

Ruth's Called Shot home run in the 1932 World Series. Soon after, Povich decided that he'd become a "hero worshipper, a romanticist" as a sports columnist, guilty of overwriting and trying to make the game more than it was. In a story in *Sports Illustrated* in September 1958, Povich, a romanticist no more, mocked the NBA, writing, "Basketball is for the birds—the gooney birds. The game lost this particular patron years back when it went vertical and put the accent on carnival freaks who achieved upper space by growing into it. They don't shoot baskets any more, they stuff them like taxidermists. . . . These fellows are biological accidents who ought to be more usefully employed, like hiring out as rainmakers and going to sow a few clouds." Povich, slightly built and only about five-foot-eight, decried the NBA's rules and wild-eyed referees and wistfully recalled a bygone era when a professional basketball team won a game comfortably by scoring a total of 26 points. The Knicks had averaged 112 points during the previous NBA season and finished last, and that troubled Povich. He wrote that basketball had degenerated "from a game to a mess." Inflamed by Povich's story, Bill Mokray, the Celtics statistician who had observed basketball for decades, dashed off a letter to the editor of *Sports Illustrated*: "If Mr. Povich ever elects to attend a game, he will quickly realize that today's Bill Russells, Bob Pettits, Kenny Sears, etc. are universally admired for their gracefulness rather than known for the awkwardness that was associated with their predecessors of fifteen to twenty years ago."

Cousy had his own thoughts about how to strengthen the NBA. When sportswriters asked, he answered candidly. For one thing, Cousy said, the NBA season was too long. By playoff time, he said, teams had already played about a hundred games, including intrasquad exhibitions at dedications of high school gymnasiums. Cousy wanted to cut the regular-season schedule from seventy-two games to sixty. "That's not a gripe," he said in December 1958. "We like the game and we like its rewards. But the newspapers sometimes hint that [late in the season] we are a little tired and stale." Besides, if properly promoted, fewer games might mean more money for the league, he said. A year later,

Cousy spoke of the personal cost of a long season: "It isn't the game itself so much as the traveling, the irregular eating, the sleeping wherever I happen to rest my head, the amount of time I have to spend away from my wife and two daughters in Worcester, the abuse of the fans when we're on the road. It all seems harder to take than it used to."

Leonard Koppett of the *New York Post* knew the NBA as few other sportswriters did. As a twenty-three-year-old stringer, Koppett had covered games in the old BAA in 1946, its inaugural season. Later he became, for the *Herald-Tribune*, the beat writer covering the Knicks at the 69th Regiment Armory, by his measure the third-tier basketball assignment behind the college doubleheader at Madison Square Garden. Koppett moved in 1954 to the *New York Post*, an afternoon tabloid with a sizable, liberal Jewish readership that cared deeply about basketball. In 1947, a veteran baseball writer, sitting with Koppett on press row of a Knicks game, had asked, "Think this sport will ever be big league?" "Sure," Koppett answered. A decade later, the two men sat together again on press row, and the baseball writer posed the same question. This time, Koppett wasn't sure.

He clinically dissected the NBA in a *Saturday Evening Post* story in December 1958, "Does Pro Basketball Have a Future?" The NBA was at a crossroads, Koppett wrote, and needed to address three major problems: 1. Refereeing; 2. Scheduling; and 3. Packaging, or, as he wrote, "the numerous details of operation and intangibles of attitude that create a big-league atmosphere."

Among current referees only about one third were top-flight, Koppett estimated; he called for the league to increase the training and pay scale of referees and to alter their assignments so they wouldn't get the same team for six games out of seven, as some had that season.

Koppett agreed with Cousy that the NBA schedule was too long, roughly four games per week, and even more during the second half of the season. Expansion would help, Koppett suggested; adding more teams with large arenas in big cities and thus better claims to choice dates would thin out the schedule.

To improve "packaging," he recommended that every team hire a trainer; only the Knicks and Pistons already had full-time trainers who traveled with their teams. Koppett noted that he had seen the unconscionable: Heinsohn bandaging his own ankle on the bench during a Celtics-Nationals game in Syracuse the previous winter.

"The owners claim they have 'a million dollars' worth of basketball talent,'" Koppett wrote, "but say they can't afford a few thousand for trainers to look after the physical well-being of that talent."

He called for improvements to inadequate dressing rooms and un-reliable stat keeping, and an end to booking games on slippery or otherwise unacceptable courts at neutral sites and even squabbles between teams about the availability of practice balls. "None of these details are critical in themselves," Koppett wrote, "but taken together they give a bush-league impression."

The pro basketball league was in its thirteenth year, which, by Old Testament tradition, Koppett wrote, is the dividing line between a boy and a man. "Will it ever grow up? That's the fascinating thing about adolescents. You have to watch and see."

Koppett might have mentioned the NBA's racial quota. Black players knew it existed—as it did systemically throughout American life—as a tacit agreement among white owners to limit the number of black players to only a few per team. Owners feared that white fans wouldn't attend games if there were too many black players, whatever that meant. To a man, black players knew the evolving ratios and whispered among themselves as they competed against one another for limited NBA roster spots. Their best basketball opportunities in the late fifties were still with the Globetrotters' two traveling teams or in the independent Eastern League, which played games on weekends across Pennsylvania in cities like Allentown, Sunbury, and Wilkes-Barre and paid some top players about fifty or seventy-five dollars per game.

In the late fifties, Lenny Wilkens, playing college ball at Providence, came home to Brooklyn and competed against black players who threw no-look passes and dribbled behind their backs. In 1958–59, the NBA's eight teams featured nineteen black players, about 20 percent of the total; those black players typically shared more meaningful friendships with one another than with their white teammates, meeting for dinners and evenings out at restaurants and nightclubs. Elgin Baylor and Hal Greer joined the league that season, and K.C. Jones came to Boston after two years of military service.

That meant the Celtics had four black players, the most in the league—Russell, K.C. Jones, Sam Jones, and rookie Bennie Swain. In another three years, the percentage of black players in the NBA would grow to one third of the total, more than double the percentages in the NFL and Major League Baseball, and five of the NBA's top ten scorers were African Americans. The game was transforming from white to black, a cultural and stylistic shift. Increasingly the game was played higher, faster, and better than ever before.

Wilt Chamberlain would be the next must-see attraction. That became evident on November 11, 1958, when the Celtics gathered near courtside at Boston Garden to watch the Globetrotters play the first game of a doubleheader. The game offered a first look at the twenty-two-year-old Chamberlain, playing for the Trotters though already scheduled to join the NBA's Philadelphia Warriors the following season. Chamberlain scored fifty points for the Globetrotters that afternoon and dominated the game athletically and aesthetically. It was only comedy, the Celtics figured. But still . . .

One teammate asked Russell, "What are you trembling for?"

BEING RUSSELL

Wilt Chamberlain's arrival in the NBA in the fall of 1959 seemed like a circus caravan pulling into town with three-headed llamas, dancing pachyderms, and blaring bugles. It had been like this for several years. "Can Basketball Survive Chamberlain?" *The Saturday Evening Post* had asked in December 1956, the month Russell joined the Celtics and when the Dipper, as Chamberlain was known, was only a sophomore at the University of Kansas. At the time, Frank McGuire, the University of North Carolina coach, postulated, "Chamberlain will score about a hundred thirty points one night and the other coach will lose his job. There might be somebody in the penitentiary who can handle him but I guarantee you there is nobody in college."

If anything, or anyone, threatened Boston's competitive future, it was Chamberlain, who in joining the Philadelphia Warriors also joined the Celtics in the NBA's Eastern Division. His body seemed a miracle unto itself: seven-foot-one and 260 pounds, "the most perfect instrument ever made by God to play basketball," Dolph Schayes declared. One writer likened his physique to "a first sight of the New York skyline." Cousy swore that the Dipper was seven-foot-four. It didn't matter what the tape measure said. "Seven-four," he insisted. Because of Chamberlain the NBA's attendance spiked by 23 percent that season.

To the eye, Chamberlain achieved the unthinkable: He made Russell appear an underdog. He was about three inches taller than Russell and forty-five pounds heavier. For the next decade they became like the *Monitor* and *Merrimack*, Civil War ironclads, doing battle in a new form of above-the-rim warfare. They would meet 142 times in the NBA, an average of 14 times per season, Russell winning 85, the Dipper 57.

They met for the first time at Boston Garden on November 7, 1959; all 13,909 tickets sold out weeks in advance. They played to a virtual draw statistically: Wilt with thirty points and twenty-eight rebounds, and Russell twenty-two points and thirty-five rebounds. Boston's 115–106 victory was due in large part to Cousy. He played magnificently, a Houdini in full, scoring twenty-four points and distributing the ball to teammates with high style. Jeremiah Tax of *Sports Illustrated* wrote that Cousy "dominated the game as he has so often done in recent years—though without adequate recognition, simply because we have all come to take this incredible athlete for granted."

Chamberlain took thirty-eight shots in the game, twice as many as Russell. "What the duel proved, chiefly," Tax wrote, "is that against Russell, Chamberlain cannot get away with the few simple offensive moves he has found so effective against lesser men. Every time he tried to use his chief weapon, a fall-away jump shot, Russell went up with him; Russell's large hand flicked away at his vision, slapped at the ball, once blocked it outright—a shocking experience for Wilt Chamberlain. All told, in this man-to-man situation Chamberlain hit exactly four baskets; the rest of his thirty points were made on tip-ins and a few dunk shots, in which, free of Russell, he stuffed the ball into the basket from above it."

Chamberlain would lead the NBA in scoring as a rookie, with a

record 37.6 points per game average. He would win the Rookie of the
Year and Most Valuable Player awards, but the Celtics would capture
bigger spoils. They won fourteen consecutive games as October became
November, averaged a record 124.5 points per game for the season, and
finished a league-best 59-16, ten games better than Chamberlain's
Warriors. Russell put together his best season and pulled down a record
fifty-one rebounds in a game against Syracuse.

Milton Gross of the *New York Post* looked to history to find their
equal. "The Celtics are unique, awe-inspiring enough," Gross wrote in
January 1960, "to be considered on a par or higher than the Yankees of
1927, the Chicago Bears of 1940 and the Montreal Canadiens of
Maurice Richard's heyday [1940s and fifties]."

Fuzzy Levane, who resigned midseason as Knicks coach, said the
Celtics cruised through games, pacing themselves, trying only to stay
close. "[They] put out just what they've got to put out to win," Levane
said. "The other teams are afraid of them. They fear the moment of
explosion."

Ed Macauley, now the St. Louis coach, said Cousy represented in
basketball the same athletic excellence that quarterback Johnny Unitas
and outfielder Willie Mays represented in their sports. "He sees things
before anybody else ever sees them and he devises ways to take advantage of the situation before anybody else thinks of them," Macauley
said. "He's just beautiful to watch. But when he does it against us,"
Macauley added with a wince, "I hate his guts."

Nearly sixty years later, Joe Ruklick, the Warriors' backup center to
Chamberlain, would remember the Russell-Chamberlain battles and
the crowd's devotion to Cousy at Boston Garden. "I can still hear that
damn noise," Ruklick says. "Cheering for Cousy, and booing Wilt.
They loved Cousy."

In the 1960 division playoffs against Philadelphia, Auerbach
hatched a plan: After a free throw, Heinsohn would set a screen on
Chamberlain down low, and Russell would slip past and run free
downcourt. The ploy proved effective and unnerved the Dipper.

In Game 2, he growled at Heinsohn, "You do that one more time and I'll knock you on your ass." Heinsohn, puffed up, replied, "Wilt, bring your fuckin' lunch!"

Heinsohn set another screen and Chamberlain delivered on his promise. He pushed him, and Heinsohn slid on his rear end across the floor. Steamed up, Chamberlain gave pursuit and threw a punch at Heinsohn just as his Warriors teammate, Tom Gola, stepped in as a peacemaker. The punch hit Gola on the side of his head, badly bruising Chamberlain's knuckles. He played through the series with his right hand bandaged.

The Celtics eliminated the Warriors in six games and once again faced St. Louis in the Finals. In his tenth season, Cousy wore down and played poorly enough in the opening games of the Finals that he publicly offered to remove himself from the lineup. "I'm completely exhausted," he said. Brown said, "Heck, I died a thousand times a game—and it's even worse when a player like Cousy is in a slump. It just kills me to see him have a bad night." About Cousy, Auerbach told reporters, "I'll never pull him out."

In Game 5, Heinsohn scored thirty, and Cousy restored the luster to his game with twenty-one points and ten assists and left to a standing ovation in a 127–102 victory.

After the Hawks took the sixth game to even the series at three games apiece, Russell sipped tea in the Boston Garden locker room prior to Game 7. "Will you all look at Russell's little pinky?" Auerbach said to his players, trying to seize a motivational moment. "Isn't he delicate? Aren't we lucky to get his lesson in etiquette?"

A pressure valve released. The Celtics led by seventeen at halftime and, with the usual scoring balance, blew down the Hawks, 122–103, for their third NBA championship in four years. Fans carried Cousy from the parquet court and tried with Russell, who contributed twenty-two points and thirty-five rebounds, but couldn't lift him.

"He played," Bob Pettit said of Russell, "what could be called one of the truly great games of all time."

"I've won all these titles," Russell said, "and some men never win nothing. I'm lucky."

After his rookie season, Chamberlain, in spring 1960, announced his retirement from the NBA. He partially blamed race at a time when about one fourth of the league's players were black. He said opposing big men physically mauled him on the court and that if he responded in kind "it would reflect on me and then indirectly on my race."

Auerbach told the press that Chamberlain was a crybaby, saying Russell took an even greater pounding as a rookie, kept his mouth shut, and persevered.

"In my ten years in the NBA, I never saw any evidence of racial prejudice," said Cousy, who had seven black teammates during that decade; his comment revealed that he missed much roiling beneath the surface. "There are over one hundred Negro players who have either tried out or made positions with clubs in the league, and I have never heard such a complaint from them," Cousy said. "Wilt is the biggest complainer ever to hit the NBA."

Chamberlain brushed it off, saying, "Maybe if Bill Russell said it, I'd pay attention. But Cousy has never encountered the problems that we have." Russell remained silent on the subject. Chamberlain's retirement didn't last long. He toured that summer with the Globetrotters and then returned to the Warriors in the fall with a new three-year contract.

Off the court, Russell and Chamberlain shared a friendship. Rose and Bill hosted Chamberlain for dinner at their home when the Warriors came to Boston, and the Dipper reciprocated by inviting Russell to Thanksgiving dinner at his parents' house in Philadelphia.

Chamberlain was right that Cousy had never encountered *the problems that we have*. Russell had been turned away at segregated diners in St. Louis—to him "the loneliest town in the world"—and at Kiel Auditorium heard venomous catcalls: "BABOON! BLACK GORILLA! NIGGER!" Russell had met prejudice when he tried to buy a home in Boston. He purchased a modest ranch house on Main Street in suburban Reading that vandals broke into three times. Reading policemen habitually followed Russell as he drove through town.

Sportswriters didn't write glowing personality features about Russell as they did Cousy. Most white sportswriters by the sixties had moved past the physical stereotyping of black athletes favored by earlier generations and exhibited by Bob Considine of the International News Service in 1938 when he described heavyweight Joe Louis as "a big lean copper spring . . . his nostrils like the mouth of a double-barreled shotgun." White sportswriters in Boston peppered Russell with questions when he first arrived about why he wore a beard, a rarity at the time. Russell spent three or four months explaining why he should keep his beard and then, "the more they questioned, the more I dug in my heels."

By and large Boston sportswriters wrote respectfully about Russell. But McHugh, the Celtics' publicist, noticed that when the usual crew of sportswriters surrounded Cousy in the locker room after every home game, it grated on Russell; he said Russell believed they didn't come to him because he was black. Russell was well read, a deep thinker, and outspoken, and in the years ahead, with the black freedom struggle surging, he would lead the league in outspokenness, and engagement, in matters of race.

If white sportswriters didn't freely turn to Russell, young black athletes did. They looked to him as a proud statesman. The Red Sox became Major League Baseball's last team to integrate—a dozen years after Jackie Robinson broke in—when they promoted infielder Elijah "Pumpsie" Green in July 1959. Russell liked Green, who was also from the San Francisco Bay Area, and sometimes brought him home for dinner. He drove Green around Boston, showing him where to go, and where to avoid, including clannish Irish-Catholic enclaves like Southie, as locals like to call South Boston. Almost immediately Russell saw through to Boston's deep-seated racial resentments in ways many black Bostonians did not. He told Green that Boston was the most segregated city he knew. A year later, a freshman center at

Bowling Green State University named Nate Thurmond met Russell for the first time at a pro-college all-star game. Listening to Russell talk about race relations, Thurmond, six-foot-eleven, felt like a little kid. "To sit there and hear Russ expound," Thurmond says, "I was in awe. Just of how he spoke, and what he spoke of, his sincerity." Stardom gave Russell a platform, and he used it.

Russell and Chamberlain couldn't have been more different in that regard or, for that matter, in almost any regard. Though he played in Philadelphia, the bachelor Chamberlain soon lived alone and glamorously in an Oriental motif apartment on Central Park West in New York City. He drove a white Cadillac convertible, which he later traded for a Bentley. In Harlem, his playpen, he co-owned a historic nightclub, renamed Big Wilt's Smalls Paradise, where in the smoky light he eyed women in the interracial crowd and gauged their availability and shared laughs with performers such as Etta James and Redd Foxx; as the club's luminous greeter, Chamberlain once introduced Russell and K.C. Jones to singer James Brown. Chamberlain drove to Philadelphia for practices and games, and hardly knew his white teammates. About the civil rights movement, Chamberlain said little.

By contrast, Russell in 1959 was married, with a toddler son nicknamed Buddha, and in his basement had arranged a large, elaborate electric train set, which he had always wanted as a boy. He and Rose hosted Christmas parties for the Celtics and their families, and made sure to buy gifts for everyone, typically ties or cologne for his teammates. For Russell, business and race merged. He bought into Slade's Barbecue Chicken on Tremont Street in Roxbury, a black district; it did not prove a good investment. After the 1959 season, Russell gave a basketball clinic for the U.S. State Department in Monrovia, Liberia. A year later, he bought a rubber plantation near there, which also proved a poor investment.

"I'm a Negro, but I'm no causist," Russell said at the time. "I love this country [the United States] even if I don't like a few things about it. America is like a wife. She doesn't have to be perfect for you to love her. I'm proud to be an American and I'll fight anybody who knocks this country. But some things upset me and you know what they have been." Someday, he suggested, he and Rose might move to Africa. He added, "Know why it's easy for me to love Liberia? That country is America in Africa. It was founded by freed American slaves in 1822."

Cousy read the Boston newspapers. He saw Russell's energized comments about race. But the captain did not engage him on the subject. Cousy was too busy being Cousy. Two of the Warriors' white stars, Paul Arizin and Tom Gola, shared a similar distance in their relationship as teammates with Chamberlain. All had grown up in Philadelphia, but as Gola would say of the Dipper, "He had his agenda and I had mine." Once, Gola absentmindedly tossed a basketball against the locker room wall and cynically explained what he was doing: "Practicing our offense—throw the ball to Wilt and then stand there."

Cousy's conversations with Russell in the locker room were about basketball or a part of the usual team banter. They roomed together during one trip to New York. It didn't work well for Russell. He liked to take afternoon naps. Cousy went out that afternoon and, by Russell's count, the phone in their hotel room rang for Cousy thirty-one times. Then Cousy returned and Russell heard him speaking French on the phone for the next forty-seven minutes. A long-distance call, Russell figured, but only until Cousy said, "Okay, Momma. See you soon," and hung up. "We just never seemed to be able to initiate anything other than a few passing comments," Russell would say about his relationship with Cousy. After games and practices, they went their separate ways.

The lights had dimmed on Russell's marriage by 1959, and he sought physical pleasures elsewhere. His fidelity to Rose lasted only two seasons in Boston. It would take another twenty years before Russell, in his second memoir, written with Taylor Branch in 1979, told the public about his relationship with a woman he called Iodine, "the queen of streetwise . . . black, with light copper skin and red hair . . . she was such strong medicine that she could clean all my wounds if I didn't mind the sting." Iodine treated him so well, Russell wrote, "that sometimes when I was making love with her the tears would roll down my cheeks."

As he told it, Iodine knew pimps, gangsters, whores, union bosses, liquor dealers, and loan sharks as well as the police, Irish pols, WASPs, and Italians who made Boston run. As a black man with handsome earnings, Russell discovered that his financial peer group among blacks in Boston consisted mostly of gangsters and pimps.

His relationship with Iodine became contentious and at times violent, Russell wrote. Angry that Russell had been eyeing another woman, Iodine, in her Mustang automobile, once secretly waited for him past midnight outside of Slade's. She followed his car for some time and then, at a stoplight, rammed it from behind. An eighty-miles-per-hour chase through Boston's streets ensued, their cars jumping curbs. Back home later, Russell got a call saying Iodine had slammed her car into a building at fifty miles per hour and police arrested her for drunk driving. It cost Russell three hundred dollars before police agreed to let her go and keep his name from the newspapers.

During another argument, in the middle of the NBA playoffs, Iodine stabbed him just below his shoulder with scissors, driving the blades deep into the bone. A doctor treated his wound and agreed to tell no one; Russell later explained his bandage to sportswriters by saying he had received immunization shots for an upcoming trip overseas.

Over time, Iodine disappeared from his life—"Fuck off, motherfucker!" she shouted into the phone before she hung up on their last conversation—and was replaced during a lull in 1960 by Kitty Malone, a white stripper in New York, by Russell's description, "a tall, stately brunette, with green eyes and skin you could almost see through." Six or seven years older than Russell, Malone appeared tired and worn to Russell, but when she laughed "it was like opening a bottle of champagne."

Together they talked about politics and history. They shared a love for books, which he saw stacked high in her apartment. She sent him books wherever he traveled, including *The Wretched of the Earth*, a book about how empires dehumanize their colonial subjects by Frantz Fanon, an Afro-Caribbean psychiatrist. When Russell returned home after four months in Liberia, he discovered that Kitty had moved—where, he didn't know. Strippers, he was told, couldn't remain in one place for too long. It took five years before he heard that Kitty had died; one story said she had died in a car accident, another by heroin overdose. All the while, as the NBA championships accumulated, Russell worked to keep up the appearance of a home life with Rose. Cousy knew little about this part of Russell's personal life.

Heinsohn believed writers and fans in Boston didn't understand the nuances of the game and how Russell's rebounding and defense affected the outcome. "They can't *see* it," Heinsohn says. "But Cousy was flashy. They could immediately attach to what he was doing."

To McSweeny, game stories in Boston newspapers struck a repetitive note during the championship seasons: "It was always Cousy made twenty-four points, and Russell blocked sixteen shots. It was always, *Cousy made, Russell blocked*." In Boston Garden, where there were relatively few African-American fans, the cheers for Cousy seemed louder, longer, and more affectionate than those for Russell. "There was something different about Cousy. He was part of the crowd," McSweeny says. "He was one of them."

Cousy saw McSweeny, in his tailor-made suits, as a gentleman, "not a raucous type. He was a cut above." McSweeny developed a strong rapport with Cousy, as did most of the beat writers, and he grew close to Russell, in part due to his abiding interest in civil rights. McSweeny's young children were about the same age as Russell's, and their families shared cookouts at Russell's house in Reading or at McSweeny's in

Medford. When Russell needed a writer to help with his first memoir in 1965, he would choose McSweeny, whose interest in politics exceeded his own interest in sports. McSweeny worked part time on statewide political campaigns. After John Collins became mayor of Boston in 1959, he created a committee to create educational and recreational opportunities for black children in Roxbury and named McSweeny as chairman. In New York City for a Celtics game that same year, McSweeny and Russell, at the suggestion of Rose Russell, took a subway to Columbia University to hear a lecture by Dorothy Height, head of the National Council of Negro Women; impressed by what Height had to say, McSweeny and Russell paid dues to join her organization.

McSweeny recognized a historic turning point in sports. For the first time, he thought, black athletes were coming along who were college-educated and had participated in the Olympics, they'd been in the world and, at least in Russell's case, were willing to speak out against social injustice. In their own way, he believed, these Negro athletes were sending out word that the American black man was equal to the white man in every way. McSweeny gravitated to their narrative and privately found joy in their success as Celtics.

As best McSweeny could tell, the racial awareness and tolerance among Celtics beat writers and Boston sports columnists was, by percentage, about "seventy-thirty: seventy [percent] acceptable, the other thirty muttering, and then finally down to only one or two" who were opposed to integration. McSweeny says, "Russell had had enormous disappointments in his white relationships all the way coming up there. He had to learn, too. He had to learn that you couldn't always get angry at some sportswriter that didn't understand you."

Though Russell sat down to dinners with Chamberlain, he didn't with Cousy, except when other teammates joined them. Cousy and Russell shared the fast break and mutual respect, but little else. Missie and Rose were closer than their husbands. Cousy often seemed somber and spent a lot of time on the road in his hotel room with Sharman, reading or watching television. Russell had a big personality, was an inveterate teaser, and had a laugh that Auerbach described as being "like a hyena in full throat. . . . It started as a giggle, quickly escalating into a booming whinny that could be heard for city blocks." Checking in at hotel registration desks with Russell standing nearby, Cousy deadpanned, "Put this guy on the third floor. Put me on the first. His laugh will penetrate cement walls."

Away from the court, Russell fought strenuously against stereotype. "You know, they think that every time a colored man goes places, the first thing he does is get himself a Cadillac," he said in a 1958 interview. Russell made sure to buy a Chrysler instead. Similarly, tall men typically wore clothes that seemed too small, he said. When Russell bought suits, he said, "I get 'em made too big, too long all over . . . I always try to do things people say I won't do or I can't do."

Since his segregated childhood, Russell believed whites were "distant, cold and oppressive," and what he saw on television and experienced in college validated his view. But during his time in San Francisco in the mid-fifties, at coffeehouses in the Italian section of North Beach, and at the hungry i nightclub where he saw performances by iconoclasts such as comic Mort Sahl and singer Pete Seeger, Russell saw that "whites were capable of protest and sadness, too." It was a breakthrough for him because he realized that "at least some whites got the blues, were irreverent and weren't tight-assed."

Perhaps only in sports or combat could you create a triumvirate of such startling diversity as Auerbach, Russell, and Cousy. They each had a theatrical calling card—Cousy's no-look pass, Auerbach's cigar (originally he smoked Robert Burns, two for twenty-seven cents), and Russell's slow march onto the court during pregame introductions, arms folded, face fixed in a scowl. "Why run [onto the court] when you're going to run for forty-eight minutes," Russell once said, explaining his grand entrances, "and besides it irritates some people."

Auerbach was a fiery Jew, son of an Old World Russian who ran a dry cleaner in Brooklyn. He grated on opposing coaches and fans, led with flying fists, and spewed his volcanic lava over referees. He was that rare coach who sold tickets through charisma, same as Stengel, Durocher, Lombardi, and Joe McCarthy. For good measure, Auerbach added ballsy hubris. Every season, in opposing arenas, he led the league in boos. Once he told Russell, "I'm a Jew." Russell didn't know what that meant exactly. "Russell," Auerbach clarified, "a Jew is a *Jew!*"

Russell, the Louisiana-born center raised in an Oakland housing project, was the league's eighteenth African-American player but its first real black superstar. He demanded respect in ways the more accommodating Joe Louis and the Harlem Globetrotters never did; they played and kept quiet. For black athletes in Russell's time, though, the battle for access had progressed into a battle for dignity and respect.

As point guard and team captain, Cousy was an inwardly intense Catholic from the slums. He rarely smiled on the court. His demeanor spoke for him: *This is who I am, this is how I play, and we will win.* He controlled the basketball court in ways he could not control life. As Cousy saw it, he was the point guard and master distributor, doling out rewards and punishments on a brightly lit stage. From out of the smoky darkness he heard the applause.

As Cousy's first black teammates, Chuck Cooper and Don Barksdale had been quieter role players and in personality blended into the team. Russell was different. He stood out. He stood his ground. He issued challenges. Cousy didn't fully understand him. For one thing, Russell wouldn't sign autographs. Cousy signed freely and thought he owed that to the game. Over and over, Cousy saw the same scene play out: Russell reading a newspaper in a hotel lobby, a fan approaching to say what a great man he was and "Please, may I have your autograph?" Russell didn't look up from his newspaper. He glowered and said no. Heinsohn didn't understand it, either. Sometimes Russell offered to shake a fan's hand instead. He saw a handshake as more meaningful and respectful than an autograph, and explained that to fans at length.

"For Christ's sake, it takes you ten seconds to sign," Heinsohn said to Russell one day. "And you are going to take ten minutes out of your life to explain this?" Once, Heinsohn asked Russell to sign an autograph for a family member, and Russell refused, saying if he signed one he'd have to sign them all. Heinsohn fumed. He says, "This was about him as an individual. That's what it was about. But people didn't take it like that, all right? He could be totally rude."

Cousy knew early on that Russell didn't like to practice. Russell horsed around at team practices, didn't put out too much effort. That got on Cousy's nerves. Still, he told Auerbach, "Arnold, just let him sit and read the newspaper in the stands," and on occasion Russell did that. Cousy knew Russell saved his best for games. "Everything is overlooked when you have the kind of talent that Russell obviously developed," Cousy says. "When you've got a guy who is going to take you to the Promised Land . . ."

Cousy watched Auerbach carefully manage his relationship with Russell. Early on, Auerbach quietly had accepted the rookie Russell's invitation to dinner at his home; he'd never done that with one of his players, preferring to keep at a distance. Auerbach sought to demonstrate to Russell "that his color didn't mean a damn thing in our relationship." Prior to the start of training camp in 1958, Russell's third season, Auerbach had pulled his center aside and asked for permission to scold him in front of the team. "I want to scream bloody murder, insult you any way I can. Be up your ass," Auerbach told him. "If I can't yell at you once in a while, I can't yell at them or they'll feel persecuted." Russell agreed to it.

Years later, Auerbach would say, "The real Russell is a very difficult man to know, but one worth knowing."

Russell praised Cousy in the sports pages, including in February 1958, saying, "You know why he's the greatest? Two reasons. First is his imagination. No matter what the situation is, he'll think of something new to try. He'll try anything. And he'll make it work for the second reason. His confidence. He knows it's going to work. . . . Some sportswriters say it must be tough to play with Cousy; he does all those wild things, surprises you, fools you and all that jazz. I'll tell you, he's the easiest to play with. You know why? When he passes you the ball, there's always something you can do with it, that's why. Some guys, they pass you the ball and there's nothing you can do with it except pass it back or eat it if you're hungry. When Cousy gives it to you, there's a reason."

Cousy, meanwhile, filled sportswriters' notepads with high praise for Russell: "What has Russell meant to us? He's meant everything," Cousy said early in 1960.

With Russell's rise to stardom, writer Ed Linn wondered in a *Sport* magazine cover story in January 1960 if the center was "beginning to resent Cousy's salary and publicity and endorsements." "There is no doubt that Cousy saved basketball in Boston," Linn wrote, "and there is little doubt that he, more than anybody else, lifted the professional game to its current status as an acknowledged big-time sport." It wasn't, as some suggested, that Cousy couldn't win a championship until Russell arrived, Linn wrote, because Heinsohn and Ramsey had arrived with Russell, and thus the Celtics were no longer the same team Cousy had known.

Linn cautioned, "There is no need to build up Cousy by tearing down Russell. The first is unnecessary and the second is impossible."

Russell's guy. That's how Bill McSweeny was known among beat writers. Sometimes, he played gin rummy or hearts with Russell, Heinsohn, and Cousy in the back seats of an Electra turboprop. Russell trusted McSweeny and talked with him more often, and more candidly, than with the others. McSweeny's affinity for civil rights— and for Russell—set him apart from competitors on press row such as the *Globe*'s Clif Keane. One beat writer, Phil Elderkin of *The Christian Science Monitor*, says Keane often tried to prompt Cousy or Auerbach to criticize Russell, but neither took his bait.

Once, McSweeny approached K.C. Jones after a press conference at Boston Garden. Jones sat on a couch and spoke softly so McSweeny, wanting to be sure he heard every word, went to one knee in front of Jones. Looking up at him, McSweeny asked follow-up questions and jotted notes. Several days later, in a small press area near the Celtics' dressing room, Keane gave him hell for it. Sharply, Keane asked him how, as an Irish kid from Dorchester, McSweeny could kneel in front of a "black bastard." They exchanged words and then Keane shoved him. McSweeny, about three inches taller and an erstwhile rifle company commander in Korea, shoved him back. Their altercation ended almost as quickly as it had started.

One famous sportsman who shared McSweeny's appreciation for Russell was Ty Cobb. McSweeny met Cobb, the legendary "Georgia Peach," at a Baseball Hall of Fame dinner in New York City in 1959. They talked about baseball and politics, and struck up a friendship. In conversations and letters penned in green ink, Cobb, then in his early seventies, told McSweeny of his appreciation for Russell as a great professional and athletic champion. Cobb said he enjoyed watching Russell on television. Though Cobb, from rural Royston, Georgia, was known for having unenlightened racial views, McSweeny heard none of that from him about Russell. "He just had admiration for him," McSweeny says. Cobb was in New York once when the Celtics came to play the Knicks. He told McSweeny, "I've got to see this guy play." McSweeny phoned Madison Square Garden and arranged for Cobb to get box seats. Back at his hotel room after the game, Cobb, a proud man who would die in 1961, talked about Russell as a "money player." He told McSweeny that Bill Russell impressed him as probably the greatest money player of any professional athlete he had ever known, "other than myself."

LOCKER ROOM PULSE

Twenty minutes before a big game, here was the Celtics' crammed locker room at Boston Garden, a dimly lit dystopian dungeon that dated to the days of vaudeville: The smell of sweat, encased here since the Depression, mixed with Buddy LeRoux's Tiger Balm and assorted elixirs. To Cousy it was a musty, unfortunate place. When Heinsohn's cigarettes and Auerbach's cigars were lit simultaneously, Cousy waved his hands to fan away the smoke so that he could see teammates across the room. Sharman, answering to his own internal drumbeat, stretched out on the cold floor to do his push-ups and sit-ups, Cousy nearby thinking, *Why does Willie want to do that? We've got to go out and run for forty-eight minutes!* Per usual, Russell was at the toilet, stooped over, vomiting from nerves. Cousy looked virtually homicidal as he conjured contempt for the opposing point guard. This was Walter Brown's building, and now Brown, ruddy-faced, and wearing a drab gray suit, wished his boys well, reaffirming *total* belief in them even as he carried a St. Christopher's medal in his pocket for extra good luck. Brown moved past the huddled Boston sportswriters, granted access to the locker room only until Auerbach waved them away. McSweeny says, "You could step into that room and sense the electricity of that team." The newspapermen shooed off, Auerbach began his pregame oration in gruff Brooklynese that, between cigar puffs, echoed in the chamber.

Now in his eleventh NBA season, Cousy moved through the Celtics' locker room with the quiet confidence of a ten-time all-star. He cracked an occasional joke but usually didn't say much, least of all to rookies. Teammates viewed the captain's personality as serious, intense, and at times withdrawn, the antithesis of the whimsy, flash, and centrality of his playing style.

With Cooz, they knew, there was ego. All great athletes have egos, or they wouldn't be great athletes. Early on, Cousy fell in love with what he could do on the court. He loved the showmanship, the stardom, and the idea that he was Houdini, and he played to all of that. He made his name from an exhibitionist's passing and dribbling, all of which (intentionally or not) drew attention to himself. As a defender he was at best adequate; that, he knew. His career shooting percentage in the NBA, just 37.5 percent from the field, was roughly the league average and wouldn't stand the test of time. At times on the court he swooned with exhaustion and tears, and teammates couldn't be sure if it was fatigue or showmanship or both; it was just Cooz being Cooz. At a game's biggest moment, he wanted the ball in his hands. He projected strength on the court but also vulnerability, anxiety, and pain deeply felt. Each performance became a personal drama, and if that made him a bit of a curiosity to teammates, it also made him a box-office sensation.

As captain, Cousy expected his teammates to perform. Rookie

Tom (Satch) Sanders learned during fall 1960 that Cooz wasn't above sneering at a teammate who dropped his unexpected, well-placed pass. A perceptive, self-aware African American, Sanders arrived at Celtics camp as the first-round draft pick, a pivot man from New York University hoping to earn a spot on a team that had won three NBA championships in four seasons. He was six-foot-six, 215 pounds, and confident that he was good enough for the NBA even if some back home in New York City had doubts. Sanders wore glasses and cumbersome kneepads on the court. To Auerbach, that didn't look right; it smacked of unprofessionalism. He got Sanders contact lenses and made him get rid of the kneepads, and played him as a forward facing the basket. Sanders's boyhood affinity for baseball pitcher Satchel Paige had long ago earned him the neighborhood nickname "Satch"—that, Auerbach let him keep.

In Celtics scrimmages during training camp, Sanders played with a fury because he believed that was the only way to prove his value to Auerbach. He dove for every loose ball, fouled veterans hard, engaged in fights, and proved his points. He roughed it up underneath the basket with Loscutoff, who was threatened by the rookie's presence, and with an African-American forward from the College of Steubenville in Ohio named Jimmy Smith, just out of the army, big and thick and seemingly without a neck or anything to lose.

Finally, K.C. Jones pulled Sanders aside and offered some guidance: "Not so rough, Satch." Jones told him the veterans didn't like it. In short: Loosen up. Two weeks before the start of the 1960–61 NBA season, Auerbach, cigar twirling in his saliva, told Sanders, "Hey, kid. Don't worry. You made it."

Though Sanders ran well and often gained a two-step advantage on opponents during a fast break, when Cousy whipped long passes to him, it presented problems. "Some were curves," Sanders says. "Some were sinkers. He just slung it! It was comin'! Some had a screwball thing, and curved out. And he would throw the long bounce pass. You had to recognize the ball would hit the ground and take off a little faster because that ball would spin."

Sanders concentrated on catching these passes. If he failed, he knew Cousy wouldn't pass him the ball again anytime soon. His contact lenses made the task more challenging. His eyeballs moved, but his contact lenses didn't always move with them. Sometimes Sanders misjudged Cousy's passes. When that happened, Cousy, during the next time-out, all but growled at him.

"He cursed me out in French," Sanders says, or at least that was what he assumed Cousy was doing, though Sanders couldn't be certain because he didn't understand French.

A team of Massachusetts scientists in 1961 studied athletes, including the Celtics, in an attempt to understand the physiological elements involved in the competitive spirit. They found that Cousy's adrenal glands produced ten times as much epinephrine, a hormone related to "vigilance, alertness and self-control," as his teammates', and that, moments before tip-off, he had a higher level of norepinephrine, the hormone associated with aggression, anger, and combativeness, than any hockey player studied.

Cousy typically attributed his ability to *see the floor* to superior peripheral vision. Fans would say, "Cousy has eyes in the back of his head." A half century later, though, studies of perceptual-cognitive expertise in elite athletes suggest that it likely wasn't what Cousy *saw* on the court with his eyes but rather how he interpreted that information in his brain.

"Because we are talking about visual cues, people think, 'Ah, it's how well people see,'" says Jocelyn Faubert, a University of Montreal psychophysicist who directs various studies of athletes' vision. "But *seeing* is an ill-defined word. People think that seeing is detecting. Detecting is detecting. Seeing is something else. Vision is interpreting, and making sense. And that's the brain, it's not the eye."

Faubert says that for audacious playmakers such as Cousy, "They optimally fit and are really geared toward what they need, which is making decisions about dynamic scenes and dynamic movement. It's a form of brain capacity."

These Celtics had their quirks on the court and off. As different as Cousy and Russell were, both led through the force of their personality and talent. At training camp Sanders noticed Russell's big laugh and thought he couldn't possibly be cantankerous, not with that laugh. So he asked Russell if he could tag along with him that night, and the center replied, "No. Hell, no! Certainly not!" Sanders deflated, furious for exposing his own vulnerability, but only until Russell smiled and told the rookie he was only kidding.

Humor cut through tensions, not only the natural competitive tension created by the rise of the Lakers and Wilt's Warriors, and the always-there St. Louis Hawks, but the rising tensions of race relations in America. Russell teased teammates all the time. That was his nature. If a teammate's shirt collar was upturned, or his hair uncombed, Russell seized his opportunity. Sometimes, he wouldn't let up, and the more sensitive Celtics swallowed hard and dealt with it.

Once, Ramsey and Sanders became his foils, Russell saying in a slightly hushed voice in the locker room, "Satch, you like Frank, doncha?" Ramsey, the Kentuckian, sat only a few feet away.

"Yeah, Frank and I get along very well," Sanders answered, his tone serious.

"Whatever you do, don't open Frank's trunk," Russell said. "You'll see all those sheets in there!"

Sanders arched a brow: "Huh?"

"The Ku Klux Klan!" Russell said. "He doesn't want you to know. So don't open his trunk!"

As Russell squealed with delight, Sanders heard Ramsey, his border-state drawl amped to a shriek, say, "You ought to stop that bullshit, Russ!"

On another occasion, Ramsey extended Russell a postseason invitation: "Why don't you come down and spend a week with the guys in Kentucky?"

"Frank, you're a good guy," Russell said, "[but] there's no way in hell I am going to spend no week in Kentucky."

Then there was Heinsohn. He had a brawny game and personality, though he had a more cerebral side. Gene Conley, his roommate, watched Heinsohn paint streetscapes with watercolors and thought, *He's just a man of many ideas*. Of course, the players knew Heinsohn as Auerbach's preferred target. Sometimes, Ack-Ack pushed back. Once, he had a big-scoring first half, and when Auerbach came into the locker room at halftime, Heinsohn, happily smoking a cigarette, chirped, "What'd I do wrong this time, Red?" Teammates broke up laughing.

When Cousy and Heinsohn arrived at practices after the drive from Worcester, Heinsohn needed to tape his ankles; that meant he would start a few minutes behind the rest of the team. Ramsey loved it and bleated, "Red! He's late!!! Heinsohn's late! That's five dollars, Red!" And the next day: "He's late again, Red! Heinsohn's late again!"

Sanders became a defensive stalwart, and Heinsohn insisted the rookie go one-on-one with him for fifteen minutes after practices. It was a hard fifteen: Heinsohn worked his moves, his hook shots, and Sanders, with his long arms, held his ground. Sanders often tried to sneak out before Heinsohn finished his end-of-practice free throws but never succeeded.

Like Arthur Fiedler with the Boston Pops, Auerbach acted as his team's energetic conductor. It would take Sanders time to get to know his coach. Once he did, he liked him. He would stop by his office before practice, and they would talk about investments or the latest news. Auerbach was easy to talk to, Sanders thought.

But as a coach? "A pain in the ass," Sanders says. "Very pushy. As a coach he had to live up to the Auerbach rep. He had to push hard. The reality was that was the only way you were going to win."

Sanders appreciated Auerbach's rule that mandated players wear jackets and ties on the road. He, Russell, and K.C. Jones developed their own intramural battles of couture, Russell, a clotheshorse, sometimes wearing capes. "Here comes Batman," Cousy called out.

In airports and train terminals, Auerbach occasionally spotted his book (*Basketball for the Player, the Fan and the Coach*) at newsstands. "Hey, look at my book!" he'd crow. Cousy and the other Celtics couldn't resist: "HEY, FOLKS, DO YOU KNOW THIS GUY?" they announced to bystanders. "THAT'S HIS BOOK OVER THERE!!" Auerbach let it go, but only until his team played poorly, and then he would explode at his men. Russell likened Auerbach to the leeches that crawled on Humphrey Bogart in *The African Queen*. "That's the way Red would get on you," Russell said, only Auerbach enjoyed it more than the leeches. In February 1960, Auerbach coached his one thousandth NBA game; he was the league's senior coach by a long shot, Syracuse's Paul Seymour next in line with 331 games.

With so much time to kill, the Celtics entertained each other in hotel lobbies, telling jokes and eyeing passing women. K.C. Jones habitually broke into song, mimicking Ray Charles or Nat King Cole, and Satch Sanders gave his best impersonation of the pensive Russell in the pose of Rodin's *The Thinker*. Waiting for the next plane to Cincinnati or out to the coast, reserve forward Gene Guarilia, a member of a country band, would start singing, and then other players took their turns. The Celtics met stars along the way: actresses Sophia Loren and Angie Dickinson, singer Lloyd Price (his song "Personality" topped the charts), the Platters, and the Four Lads. Actress Doris Day sat courtside at Lakers games in Los Angeles, and singer Johnny Mathis, a friend of Russell's, visited the Celtics' locker room a few times.

Players' family members orbited on the periphery. When Sanders's mother visited from New York, Missie Cousy got her a choice seat on Wives Row, and they chatted the night away. Sam Jones, meanwhile, convinced Russell's young son Buddha that his favorite NBA player could only be . . . Sam Jones.

In what became his anthem, Auerbach told his men, "Statistics. What do they prove?" His Celtics accepted this concept, principally because they believed their coach was smarter than other NBA coaches. He had sculpted a team with interlocking pieces, each man with an established role and purpose: Sharman, Heinsohn, and Sam Jones as shooters, Russell, Sanders, and K.C. Jones as defenders, Cousy as ball handler and distributor, Loscutoff and Conley as on-court policemen, and Ramsey as sixth man. (Lakers coach John Kundla: "That Ramsey has an angelic look on his face, but when he enters the game, he kills you.") Except for Cousy in assists, Russell in rebounds, and Sharman in free throw percentage, the Celtics rarely had a league leader in any individual offensive category. In 1959–60, the Celtics won the NBA title, and their leading scorer, Heinsohn, with nearly twenty-two points per game, ranked tenth best in the league. As Auerbach liked to point out, Russell was one of the poorest shots in the league, yet its most valuable player.

To a man, the Celtics submitted to the higher cause, submerging their egos. Once, Russell pulled down an offensive rebound and K.C. Jones, just five feet from the basket, called for the ball: "Bill! Bill! Bill!" Russell, his college roommate, spotted him, but instead passed out to the corner to Sam Jones. "On another team who would be pissed off?" K.C. Jones asked rhetorically. "The guy in my position, who didn't get the pass." But Jones didn't mind at all. With the Celtics, he had a different role.

On the court, the Celtics rolled on in 1960–61. They finished 57-22 during the regular season and won the Eastern Division, Chamberlain's Warriors a distant speck in their rearview mirror, eleven games behind. Still, the Celtics averaged little more than seven thousand fans per game, leaving the Garden only half full. They used the same team-oriented formula, with high scorer Heinsohn (twenty-one points per game) ranking just fourteenth best in the league. At thirty-two, Cousy was slowing a bit, his playing time down to thirty-two minutes a game; Sharman, at thirty-four and in his final year with the team, played just twenty-five minutes a night as the Jones Boys (Sam and K.C.) became more integral players, K.C. as a peerless defender, and Sam, smooth and effortless, as the best bank shooter in the league. (He had been taught years before to aim for a rivet in the backboard, and if a rivet wasn't there on the glass, he imagined that it was.)

Cousy remained daring. Against Syracuse, he stunned forward Cal Ramsey by throwing a bounce pass between Ramsey's legs to Heinsohn for an easy layup, a pass unlike any Ramsey had ever seen.

St. Louis rookie guard Lenny Wilkens watched Cousy from afar and admired his game: *Be able to penetrate, get to the basket, know where your teammates are,* Wilkens thought. *That's how a point guard should be.* Even so, when Wilkens stole the ball from Cousy as the Celtics captain attempted to dribble behind his back during a game at Kiel Auditorium, referee Jim Duffy whistled Wilkens for a foul.

"How can you make a call like that?" an incredulous Wilkens pleaded.

Duffy, with a steely-eyed look, admonished the rookie: "*You* can't take the ball away from a guy like Bob Cousy."

The Celtics blew down Syracuse in five games in the 1961 playoffs, though not before Auerbach and four of his players (Conley, Loscutoff, Ramsey, Heinsohn) got into a melee with Syracuse fans during Game 4 at Onondaga County War Memorial. Such was the intensity of the Celtics-Nationals rivalry, and of the local crowd, that referee Sid Borgia would say, "Officials deserved combat pay for working in Syracuse." In this instance, the melee began with Auerbach rising from the bench to protest a goaltending call against Russell and ended with Loscutoff and Conley, near the Boston bench, fending off a few fans as fists flew and police rushed in to reestablish order.

Then, in the Finals, the Celtics took out St. Louis in five games. They struck a balance with so many scoring options: In Game 1, Heinsohn led with twenty-six points, and in the next Cousy led with twenty-six. In the third, Russell led with twenty-four, and then Sanders and Cousy led in Game 4 with twenty-two apiece. The Celtics closed out the series at Boston Garden with Russell scoring thirty points, making seven shots in a row at one point.

In the final moments, the Celtics ahead by eleven, their fourth NBA championship nearly in hand, fans crowded courtside at Boston Garden, packed five deep.

Preparing for the moment, Auerbach removed his suit jacket and tie. Then his men adhered to tradition immediately after the game and drenched him in the locker room shower.

Auerbach lit a dry cigar and pointed to Russell, saying, "There's my boy. He'll make a coach of me yet."

From the opposing locker room, Pettit said of Russell, "He beat us tonight, like he's beaten us before."

NBA players voted Russell his second MVP award, and Auerbach didn't hold back: "The N.B.A. publicity has been stupid, and I haven't hesitated to say so because it has been eminently unfair. For the past four and a half months all they sent out was Chamberlain . . . Chamberlain . . . Chamberlain, like he was on the N.B.A. payroll. It got sickening."

And then the Boston maestro waved his wand and said, per usual: "Statistics. What do they prove?"

ARISTOCRATS

By the fall of 1961, with four NBA championships to their name, the Celtics were expected to capture a fifth. Pistons rookie forward Ray Scott heard the season's big question whispered across the league: "Who is going to finish second?"

To Scott, Detroit's first-round pick, fresh out of the Eastern League, it seemed as if Boston began every season with a ten- or fifteen-game winning streak and cruised to the title from there. Opposing players, he sensed, viewed the Celtics with a respect and appreciation that approached reverence.

As a young black player, Scott heard about the league's racial quotas. In Detroit, Earl Lloyd became his mentor. Lloyd had been one of the NBA's first black players, arriving in 1950, the same year as Chuck Cooper. He played nine seasons, including the last two with the Pistons, before retiring in 1960. Like a griot, Lloyd told stories of the NBA past and how it was for the black pioneers of the game, and Scott listened to every word. From Lloyd, Scott learned that as an NBA player, he served as a model for the black community, and that he must carry himself as a gentleman at all times, which meant suits, ties, and eating in the right places.

An amiable fellow, Scott introduced himself to Russell, and though the Celtics center didn't take him under his wing, Scott was grateful that the great Russell at least acknowledged him—"He didn't acknowledge a lot of people," Scott says—and involved him in conversations, sometimes over drinks.

To the rookie, Russell was a basketball statesman. "What Russell talked about primarily was respect," Scott says. "He felt that society systemically disrespected him as a person." Russell told him that he did not like living in Boston. "When he talked about Boston," Scott says, "it was never in a favorable sense."

Racial tensions percolated on October 17, 1961, in the hours before a scheduled Celtics-Hawks exhibition game at the University of Kentucky's Memorial Coliseum in Lexington. Ramsey and Hagan, former teammates at Kentucky, were to be honored at the game, and their young children awarded scholarships to the university. A few nights before, in Marion, Indiana, a restaurant had refused service to the black Celtics even as they saw vacant tables across the room; the black Celtics reported the incident to local police.

Now, after the team flew in the early morning from Wichita to Kansas City to St. Louis and then by charter to Lexington, Sanders and Sam Jones checked in with their teammates in mid-afternoon at the Phoenix Hotel without incident. In the hotel's coffee shop, though, the two Celtics were told they would not be served. Furious, they gathered with Russell and K.C. Jones.

Led by Russell, the group met with Auerbach. Russell said they wanted to forgo the exhibition game and fly home to Boston immediately.

Auerbach hedged. "Let's think about it awhile," he said. As he saw it, the university had sold about ten thousand seats for the game at which there would be no segregated seating; the university had done nothing wrong, Auerbach said, and neither had the event's welcoming committee. This, he insisted, was a hotel problem. "Why not go out there," he said, "and show them you're bigger than some two-bit wait-ress in a lousy hotel?" Auerbach insisted the Celtics had a contract and they would meet their obligation.

Russell did not hedge. He said it would be better if the black players went home and white Kentuckians got the segregated game they wanted.

The conversation lasted about two hours before Auerbach finally yielded and drove his black players to the airport; the Hawks' black players also boycotted the game. The Celtics performed that night with seven white players, including Cousy, who made no public state-ment about the incident at the time.

Later that night, Brown, by phone, told Auerbach, "I wouldn't have played it. I don't give a damn about the money." In comments to sportswriters, Brown supported his boycotting players. "I don't blame them a bit [for leaving]," he said. "I will never subject my players to such an embarrassment again."

Ramsey made his position clear to sportswriters: "I was one hun-dred percent behind Bill Russell and the other boys. No thinking per-son in Kentucky is a segregationist. I can't tell you how sorry I am as a human being, as a friend of the players involved and as a resident of Kentucky for the embarrassment of this incident."

Boston newsmen awaited the black players when they arrived at Logan Airport that night. "All Sam and Tom wanted to do was to get something to eat," Russell said. McSweeny reached Russell by phone at his home in Reading the following day. "If I can help it I will never again play where there is segregation," Russell said. "I think of athletes as entertainers. One of the ways the American Negro has attempted to show he is a human being is to demonstrate our race to the people through entertainment, and thus become accepted. I am coming to the realization that we are accepted as entertainers, but that we are not accepted as people in some places. Negroes are in a fight for their rights—a fight for survival—in a changing world. I am with these Negroes."

Cousy believed his black teammates acted appropriately under the circumstances. Later a few NBA referees privately told him they thought the black players had considered only themselves and not the league. "If they don't think about themselves," Cousy countered, "I don't know who else is going to."

The 1961–62 season, a breakout time for scoring in the NBA, statistically belonged to Chamberlain. He averaged an astonishing fifty points per game and threw down a one-hundred-point thunderbolt against the Knicks in Hershey, Pennsylvania, a revolutionary act that symbolically blew the quota to smithereens and announced the NBA as a white man's enclave no more. Russell heard about Wilt's hundred the next morning and told Sanders, "The Big Fella finally did it." Five days after Chamberlain's big night in Hershey, playing out the regular season, the Celtics beat Wilt and the Warriors by fifty-one points, 153–102, the Dipper limited by Russell to thirty points.

As Boston swept to a 60-20 mark, Russell expanded his empire. "The Celtics are the aristocrats of basketball—arrogant perfectionists who play with almost insulting contempt," Jim Murray of the *Los Angeles Times* wrote.

"They come on court with the Emperor of Basketball, Bill Russell, and the score is psychologically 20–0 before the tip-off."

It was not a season without problems, though. In early February, Auerbach heard a morning knock at his door at the Syracusean Hotel. Dressed in a white T-shirt and underwear, his hair a matted mess, he opened the door and was handed a summons just as a camera's bulb flashed—a newspaper photographer, his resulting image of a surprised Auerbach sent out on the wires and published in newspapers across the land. The Syracuse fans who fought with Auerbach and his players in the 1961 playoffs had lodged lawsuits seeking $750,000 in damages against the coach, his players, the NBA, and the arena. WHAT A WAY

TO WAKE UP, the *Daily Record* caption read. Auerbach let the lawyers handle it and focused on the season.

Television ratings were a bigger problem. Ratings for the weekly Saturday afternoon NBA games had slipped to 4.8 (roughly nine million viewers) compared with NFL ratings on Sunday afternoons of 10.4 (fifteen million viewers). Having a weak team in New York did not help the NBA. After seven seasons, NBC had already decided not to renew its contract with the league. Attendance remained a problem, too. The NBA averaged 4,566 fans per game in the 1961–62 season, only about a thousand more than in Cousy's rookie season eleven years before. At least the league's franchises had migrated since that time to bigger and greener pastures—from Fort Wayne to Detroit, Tri-Cities to St. Louis, Rochester to Cincinnati, and Minneapolis to Los Angeles. The NBA had become big-city, if not big-time.

Cousy told Missie he wanted to retire at season's end. At thirty-three, he was a step slower now and knew it. To compensate, his competitive instincts drove him doubly hard. He no longer felt indispensable. Since Sharman was gone, he roomed alone, typically given a suite in each city. He closeted himself in his hotel suites, took room service but no phone calls. He read a lot. The walls closed in.

Missie liked the idea of his retirement; their daughters would have more time with him. Boston College had offered Cousy its head coaching job, and finally he had accepted. He told the press, "It's not like a Russell would be leaving."

But then Auerbach asked him for one more year and insisted, as only Arnold Auerbach could, that it was for Cousy's own good. At the team's Boston Garden offices on March 21, 1962, a horde of sportswriters and radio and television broadcasters waited as Cousy spent a half hour with Auerbach and then fifty minutes with Brown. When Cousy and Brown finally emerged, Cousy stared into the cameras and said, "I guess you'll be seeing me running up and down the floor again next year." He would play one more season.

Russell and Chamberlain did battle again in the 1962 playoffs. The games between their teams that season had been tense, physical. On offense, Warriors rookie Tom Meschery had driven into the lane and encountered Russell. "Bill looked like a big bird, arms in the air, in the crouched position. As you approached he was ready for you," Meschery says. "He never left the ground until you committed. That was his great skill." On defense, Meschery covered the burly Heinsohn. "He was an irritating son of a bitch," Meschery says. "He would get after you and elbow you. I wasn't about to back down." In one game he scuffled with Heinsohn, at which point Loscutoff pinned back Meschery's arms, and Heinsohn struck him above the eye with a right cross. Meschery needed six stitches to close the gash.

Now, in Game 5, the playoff series even at two games apiece, Chamberlain exchanged words and shoves with Sam Jones. Taking no chances, Jones picked up a photographer's stool near the baseline to fend off the opposing giant and waved the stool at him. John Havlicek, the team's new top draft pick, was there to watch the Celtics play that night, the first time he had ever been to Boston Garden. Havlicek starred at Ohio State, and his dorm-mate Bobby Knight told him the Celtics were the perfect NBA team for him, the way they ran the fast break and played defense. "You should go kiss Red Auerbach's ass when you meet him," Knight advised. Sitting in the crowd, though, Havlicek couldn't believe what he was seeing. Ohio State had magnificent facilities. By comparison, Boston Garden was old and decrepit, its locker rooms sad. Now Havlicek watched veteran Carl Braun, acquired by the Celtics that season, rush in to help Sam Jones, at which point Warriors guard Guy Rodgers threw a punch that busted Braun's lip. Seeing this, Loscutoff flexed his muscle and rushed at Rodgers, who turned and ran. Incredulous, Havlicek thought, *What have I gotten myself into?*

The series extended to Game 7, the score tied 107-all, eleven seconds remaining, the Celtics with possession. In the Warriors' huddle during a time-out, Gola asked to cover Sam Jones. Coach Frank

McGuire shook his head, saying that Rodgers would stick with Jones. "No, they will go to Sam Jones," Gola pleaded, "and Guy can't cover him." In a moment, Sam Jones had the ball, and the series, in his hands. He moved behind a Russell screen near the free throw line and made a jump shot. One second remained. Philadelphia inbounded from halfcourt to Chamberlain, who caught the ball, turned and shot.

Russell rose with him and blocked it—series over.

Boston moved on to the first-ever bicoastal NBA Finals against the Los Angeles Lakers. Even with the U.S. Army allowing Private Elgin Baylor a special pass to play the entire series, and Jerry West performing like the star that he was, the Celtics won another tense seven-game series. The Lakers had a matchup problem. They had no center to compete with Russell—they had only Jim Krebs and Ray Felix—a riddle they would fail to solve, at least until 1968, when they traded for Chamberlain, and even that didn't work.

In Game 7, Los Angeles guard Frank Selvy had his chance. With three seconds left, the game tied, and Cousy bearing down on him, Selvy took a ten-foot jump shot that would have won the series. But he missed it, and when Russell grabbed the rebound as time expired, he wrapped his arms around the ball protectively. In overtime, Russell played with force. When Ramsey fouled out, Guarilia covered Baylor, a mismatch. Cousy cupped his hand over his mouth and advised Guarilia that Baylor liked to back in and turn to his left for shots. "See if you can step in front of him and make him go to his right," Cousy said. Guarilia did that, and Baylor missed a couple shots and then fouled out. The Celtics, playing their fourteenth playoff game in twenty-five days, built a seven-point lead.

Their fifth NBA championship ended famously with the ball in Houdini's hands, Cousy stalling out the final seconds, dribbling on the parquet floor this way and that way, like a mouse loosed, Lakers defenders Selvy, West, and Tom Hawkins unable to quarantine him, big Ray Felix lunging at him hopelessly, and then, even before the final seconds expired, two young Celtics fans on the parquet floor reaching for him, wanting only to embrace him, even as he dribbled on. Braun raced onto the court to rescue Cousy from the enveloping crowd and to let him know the game was over. Disconsolate, West walked down narrow steps toward the visiting locker room, "like descending into the catacombs of hell," he would say. Even worse, Felix, unaware the series was over, tried to be inspirational, calling out to his teammates, "That's okay, boys, we'll get 'em on Tuesday!"

As a commercial photographer, Tom Kelley carried impressive credentials. In Hollywood across the decades he had shot Gable, Garbo, and Dietrich. He had also photographed world leaders, among them FDR, Churchill, and JFK. When a struggling actress named Marilyn Monroe in 1949 posed nude in suggestive positions against a red velvet backdrop, Kelley's camera famously captured it. For these photos, Monroe got fifty bucks, and Kelley got his calling card.

Now, shooting for Jantzen sportswear, Kelley posed Cousy, in ball cap, bright yellow knit shirt, and outrageous four-color duck pants, standing upright, barefoot and proud, on a small outrigger named *Bloody Mary*, left hand at his hip as he looked to shore in his role as the so-called director general of the Jantzen International Sports Club. In this photo, shot at the Hanalei Plantation on the Hawaiian island of Kauai, Cousy's football buddies Frank Gifford and Paul Hornung pull the outrigger ashore while professional golfer Ken Venturi, aboard in his white duck knee-choppers, splashes his paddle in the water.

Each off-season, Cousy looked forward to these Jantzen photo shoots, usually conducted over ten days at an exotic beach location such as the Bahamas, Jamaica, Maui, and a few times at the Royal Hawaiian Hotel on Waikiki. He brought Missie each time and, once or twice, their daughters came, too. Kelley was meticulous, a perfectionist. If the photo session was to start at six-thirty in the morning, then Kelley showed up hours earlier, calibrating lighting and other details. In one ad, Cousy sits atop a surfboard carried above the surf by four athletes; in another, he sits surfside, holding on to rocks, water splashing around him, as Venturi pours a bottle of Coke through a snorkel into Cousy's mouth and Gifford and surfer John Severson stand nearby smiling (caption: "Cousy on the Rocks"). These images reflected young white athletes, in their masculine prime, sharing in beachside fun and frivolity.

To Cousy, the Royal Hawaiian was the Waldorf Astoria of Hawaii, an elegant place for the older, moneyed set. Taking Kelley's directions, Cousy and Gifford posed in the early-morning light at the Royal Hawaiian on the back patio or on the beach for two or three hours for national magazine ads. Then they rushed off to play eighteen holes of golf. They were back with Kelley in the late afternoons to shoot the style folders for Jantzen's catalogues, wearing handsome menswear, including colorful turtleneck sweaters and slacks meant for the young, hip crowd. They changed outfits often, each time walking downstairs from the hotel lobby to the men's room. Finally, tired of climbing stairs, they hid behind huge potted plants in the lobby, Cousy and Gifford bare-assed as they changed from one swimsuit into the next.

If Cousy served as an exemplar of how a white star athlete reaped the spoils of celebrity, Russell represented the same for a black star athlete. Few endorsements came his way, even after he won five NBA championships and three league MVP awards in six seasons. In summer 1962, Russell drove south to Louisiana to take his young children to see his grandfather, Jake Russell, a man he respected and loved deeply. He knew about Jake Russell's life odyssey, how he was part of the first generation of Russells born free in America and how, as a young man, he had worked a mule on a farm near West Monroe. Jake Russell had raised money among impoverished blacks in the area to build a schoolhouse and pay for a teacher, stirring the enmity of the local Klan. He had seen a lot and accomplished plenty and, as his grandson viewed it, was worthy of every man's respect. In a few years, Jake Russell would attend a Celtics exhibition game in Shreveport, and in the postgame locker room see Sam Jones and John Havlicek in the shower together, a black man and a white man passing a bar of soap back and forth and alternating turns beneath the splash of the lone shower head. Jake Russell, wide-eyed, would say, "I never thought I'd see anything like that."

As an NBA player, Bill Russell had endured slights and catcalls. Later he would say it made him want to scream, "I MUST HAVE MY MANHOOD."

In 1962, he drove his children deep into the South, heading to see Grandpa Jake. His children became hungry and tired. Because of segregation, he could not stop at most restaurants and motels. From the backseat he heard the voices: "Daddy, can't we stop?" "Daddy, I'm hungry." Bill Russell was a world champion, a most valuable player. Only too well, he understood that race had been, still was, and always would be a factor in a black man's life.

Bob Cousy Day, 1963

LA FERME DES COUSY

His palms turn upward, and there is a plea in the old man's voice. "I never had this long a discussion in my life with my father," he says. In his favorite chair at home, remembering Bob Cousy Day, he is reminded—by the presence of his parents on that afternoon—of his roots, and of how far he traveled from *sale Boche* to that seminal moment in Boston Garden when the people who gave meaning and definition to his life (Missie and the girls, Auerbach and Russell, his parents) were all there. At some level, pro basketball is about manhood. On the court he projected a classic masculinity. He shed tears, too, revealing a deeper sensitivity, but mostly he swaggered in a way his father never did. He can still see Joe Cousy in his mind's eye, in front of their little house in St. Albans, shining the chrome on his taxi, as if making love to it. They hardly spent any time together, father and son. He says, "I never knew the little guy." His eyes project sadness, regret. He is left with many questions, too late to ask: He would ask about his father's early life in France, and about the family farm, his first wife, and serving in the German army during World War I. *What was that like?* He would also ask about *sale Boche*, and why he sat silently when his wife hit him. "She's irrational about the French-German situation" is what he imagines his father would have replied. The answers to all of these questions matter to him now more than they ever did as he attempts, with some stumbling, to shape and understand his life's narrative. He didn't make it to his father's deathbed in time and isn't sure what he would have said, anyway. "What do you say to a father that you've never had a profound conversation with?" he asks now. He shifts uncomfortably in his chair. "How do you try to sum it up in a few last-minute words?" He considers the magnitude of that task, quivers, and then says softly, as if to himself, *"God . . ."*

In spring 1962, Cousy traveled to the Old World and found his way into his family's past. He struck a deal with the Gillette Razor Company to spend five weeks on a promotional tour of France, giving basketball demonstrations in fifteen cities; Gillette agreed to pay full expenses for Missie and the girls. First, the Cousys stopped in Rome. The archdiocese of Worcester had arranged for the family to have a private audience with Pope John XXIII at the Vatican, which meant they would receive papal blessings as the pope mingled briefly with a group of about thirty people. The Cousy girls, just ten and nine, had practiced genuflecting in preparation to kiss the pope's ring but never got the chance. As their group crowded near the pope, someone accidentally brushed against little Ticia. She stumbled and, in attempting to keep her balance, grabbed the pope's robe. Pope John XXIII turned and gently patted Ticia's head. The Cousys stopped at Lourdes, in the foothills of the Pyrenees, where the apparition of the Virgin Mary is said to have appeared in 1858; Missie filled two plastic jugs with holy water to take home.

They landed at Orly Airport in Paris on May 1, 1962. "Excuse me," Cousy said to a sportswriter from *L'Équipe* at a press conference on the Champs-Élysées, "but it will take me two or three days to find my French vocabulary."

At the elite National Institute of Sport near Paris, Cousy wore a T-shirt that read BOB COUSY FRANCE GILLETTE and demonstrated dribbling and shooting. He showed off his famous arm-roll, which once had embarrassed Sweetwater Clifton, and wowed his audience by dribbling behind his back. During clinics, he spoke English; in question-and-answer sessions, he spoke French. He watched young French players and said, "I think they are a little delayed in their physical advancement. They do not make their moves naturally." In Le Mans he played two-on-two and showed a film of the Celtics' fast break.

Missie told him he went through a personality change in France. For one thing, she said, he used his hands more when he spoke, and at night he chattered in his sleep, which wasn't unusual, except now he chattered in French. Even as Cousy stumbled to regain command of his first language, Ticia marveled at her father's ability to converse. It was almost as if she were watching a different person. With a child's rich imagination, Ticia pretended to be a little girl from a French family. She knew that if no one in her family spoke other than her father, everyone would assume they were French, and she reveled in her secret. In one photo from this trip, the four Cousys walk hand in hand on a Parisian street, the girls in matching floral dresses and Belgian loafers, Missie in a classic houndstooth suit, and Cooz in a worn sport coat and slacks, the stub of a cigar in his mouth.

They moved through France in two cars driven by Gillette representatives. Heading northeast, not far from the German and Swiss borders, Cousy studied a map and realized they were close to his father's old family farm in Lachapelle-sous-Rougemont. Only now did he think to pay a visit.

Near Mulhouse they diverted from their path and found their way to a farming village with fewer than five hundred residents. Cousy sought directions to the farm from the parish priest. He asked, *"Mon père, où se trouve la ferme des Cousy?"*

The priest smiled at him and pointed down the road.

In a short distance they came upon a ramshackle farmhouse. Cousy went inside and introduced himself: *"Je suis Robert, fils de Joseph."* ("I'm Robert, son of Joseph.") His unannounced arrival startled his relatives. Cousy's father, still in St. Albans, was now seventy years old and had not spoken of the people he had left behind when he and Juliette boarded the *Mauretania* in 1927.

Now, thirty-five years later, here was Cooz sizing up his uncle Eugène, an old and stooped French farmer, his hands gnarled from his life's work. The farmhouse, spare with an earthen floor, had more modern living quarters upstairs. His relatives went outside, milked a goat, and returned with a bowl of fresh milk, still warm. Raised to be polite, Marie read her mother's expression: *You have to drink some of that!* They served bread and cheese, and when Missie and the girls needed to use a restroom, they were directed to a barn. It was dark inside, and when they saw a hole in the floor and realized what it was for, the girls laughed.

Cousy and his uncle Eugène shared wine. Eugène asked about his brother, Joe: *"Comment va le playboy?"* ("How's the playboy?") This confused Cooz. *My poor father,* he thought. *From the minute the boat landed at Ellis Island he worked two or three jobs. Playboy?* He saw that Joe wasn't appreciated on the farm. Joe worked hard throughout his life, and still his brother seemed to disparage him as a playboy.

Now he understood why his father had left this farm that had been trampled during World War I. He was thankful that Joe Cousy had taken that risk. Moving through this broken-down farmhouse, and on the brink of playing his final NBA season, he had an epiphany: If his father hadn't boarded the *Mauretania*, Cooz might've become an obscure French farmer just like his uncle Eugène.

No Celtics, no NBA championships, no Houdini.

HIGH-STRUNG

Some things would never change: Arnold Auerbach, for instance. Cousy played more than a thousand NBA games for his coach. He knew Auerbach's quirks, tics, and halftime motivational speeches ("What the hell is going on? What do you think this is—*a prom*, or something?"). Here was a quintessential Auerbach truth, born of his Brooklyn upbringing: You don't get anything in life that you don't fight for.

Cousy admired the man for his will to win. Thirteen years later, he recognized that Auerbach retained every bit of his scorching intensity even as he created more enemies along the way. Once the rookie Havlicek noticed his coach favoring his left hand at practice. "Who'd you punch?" Havlicek asked. The guy on the highway who cut him off at a red light, Auerbach replied. "I got to him," Auerbach said, "and I punched him."

No surprise then that, moments after the Celtics defeated the Cincinnati Royals 128–127 in overtime at Cincinnati Gardens on

December 2, 1962, an enraged Royals fan—a service station attendant by profession—strode up to Auerbach and shouted, "Sauerback crybaby!" and kicked the Celtics coach in the shin. Auerbach whirled and punched the fan in the mouth, knocking out a tooth. The fan pressed assault charges; after the game, Auerbach was escorted to a local police station, where he saw the aggrieved fan holding a handkerchief over his mouth. Auerbach stomped and fumed, especially after realizing he didn't have enough money to post a $300 bond. Cousy and LeRoux came to his rescue. Cousy pointed at his coach and said, "You can't put that man in jail"—here, he winked—"because you don't have Chinese food." Auerbach kept fuming as Cousy and LeRoux handed over the additional money he needed.

Later, in an out-of-court settlement, Auerbach would pay $250 for the fan's dental bills and $200 in assorted expenses. On a cold winter night in Cincinnati, Cousy and LeRoux got their coach out of his latest predicament, and the Boston Celtics, bound for game twenty-three in an eighty-game schedule, headed for Detroit.

Another hotel room, another mirror: A nerve was jumping beneath Cousy's left arm. He felt it, the twitch strong and fast, but he couldn't see it. He removed his shirt, raised his arm, and studied his torso in the mirror's reflection. He expected to see movement beneath his skin's surface, like a mouse under the covers. He saw no movement at all, nothing. *Where the hell is it?* Now another nerve twitched beneath his left eye. This was his usual pattern: first one twitch, and then the other, first the arm, and then the eye. It had been like this for a couple months. The twitching lasted only a few minutes each time. He looked beneath his left eye and saw no movement. *Where the hell is it?* He expanded his view. He studied his face in a more holistic way, as if for the first time. He saw exhaustion. He saw that his hairline had receded into a widow's peak, and that his eyes, always deep set, had hollowed out, like caves. His face, always long and thin, seemed longer and thinner.

This was not the natural progression of age. It was the product of inner tumult and pressure—pressure to win another championship, pressure to be Houdini, pressure to be gracious to every autograph-seeking fan who came at almost any moment to his hotel breakfast table or the front door of his house, and pressure from an FBI man who quietly pulled him aside after a practice and told him that one of his social friends from Springfield was a known gambler with ties to the mob and advised Cousy to stay away from him.

A perpetual worrier, Cousy fretted over his imminent life transition. Would he even be a good coach next season at Boston College? A psychiatrist told him the twitching resulted from his inner turmoil and would disappear at some point. In his reflection, Cousy saw his eyes peering back at him. He considered himself a high-strung man.

This was it for Cooz, the final go-round. He was tired of the NBA grind, all of it—except for the games, that was the easiest part, though now he only played a little more than half the time. He felt as if, physically, he could play two more seasons, but mentally not even two more minutes. As the Celtics headed toward another Eastern Division title, Cousy, at thirty-four, showed signs of creeping age. He fatigued more easily. Auerbach always knew when to pull him from the game, typically calling for K.C. Jones as his replacement.

When Charley Wolf, Cincinnati's coach, accused Cousy of using rough tactics against his guards, Walter Brown howled, "For thirteen years, I've seen Cousy drive and get murdered!" Brown's words were heartfelt—as always, he was protecting his star—but Cousy played more physically as a way to hold his ground against younger, faster opponents. Some came after him hard. They were twenty-three or twenty-four years old, aggressive, and looking to make their names against him. Cousy was fighting not only against them but against time. He averaged thirteen points a game (a career low) and nearly seven assists, numbers that represented strong production for a guard playing twenty-six minutes a night.

Forever in motion, the rookie Havlicek discovered that as soon as he got open, Cousy delivered the ball to him. "He was uncanny in that way," Havlicek says.

Cousy knew fans still expected to see his old tricks, so he threw a no-look pass or executed a transfer around his back on a drive to the basket, and when he heard the *ooh*s and *aah*s from the crowds, it pleased him, maybe more than it had earlier in his career, because it reassured him that he was still there, still alive, still the Man.

As the long season wore on, Cousy couldn't bear being away from home. Each day on the road played out slowly, the clock ticking monotonously. *Eleven A.M. . . . Noon . . . One P.M. . . . Two P.M.* He sat in his hotel room dreading the moment he would leave for the arena. He had too much time to worry. Already he had missed half of his daughters' formative years. Missie was a stabilizing force at home. For the girls, she created play stations and a make-believe kitchen, and on a phonograph played songs from Broadway shows, *The Sound of Music* and *My Fair Lady*. It was a contented home for the girls even if their father was hardly around. Each day, Missie talked to them about where he was, and how the Celtics had played the night before—she tried to keep him vibrant and present in the girls' daily lives—but still he wasn't there. The truth was that he belonged more to Celtics fans than to his daughters. The girls didn't understand that. How could they?

Marie and Ticia were growing up, Cousy realized, while he was sitting in hotel rooms in Syracuse, St. Louis, and Detroit. Ticia, a shy girl, did not tell her classmates in Worcester who her father was, but they all knew anyway, and she hated that because she preferred anonymity. Once Marie told him, only half joking, "Daddy, why don't you break a leg so you can be home more?" Her question worked like a corrosive in his thoughts.

In his hotel rooms, Cousy felt like a soldier in combat looking up at a hill each morning and knowing that sometime that night he would need to take the hill. There are just so many nights in a man's life that he is capable of taking hills. Cousy wished he could be anywhere else or be anyone else. To occupy his mind, and pass time, he read voraciously: an Allen Drury novel; Theodore H. White's *The Making of the President, 1960*; a nonfiction book about Communist plans to dominate the globe; and Harper Lee's *To Kill a Mockingbird*. He considered Lee's novel profound; it struck an emotional chord with him. He thought it admirable that the fictional southern lawyer Atticus Finch fought for an African-American underdog.

To stoke the embers of his competitiveness, Cousy played mind games. He believed he needed to rouse himself from fatigue and dread and complacency. He imagined each night's opponent as a mortal enemy. One night that enemy was Richie Guerin of the Knicks, another night the Lakers' Frank Selvy or Dick Barnett, another the Pistons' Gene Shue. By opening tip-off, Cousy fed off this contrived hostility. It lifted his game. If his opponent said hello on the court just before the opening tip, Cousy wanted to kick him in the groin.

Sometimes Cousy would run a hot bath in his hotel suite in the early afternoon. He would soak his tired bones and muscles in the tub, all the while thinking about his opponent's moves and tendencies. In his mind, Cousy saw Selvy distributing to West and Baylor, and the images were so vivid it was as if Selvy was in the bathtub with him. Grimly Cousy asked himself: *How long can you go on putting yourself in a trance?*

With Sharman as his roommate, he'd always had someone to talk to. Once they created a list of fifty jobs they might try after retirement, though both admitted coaching seemed most likely. Together they passed time, though never talking about current events, never discussing Ike, Khrushchev, or civil rights. Instead they fell into their habits, with Sharman a virtual slave to his eating and exercise regimens.

Rooming alone now, Cousy became like a hermit. He wondered if his teammates thought him odd. If Heinsohn called, he might go out after a game to have a beer with him. More often than not, though, Cousy ordered room service—much less disruptive that way, no need to leave his bunker. If he went to the coffee shop for breakfast and saw one or two teammates there, he sometimes sat alone at another table, and he figured they understood.

Several times during his final season, postmidnight, his hotel room phone rang, K.C. Jones on the line, saying, "Cooz, can I come up?" Jones needed to vacate his room because Russell, his roommate, wanted to be alone with a woman, or at least that's how Jones explained it to Cousy. Each time he called, Cousy got up and unlocked the door to his suite, and a few minutes later, he heard Jones walk in and slide quietly into the other bed.

No one could persuade Cousy to play another NBA season, not this time. He had agreed to become head coach at Boston College when the Celtics' season ended and had signed a three-year deal. Instead of making $35,000 as an NBA player, Cousy, though still earning a handsome amount from endorsements, would make only $12,000 as a college coach. That's in part why he accepted a couple thousand dollars to fly to New York in 1962 to be photographed for an advertisement for Kent cigarettes. He did it for the money. The resulting image of Cousy, with a cigarette between his fingers (next to his 1957 NBA championship ring), appeared in national magazines and on posters on city buses and in pharmacy windows. He saw the ad and shuddered. Cousy thought it looked unnatural. He wasn't even holding the cigarette properly, and for good reason—he smoked an occasional cigar, but never a cigarette. (Missie, on the other hand, sometimes had multiple cigarettes going simultaneously in various rooms of the house.) From the first moment he saw that cigarette ad, he knew his participation was a mistake. It was as if he had said the F-word in public. When he received letters expressing disappointment that he promoted cigarettes, Cousy asked for the ad to be pulled; he even offered to return his endorsement money. It was too late for that, though, and the ad ran for about a year.

His final season with the Celtics generated fawning, reverential coverage. National magazines and newspapers wrote about the grand old man of pro basketball. He made a victory tour through the league's other cities, a repetitive farewell night of appreciation at each stop. He suspected these nights were promotional gimmicks to help those teams draw an additional few thousand fans. He didn't mind waving to fans at halftime, but he thought all the speeches and gifts over the top. He played along with it, deciding that he owed the NBA for all that it had given him. The Celtics would host a Bob Cousy Day on St. Patrick's Day, before the regular-season finale, and that would be more significant and personal to Cousy. Boston Garden was home; the Celtics fans were old friends.

The writer Herbert Warren Wind spent a few days with Cousy in January 1963 to research a profile for *The New Yorker* to coincide with Bob Cousy Day. Wind was an elegant stylist and premier golf writer who coined the name "Amen Corner" for the eleventh, twelfth, and thirteenth holes at Augusta National Golf Club. In his tweed jacket and cap, Wind always seemed like a British lord to Cousy. Together they sat in a hotel coffee shop in Cincinnati in mid-afternoon, the Celtics about to play their ninth consecutive road game in a span of fifteen days.

Suffering from a thigh injury, Cousy, over a bowl of vegetable soup and a grilled cheese sandwich, told Wind, "It was a good thing this trip turned out to be so rough. The first couple months of the season, everything went so smoothly that I was wondering if I really wanted to retire. Well, I'm sure of it now. The schedule's just too brutal and the season's much too long. This is a game where you've got to put out your top effort every second. You're head to head with your man. In the final analysis, it's how much better you can sustain your drive, your purpose, than he can. That's what makes a man, and a team, superior."

The next night, Wind took in the game against Syracuse at Boston Garden and then joined Cousy and Missie on the drive back to Worcester. He spent two nights at their house. One morning, he observed

Cousy with his daughters and answering phone calls about charity work and various business deals. On the second morning, Wind accompanied Cousy and Heinsohn in their car, bound for a Sunday afternoon home game against the Chicago Zephyrs. Driving along Route 9, they passed a restaurant that Cousy and another man wanted to buy. "My partner wants to call it 'Bob Cousy's Abner Wheeler House,'" Cousy said, "but I'm sort of partial to 'Abner Wheeler's Bob Cousy House.' More class." Heinsohn replied, "If you're still thinking of taking up the piano next year, it might cut down your overhead. You could be featured in the lounge—playing 'Chopsticks.'" This was the essence of the Cousy-Heinsohn friendship: one zinger followed by another, their humor puncturing the demands and pressures of another long season. "He has made his farewell season a suitably triumphant one," Wind would write of Cousy. "This does not come to pass very often in sports."

That the Celtics and Lakers would meet in the 1963 NBA Finals seemed a foregone conclusion. Even before the season, William Leggett of *Sports Illustrated* had suggested a "great basketball dynasty is abuilding"—and he meant the Lakers, with Baylor's full-time return from the army and West's rapid maturation. "This," he predicted, "is the season it should take over."

In early February, the Lakers had a league-best 46-14 record, the Celtics next best at 43-18. To the Celtics, the Lakers were too wrapped up in themselves and Hollywood, especially with L.A. newspapers touting Los Angeles as "the basketball capital of the world."

"The Lakers aren't the champions of anything," Auerbach said, spitting out each syllable. "Los Angeles has been in this league for two years and it's the basketball capital of the world?" Auerbach shook his head and muttered an obscenity.

To the Lakers, the Celtics were old and arrogant. Coach Fred Schaus thought Auerbach arrogance personified. Schaus turned his back whenever they were in the same room. "I respect Auerbach as a coach," Schaus said. "But I don't like him. I just plain don't like him."

In pregame talks, Schaus told his players that, by defeating the Celtics, they would symbolically shove that cigar down Auerbach's throat.

The two teams met on back-to-back nights in mid-February, first in the opening game of a doubleheader at a neutral site, Detroit's Cobo Arena, and then at Boston Garden. Entering the locker room at Cobo, Cousy looked all business, wearing his green team blazer, carrying a briefcase and a copy of that day's *Boston Traveler*, which featured this headline: L.A. FEELS CELTS ARE WASHED UP. Russell, Ramsey, and Sanders crowded close and read the accompanying story over Cousy's shoulder, Satch whispering to Russ, "Oh, great and noble, bearded one: We have a job to do tonight." Elgin Baylor saw a few Celtics warming up on the court as he walked into the arena that night; pure showman, Baylor smiled, unbuttoned his fancy overcoat, took a penny from his pocket, and tossed it at the Celtics on the court, a gesture once used by vaudeville customers to force bad acts from the stage.

Once the real show started, Cousy stirred the crowd with his passing, once tossing the ball, discus-like, the length of the court to Russell, who leaped and tipped the ball into the basket. Just before halftime, Cousy became winded and called to Auerbach, "Get me! Get me! I've had it." The Celtics led by twenty-one points at the half and won 120–93.

"This is the kind of victory I could savor for a long, long time," Cousy said, but he didn't have that luxury.

The next night in Boston, the Celtics led by twelve points with seven minutes to play, but the Lakers ran off a 13–2 streak; Heinsohn got a technical with thirty seconds to play for cursing at a referee, and the Lakers won 134–128.

In the quiet Celtics' dressing room, Cousy, looking ahead to the playoffs, told the gathered sportswriters, "Just wait."

"TAKE IT EASY, BABY"

The black freedom struggle convulsed the nation with spasms of racial tension across the South: Freedom Rides, freedom songs, sit-ins, and Alabama governor George Wallace, like a gargoyle at the gate of the Old South, saying in his January 1963 inaugural, "Segregation now, segregation tomorrow, segregation forever." Black leaders looked with hope to Washington but were losing patience with the Kennedy administration, slow to move on civil rights.

"We think that the president is a fine man, like we said," Jackie Robinson, the retired ballplayer turned businessman, wrote in frustration in his ghostwritten column in the *Amsterdam News* in Harlem. "But Abraham Lincoln he ain't."

Having no time for flippancy, James Baldwin excoriated white America in his 1963 book, *The Fire Next Time*, in which he published a letter to his young nephew decrying the diminishment of black life. "The details and symbols of your life have been deliberately constructed to make you believe what white people say about you,"

Baldwin wrote. He added, "You must accept them and accept them with love. For these innocent people have no other hope. They are, in effect, still trapped in a history which they do not understand; and until they understand it, they cannot be released from it."

January 31, 1963. Mid-morning, the calls went out to Celtics players in their hotel rooms: a White House group tour. Wear coat and tie. Meet in the lobby. The Celtics would play the Cincinnati Royals at seven-thirty at a neutral site in nearby College Park, Maryland; the NBA scheduled such games at neutral sites in hopes of developing new fans in other cities. Late morning, Cousy put on a blue blazer and gray slacks; Russell, with a do-not-disturb request on his hotel phone, did not get the message and missed the tour.

At the White House, a side door opened, and the arriving Celtics spotted First Lady Jacqueline Kennedy with her two young children, Caroline and John, along with her sister, Lee Radziwill, and Clipper, the Kennedys' new German shepherd, a gift from the president's father.

Cousy had voted for JFK in 1960, though he kept his politics mostly private. For years, Auerbach had made it clear to his players that they couldn't afford to alienate fans by aligning with politicians or causes, at least not publicly. Auerbach wanted to fill the Garden, not empty it.

But when Teddy Kennedy, the president's thirty-year-old brother, running for his big brother's vacant U.S. Senate seat in Massachusetts, stopped by a Celtics practice in autumn 1962 to ask Cousy to campaign with him, Cooz, though not enamored of the idea, figured he couldn't turn down the president's brother. So he campaigned for two days along the North Shore, sitting in the back of a limousine with Teddy and his campaign aides, hearing them discuss strategy, including which local politicians to cite in speeches and which ones not to cite ("We don't mention that prick!"). Together, Cousy and

Teddy took their places behind a high school marching band and paraded into view. They hopped up onto a sound truck, one at a time. Teddy swept to election, though Cousy, for his part, hated every second of campaigning.

When a White House staffer earlier had asked Dave Powers, a presidential aide and JFK intimate from Boston, if the president might meet briefly with the Celtics during their tour, Powers, an avid sports fan, said no. "If it ever gets in the newspaper," Powers said, "then every sports team in the country will want to come in and have their picture. We just can't do that."

But as the Celtics toured the White House, Powers showed up to say the president would say a quick hello, after all. The Celtics waited for him in the Cabinet Room, the players studying the nameplates as they sat in the chairs of the various cabinet secretaries: Dean Rusk, Bobby Kennedy, Robert McNamara, Luther Hodges, and others. Was it Heinsohn who as secretary of defense suggested an invasion of another country, and Loscutoff, as secretary of the treasury, who mandated that a million dollars be given to every NBA player, or vice versa? Some Celtics, Cousy included, pocketed the matchbooks on the table that featured the presidential seal on one side and a picture of the White House on the other. (A few weeks later, Heinsohn playfully accused Cousy of becoming "the only match dropper in the world. He won't go anyplace without them.")

Kennedy came in. Around the table he went, smiling, shaking hands, and asking players where they'd gone to college. He revealed some knowledge of the team: He asked Auerbach if he had been thrown out of any games lately. Cousy thought JFK smooth, at ease, like one of the boys.

The president escorted the Celtics into the Oval Office, where Ramsey spotted the rocking chairs he had read about. Four weeks hence, Kennedy would address Congress and say that a century had passed since Abraham Lincoln's Emancipation Proclamation. He would say that blacks in America were in despair, living seven years less than whites on average and twice as likely to be unemployed; it was time, Kennedy would tell Congress, "for a sober assessment of our failures."

Nine Celtics players (six whites, three blacks) stood with the president in front of his desk and posed for a photographer, Auerbach between Kennedy and Cousy. The next day's *Boston Globe* published this photo, as did other newspapers, and reported that Russell had overslept and missed the visit.

As they prepared to leave, the Celtics formed a line, one by one shaking Kennedy's hand. Cousy stood in back, behind Sanders, and noticed his young teammate's nervousness. In September 1960, Sanders had cheered with the enthusiastic crowds outside the Hotel Theresa in Harlem when Cuban president Fidel Castro lodged there before addressing the United Nations. At the Theresa, Castro met with Nikita Khrushchev, Malcolm X, and others. "The happiness that I had," Sanders says, "was that he was a prominent figure that didn't stay downtown; he came *uptown*." Sanders's college teammates swore that Satch stood fully upright, ramrod straight, in front of NBA scouts so they would think him taller. For that they called him "Posture." His Celtics teammates considered Sanders quiet and likable, off the court a gentle spirit. Much later in his thirteen-year NBA career, by which time his game and his confidence had grown, Sanders heard fans at courtside during road games shouting racial epithets at him. Stepping toward the hecklers, he would ask, "What time did your wife get home last night?" And then: "It was kind of you to share her." That response shut up several audiences.

But now, just twenty-four years old and awed by the setting, Sanders shook Kennedy's hand and, uncertain what to say, blurted out, "Take it easy, baby."

Cousy saw the nation's thirty-fifth president double over with laughter.

Boston, Kennedy's hometown, was suffering its own racial turmoil. That was a problem for the president because in politics appearances mattered. Kennedy hoped to pass through Congress a civil rights bill, which he would use to his advantage in his 1964 reelection campaign; southern Democrats called him a hypocrite and fought hard against him. Boston's black population had nearly tripled since 1940 to more than 64,000, most of the newcomers arriving from southern states and living in Boston's poorer areas. Even so, blacks represented only about 11 percent of Boston's population, small for a major northern city.

In spring 1963, after a study revealed that fifteen public schools in Boston—in a geographical half-moon from the South End through Roxbury to a portion of Dorchester—had black student enrollments that exceeded 90 percent, the local NAACP demanded an immediate public acknowledgment by the Boston School Committee that its system suffered from "*de facto* segregation." The school committee balked.

Russell willingly entered the fray. About half of the more than five thousand African-American students in Boston's public junior and senior high schools would stage a one-day "Stay Out for Freedom Day" boycott in June, with Russell addressing a "Freedom Workshop" at the St. Mark Social Center. Wearing a colorful sport coat and tie, Russell urged black students to conduct themselves as "ladies and gentlemen" and to "wear your color as a badge." Then they sang songs from the black freedom struggle. Only weeks before, Russell, with K.C. Jones at his side, had led a civil rights march from Roxbury to Boston Common, where ten thousand people massed and heard the Reverend James Bevel, an aide to Martin Luther King Jr., say, "You don't have to go to Alabama to find segregation. Just go out your back door and walk across town."

Russell knew the truth of that. Honored that month with a testimonial dinner attended by two thousand residents in Reading, where

When Juliette and Joe Cousy arrived at Ellis Island on the *Mauretania* in 1927, she was pregnant with a son, their only child.

Juliette Cousy in a photo likely taken during the 1920s.

In their dysfunctional marriage, Joe Cousy deferred to Juliette. When a decision needed to be made, he would say, "If you'll see my wife, she'll tell you."

In 1946, Bob Cousy (far left) of Andrew Jackson High School was named captain of the *New York Journal-American* all-city team.

With freshman guard Bob Cousy (front row, second from left) playing on the second platoon, the Holy Cross Crusaders, in a remarkable underdog's run, won the 1947 NCAA basketball championship.

Bob Cousy carries his bride, Missie, over the threshold at a Boston hotel in December 1950. The Celtics played later that night.

In his Texaco uniform and cap, Bob Cousy (third from right) and his former Holy Cross teammate Frank Oftring opened a service station in Worcester in 1951. Soon enough, they sold out.

Cousy drives past Dick McGuire of the New York Knicks during an NBA game in 1955. "Covering Cousy's dribble for nine years," McGuire would say, "is like trying to catch a yo-yo."

The Celtics whoop it up after sweeping the Minneapolis Lakers to win the 1959 NBA championship. Back row (left to right): Bill Russell, Sam Jones (half-turned), Jim Loscutoff, Gene Conley, Bennie Swain, and K.C. Jones. Middle row: Trainer Buddy LeRoux, Coach Red Auerbach, Cousy, and Tom Heinsohn. Front row (sitting): Frank Ramsey and Bill Sharman.

Bill Russell was the only African-American player on the 1957 NBA champion Boston Celtics. The league featured fifteen black players that season. The following season the St. Louis Hawks, the NBA's southernmost team, became the last all-white champion in NBA history.

Six years later, the 1963 NBA champion Celtics had four black players (Russell, K.C. Jones, Sam Jones, and Tom Sanders) and the number of African-American players in the league reached nearly forty percent. For Cousy (front row, second from right), this was his final season with the Celtics.

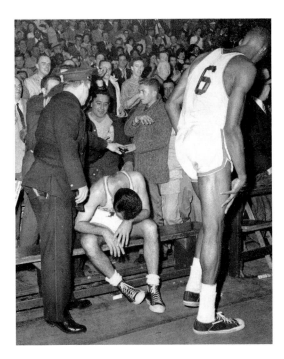

Emotion overcame Cousy after the Celtics defeated St. Louis, 122–103, in Game 7 of the 1960 NBA Finals at Boston Garden. Sitting on the Celtics bench, he wept with joy.

Moments later, emotion overcame Celtics fans, who celebrated the team's third NBA championship in four seasons by carrying Cousy from the court on their shoulders.

In November 1962, Cousy (middle row, second from right) was among twelve sports figures honored in New York as Athletes of the Decade for the 1950s. Front row (left to right): Outfielder Willie Mays, auto racer Roger Ward, jockey Eddie Arcaro, and harness racer Del Miller. Middle row: Running back Jim Brown, golfer Arnold Palmer, Cousy, and linebacker Chuck Bednarik. Back row: Hockey player Maurice Richard, pitcher Warren Spahn, and boxer Rocky Marciano. Bowler Don Carter was absent.

"Passing was my raison d'être," Cousy said. His theatricality extended to dribbling. A multiple-exposure portrait in 1955 showed his famed behind-the-back dribbling maneuver.

Auerbach and Cousy traveled the globe together as goodwill basketball ambassadors. They knew each other's quirks. In foreign restaurants, Auerbach loudly hailed waiters. "Arnold, you are the poster boy for the ugly American," Cousy told him. Once, an embarrassed Cousy moved to a different table.

A rare calm moment on the bench for Boston Celtics coach Red Auerbach. Cousy and Tom Heinsohn (at far left) watch the action with him.

In spring 1962, the Cousys visited France and strolled down a Parisian street: (from left to right) Missie, Ticia, Bob, and Marie.

The wives of Celtics players became friends, and sat together at Wives Row in Boston Garden (from left): Lynn Loscutoff, Judy Phillips, Diane Heinsohn, Jean Ramsey, Missie Cousy, and Gladys Jones.

After the final game of Cousy's storied career with the Celtics, Russ embraces Cooz in the visiting dressing room at the Los Angeles Sports Arena. Boston had just defeated the Lakers to win the 1963 NBA championship, the team's fifth in a row.

The players expected only a White House tour in January 1963, but President John Kennedy agreed to meet with them in the Oval Office. As the team prepared to leave, Tom (Satch) Sanders shook the president's hand and nervously said, "Take it easy, baby." Cousy (front row, second from left) watched JFK double over with laughter.

Joe Dillon, a Cousy fan from Southie, meets his hero before a 1963 playoff game. Three weeks earlier, Dillon had rescued the emotional Celtics captain on Bob Cousy Day by shouting, foghorn-like, from the crowd, "We love you, Cooz!"

Cousy and Russell strike a pose at the Celtics' end-of-the-season breakup dinner in April 1963. That night Russell became emotional at the microphone while talking about him: "We see each other as brothers, not as great athletes. Cousy, just by being himself, has given me so much."

Cousy enjoyed the spoils of his celebrity with commercial endorsements. Here, in a 1965 ad for Jantzen, he is carried along the surf by (from left to right) golfer Ken Venturi, John Severson (founder of *Surfer* magazine), and Cousy's buddies, football stars Frank Gifford and Paul Hornung.

Bob Cousy Day, a seminal moment in Cousy's life, became an emotional venting known as the Boston Tear Party. The next day's *Boston Globe* front-page headline read: HUB'S TEARS STIR COUSY: GARDEN THRONG WEEPS—AND BOB WEEPS, TOO.

On Bob Cousy Day, Celtics owner Walter Brown (with microphone) put it like this: "I'm the guy that didn't want Bob Cousy," he said. "What a genius!"

In nearly sixty-three years of marriage, Missie Cousy said this was among her favorite photographs.

In a 2006 ceremony in Boston following the death of Red Auerbach, Cousy joined U.S. senator Ted Kennedy, Massachusetts governor Mitt Romney, former teammate Tom Heinsohn, and others to pay tribute to his old coach and friend.

Cooz throws out the ceremonial first pitch at Boston's Fenway Park in April 2007.

Seven members of the 1962 NBA champion Boston Celtics gather at TD Garden in Boston in 2012 for a fiftieth anniversary celebration (from left to right): Tom "Satch" Sanders, Bill Russell, Frank Ramsey, Sam Jones, Tom Heinsohn, Cousy, and Jim Loscutoff (seated).

President Barack Obama presents Bill Russell with the Presidential Medal of Freedom, the nation's highest civilian award, at the White House in 2011.

Bob Cousy arrives at the second annual "Globies" sports awards night, sponsored by the *Boston Globe*, in 2016. The eighty-eight-year-old was honored with a Lifetime Achievement Award.

It was a family affair when the Bob Cousy statue was dedicated outside the Hart Center at the College of the Holy Cross in 2008. Standing with Cousy are (from left) daughters Ticia and Marie and his wife, Missie.

he lived, Russell became emotional as he expressed gratitude. But then, about a month later, word slipped out that the Russells wanted to move to a different part of Reading, and white neighbors there objected strenuously. Later, vandals broke into Russell's house and wrote racist graffiti on the walls.

"I played for the Celtics, period," Russell would say much later. "I did not play for *Boston*."

In joining the battle for racial equality, Russell acted in the manner of a proud race man. After an assassin gunned down Medgar Evers of the NAACP in Mississippi in June, Russell flew to Jackson where, protected by armed guards, he led several integrated basketball clinics. Then, in August, he stood on the mall in the nation's capital and heard MLK address the March on Washington. He stayed at the same hotel as MLK, who invited him to stand onstage as he delivered his speech; Russell declined, saying he hadn't earned that honor, and instead sat in the front row of the crowd.

Local civil rights leaders, thankful for Russell's involvement, viewed the one-day school boycott in Boston as the start of a northern freedom movement.

In taking on the Boston School Committee, Russell was also taking on its chairwoman, Louise Day Hicks, and not for the last time. It was part of Hicks's ambition to keep enrollment at schools in her native South Boston as white as it was. In the dozen years to come, Hicks would serve as a lightning rod of Irish-Catholic resistance to court-ordered busing in Boston, finding her way with pithy quotes to the front pages and once the cover of *Newsweek* magazine. To one civil rights leader, Hicks was "the Bull Connor of Boston," and to a Washington columnist "Joseph McCarthy dressed up as Pollyanna."

As a tough Boston pol, Hicks came not from central casting but from Southie, a white, working-class district filled with Catholic churches, bars, and American Legion halls; its streets teemed with laborers, city workers, cops, and longshoremen. Shaped like a dumpling, Hicks wore flowered hats, white gloves, and pink or blue dresses often accented by a string of pearls and a corsage. As a woman practicing law Hicks was uncommon, and as a woman elected to public office even more so; she first won a spot on the school committee in 1961, at forty-five, using the slogan "The Only Mother on the Ballot." In time, her slogan became "You Know Where I Stand." Her father, William Day, an important man in Southie, had been her hero, "the greatest fellow that ever walked this earth," she said. He also had served part time as a special justice of the South Boston District Court, where he was known to be lenient to friends and neighbors. Judge Day raised his family in a handsome three-story, eighteen-room house that faced the sea, and when South Boston residents met him on the street, they tipped their hats respectfully. Louise revered him. On his deathbed in 1950, she would later say, he told her, "Take care of my people."

She understood that he meant the people of Southie, nearly all white, and she took to heart his dying request.

"A large part of my vote probably does come from bigoted people," she would say. "The important thing is that I'm not bigoted."

Hicks dug in: She, and other Boston School Committee members, refused to acknowledge de facto segregation in Boston schools in spring 1963, dodging with semantics. She explained, "Segregation means to separate or set apart. This has been a way of life in the South—a way of life that I cannot accept. However, segregation is not a policy or a way of life here. . . . I will agree with you, if you say that Boston, because of its racial and ethnic groupings, has predominantly Negro schools. . . . The Boston school system is integrated, therefore it cannot be segregated." Protesters with pickets habitually massed outside the school committee's offices at 15 Beacon Street.

In the fall of 1963, Hicks would sweep to reelection as the top vote getter in a field of ten candidates for the school committee, capturing more than 78,000 votes, far ahead of the pack. Even more impressive, she outpolled Mayor John Collins, running in a separate race, by more than 21,000 votes.

Louise Day Hicks's outspoken resistance to busing had wide currency among whites in Boston.

Beaming on election night, Hicks called her reelection "a magnificent expression of confidence in my candidacy."

The children of Cousy and Russell were not enrolled in Boston's public schools. Cousy's daughters attended parochial school in Worcester; Russell lived in suburban Reading, his oldest son only a kindergartner.

But in Boston, hometown of the Celtics, the voters had spoken.

ANTICIPATING HIS DAY

With St. Patrick's Day approaching, Cousy pulled out a pen and pad and wrote multiple drafts of his speech. Per usual, the Celtics were streaking. They won all but three of their final seventeen regular-season games to sprint past the Lakers by five games and finish 58-22, best in the league. For seventeen years, including four in college, Cousy had played at Boston Garden. In his speech, he wanted to speak from the heart and thank the appropriate people, including Garden fans. He jotted down random thoughts. *"If I had to do it all over again, I can't imagine doing it any place but in Boston."* He would say that. At times as an NBA player, he had been critical of the league. He would explain himself: *"I just would like to say that it has always been with the thought of possibly improving basketball, which up to now has been my life."*

Through Auerbach's brother Zang, a commercial artist and illustrator with connections in the jewelry business, Cousy arranged to buy wristwatches to thank his friends in the Boston sports press. He engraved these watches for the occasion and would present them privately to Clif Keane, Jack Barry, Joe Looney, Bill McSweeny, and radio play-by-play man Johnny Most, among others.

Joe and Juliette Cousy weren't accustomed to the spotlight, but their son made arrangements for them to attend Bob Cousy Day. He knew they would be out of their element, and that concerned him.

He had done plenty of public speaking, but never with such a strong undercurrent of emotion. Cousy did not want to break down during his speech, no tears. He would thank the NBA and the Syracuse Nationals (the Celtics' scheduled opponent on Bob Cousy Day), his business partners and summer campers at Graylag, and the governor and the mayor, and who else? Walter Brown, naturally, and Missie and the girls, and his parents. As for his teammates, he struggled to get his words just right. *"I will say simply that the deepest regret I have in leaving is no longer being able to share the camaraderie and esprit de corps and the common bond of competition, and the inspiration I have received being captain of this team."*

Cousy was ten years old, living in a New York City slum, often playing stickball and swimming in the East River, when Lou Gehrig, on his day of appreciation—July 4, 1939, the most famous such fan appreciation day of all—stood before a sellout crowd of sixty thousand in between games of a doubleheader at Yankee Stadium. Not everyone knew then that the thirty-six-year-old Gehrig was in the grips of a terminal disease, amyotrophic lateral sclerosis. Yankees owner Ed Barrow decorated the moment as best he could, draping colorful bunting across the stadium and bringing back Gehrig's teammates from the famed 1927 Yankees, including Babe Ruth. The New York mayor, Fiorello La Guardia, and U.S. Postmaster General James Farley made brief speeches at microphones by home plate. So did Ruth, who remembered the greatness of the 1927 Yankees and urged Gehrig to catch plenty of fish in his free time. Manager Joe McCarthy recalled for the crowd the day Gehrig came to his hotel room and begged out of the lineup because he felt he had become a hindrance to the team. McCarthy turned to Gehrig and said, "My God, man, you were never that."

Gehrig, too emotional to speak, heard the crowd chanting, "We want Lou!" He shook his head, but McCarthy encouraged him. Gehrig stepped to the microphones, took a deep breath, and in a voice choked with emotion, spoke with grace of his family and teammates and then said, "For the past two weeks, you've been reading about a bad break. Today, I consider myself the luckiest man on the face of the earth."

Cousy's family, saving every penny, didn't buy newspapers then, so Cousy didn't learn about the speech until a few years later when actor Gary Cooper portrayed Gehrig in the 1942 film *The Pride of the Yankees*. At the time, Cousy and his neighborhood friends saved their dimes by sneaking into the Linden Theater in St. Albans with the help of a fire ladder. So powerful was Gehrig's speech, and Cooper's re-creation of it in the film, that when Cooper visited U.S. naval bases on a South Pacific tour in 1943, the troops called for him to deliver that farewell speech onstage, and he obliged, all but becoming Gehrig.

Cousy well knew about Ted Williams's farewell in Boston. Two and a half years before, in September 1960, on a gray Wednesday afternoon at Fenway Park, little more than ten thousand fans attended the Red Sox game against the Kansas City Athletics. In the crowd was John Updike, a young novelist who would write about the day for *The New Yorker*. In a pregame ceremony, Williams got a silver bowl and a plaque, and Mayor Collins presented a thousand-dollar check to the Jimmy Fund, Williams's favorite charity, for children with cancer. Ted being Ted, he seized the moment to throw one last verbal spear at his antagonists, Boston's sportswriters. Updike quoted him: "In spite of all the terrible things that have been said about me by the maestros of the keyboard up there"—Williams glanced up at the press box— "and they were terrible things. I'd like to forget them, but I can't." Williams paused, and then pivoted, saying, "I want to say that my years in Boston have been the greatest thing in my life." Cousy knew Williams, though not well. He admired him as a ballplayer and for having given up nearly five prime seasons of his career to serve as a

Marine pilot during World War II and the Korean War. That afternoon, Williams hit a home run on what became his final at-bat as a major leaguer.

"It was in the books," Updike wrote, "while it was still in the sky."

Williams ran the bases in a hurry, head down, same as always, refusing to acknowledge the cascade of cheers as he disappeared into the Red Sox dugout. The small crowd kept chanting, "We want Ted!" But he chose not to step out and wave in response. "But immortality is nontransferable," Updike wrote, adding, "Gods do not answer letters."

In their relationships with Boston's sports press, Williams and Cousy could not have been more different. In their final hours, Williams gave sportswriters vitriol, Cousy gave them wristwatches.

Boston, a provincial town, loved its own, and now its most celebrated luminaries were President Kennedy, Cardinal Cushing, Williams, and Cousy, the truest of household names in the Hub. A generation of hard-hearted men in Boston would cry at least twice in 1963—on Bob Cousy Day, an emotional venting that became known as the Boston Tear Party, and just eight months later, when Kennedy was murdered in Dallas. (Upon the president's death, the Cousy family physician made a house call because Cousy's mother-in-law, a devout Irish Catholic and erstwhile suffragette born as Mary O'Hanlon, became overwrought and needed a sedative.)

Cousy rehearsed his speech, made more changes, trimming it to seven minutes. He figured it might take a minute or two longer at Boston Garden because he wept a few times even as he rehearsed it.

Boston's sports pages filled with devotionals. Jerry Nason of the *Globe*, who had covered Cousy's entire career, placed him among the six greatest athletes in Boston's history, with hockey's Eddie Shore, golfer Francis Ouimet, marathoner Clarence DeMar, pitcher Albert Spalding, and prizefighter John L. Sullivan. "This is going to be a wingding," Nason wrote, "this fond farewell of an adoring citizenry to perhaps the most professional and selfless athlete Boston has ever known, and I exclude nobody. But nobody!"

With echoes of Grantland Rice from a bygone era of sportswriting, the *Globe*'s Jack Barry turned to doggerel: *"When sixty-three goes by the board / The pleasures we shall lose / All pale before the greatest one / The last year of The Couz."*

For Bob Cousy Day, the last of the 13,909 tickets sold ten days in advance, a rare sellout. On the one hand, the Celtics averaged 8,753 a game in Cousy's final season, second best in the league, just a smidgeon behind the Knicks and superior to the league-wide average of 5,053; but after winning five NBA titles in six seasons, the Celtics still averaged more than five thousand empty seats a night.

Stations in six New England cities would televise Bob Cousy Day festivities, and the game.

In Sweden to attend the world hockey championships, Walter Brown flew all night to make it back to Boston for Cousy's special day.

In a rare moment, Auerbach admitted he made a mistake thirteen years earlier, saying, "Now, if we had to go back and pick from that hat again . . ." He turned more serious when he said, "[Cousy] has never second-guessed me—never! And that's important. A different kind of Cousy probably could have created a one-of-us-must-go situation on the Celtics. . . . I have what they call a temper."

Celtics wives held an emotional gathering for Missie a few days before Cousy Day. They gave her a charm inscribed, "Love from all the Girls on the Row." She had been sitting on Wives Row—Section N, Row F—for thirteen years, and now the other wives assured her they would be there in force, and no doubt with tears, come Sunday.

Cousy told Phil Elderkin of *The Christian Science Monitor* how carefully he had considered the Cousy brand. "Actually, it's very important to me—personally and financially—to go out on top," Cousy said. "I'm quitting, you might say, with the Cousy image intact. . . . Coming back this year had to be just a little bit of a gamble. Suppose

I'd gotten hurt or suppose I found I'd made a mistake—that I really couldn't do the job anymore? To an advertiser or a public relations firm, my name wouldn't have been worth much, would it? But I don't have to worry about that now. I've proved I can still do the job." Elderkin joined the sportswriters' chorus of praise for Cousy, writing, "Getting to know Bob Cousy is a rich, rewarding experience. If there is a lot to Cousy the basketball player, there is even more to Cousy the man. Bob stopped needing the kind of publicity sports writers are privileged to give years ago, yet he still says thank you for a story; often will take the time to pen you a personal note."

McSweeny believed Cousy did not set out to build his reputation; it came to him naturally. As part of McSweeny's multipart series on Cousy in March 1963 in the *Record American*, Cousy said of his retirement, "You don't predicate a thing like this on money." McSweeny noted that Cousy clenched a fist as he spoke, and seemed nearly angry. "Realize the torment and the anguish," McSweeny wrote, "as well as the joy of being the super star." McSweeny had sat in Boston Garden about two and a half years earlier to hear John Kennedy's speech on the last day of the 1960 presidential campaign. "In twenty years of sitting in that place it was the only night I ever heard the air literally crack as a result of sheer noise," McSweeny wrote. "Maybe a few of the echoes will be left over for the Cooz. I wonder what he'll think? I wonder what we'll think?"

THE BOSTON TEAR PARTY

He awoke early on Bob Cousy Day, restless, exhausted. He had slept four hours. Auerbach was scouting college players in New York at the National Invitation Tournament, so Cousy had coached the Celtics to a meaningless victory over the Nationals the night before in Syracuse. Their plane had arrived at Logan at two o'clock in the morning after a rough flight through rainstorms. Cousy checked in to the old hotel beside the Garden, once known as the Manger and now the Madison. He ate a small breakfast, greeted people who stopped by his table, signed autographs, and kibitzed. He attended morning Mass, gave up his seat to a woman, and stood in the back of the church, the easier to avoid fans and leave more quickly.

Back at the hotel, he knew a passageway into the Garden but got locked in between the buildings. He knocked on the Garden door for several minutes. "This is going to be a great place to spend Cousy Day, isn't it?" he said to a *Newsweek* reporter, Bill Roeder, who had covered his first game at Andrew Jackson High School eighteen years before. "Locked in the catacombs."

A woman cleaning the arena called out from behind the Garden door, "Who is it?"

"It's one of the players," Cousy answered, humbly enough on this day. She let the guest of honor in.

Two hours before this regular-season finale against Syracuse, sportswriters gathered in their usual place around Cousy in the Celtics' dressing room.

The inevitable questions came: "How does it feel, Cooz?" "Any chance of changing your mind, Cooz?"

He said, "I just want to do the right things out there."

He worried about his speech, worried about the weather, worried about his parents flying in from New York. "Do you think planes will fly?" he asked. A photographer asked him to pose, and he did; another photographer asked for a different pose, and he did that. An usher wanted an autograph for his kid; he signed. Cousy told the gathered writers about his pregame pep talk the night before in Syracuse when he served as player-coach in Auerbach's absence.

"I told the boys to win it for Arnold," he said with a laugh.

Backup center Clyde Lovellette chipped in, "What a coach, this Cousy. At halftime he said, 'Can you play, Clyde?' I said sure. He told me to take my training pants off. There I sat for the rest of the game in my shorts. Never did play."

Auerbach walked in jauntily. "Arnold, I told them to win it for you," Cousy told him. "Boy, were they inspired. They want you to coach B.C. and want me to stay here." His teammates laughed, and so did the writers.

Cousy fidgeted. To an usher he said, "Be sure my mother can come up the back ramp, will you, please? She can't walk too well. I'm worried about her. Thanks a lot." The crowd of sportswriters scattered, leaving Cousy to his thoughts, mostly about his speech.

Fans filtered into the Garden. His former teammate Ed Macauley showed up. Doggie Julian, his coach at Holy Cross, came from Dartmouth. Dozens of friends from Worcester came—a business partner, his dentist, several college teammates. "I hope my nerves don't go," Cousy said. Soon, a policeman opened the dressing room door and said, "Time."

Sportswriters cleared out, and Auerbach went through the usual player assignments. The game was irrelevant with first place already clinched. Auerbach smiled, told his men to win this one for Cooz.

Cousy tucked his speech inside his warmup jersey and, as always, led the Celtics out to the edge of the court. There, Joe and Juliette Cousy sat. A stampede of photographers moved toward them. Cousy kissed his mother and shook his father's hand.

All eyes on Cousy. Here was a time-capsule Hub scene: Clouds of cigarette smoke filled the old arena built in the same year as Cousy's birth, 1928. The sellout crowd dressed for the St. Patrick's Day occasion, men in coats and ties, women in dresses, all with splashes of green. Some could almost never remember a time when Cousy had not been a Celtic. Thirteen years was an athletic eternity, slightly longer than even Franklin Roosevelt's tenure in the White House.

An era was ending in Boston sports, and no one understood that more acutely than thirty-two-year-old Joe Dillon, who sat in the balcony on the Causeway Street side of the Garden. Dillon was your garden-variety character from Southie: blue collar, loyal to his family, a neighborhood guy who would give you the shirt off his back. His Southie nickname was "Monk," earned the day he shaved the hair around the top of his head, giving him the look of a Franciscan monk. Only five-foot-eight and stout, he was a basketball fanatic who had played with a fancy style at South Boston High School and imagined himself as Cousy. He revered Cousy, knew all of his statistics dating to Holy Cross, and came to see him play at the Garden at least ten times a season. As he grew older and thicker, friends saw Dillon more as another Celtic, "Fat Freddie" Scolari. For all that, Dillon's distinguishing characteristic was his voice. It often came with the explosive force of a foghorn. He let his voice be heard at sports events with a cheer, opinion, or heckle, even at Little League games. On this day, Joe Dillon's voice would become part of the celebration in a sudden, surprising, unforgettable way.

The pregame ceremony began. It was that rarest moment when Bob Cousy stood on the Garden's parquet floor and barely moved. Head down, arms folded, he stared at his feet. Cousy wore his white Celtics warmup suit and a white towel around his neck, and a look equal parts modesty and trepidation. Nearly two dozen photographers knelt before him. Johnny Most, as master of ceremonies, introduced each speaker. In his coat pocket, Most kept a copy of Cousy's speech; if emotion overpowered the man of the hour, Most would finish the speech for him. To Cousy's left were Missie and the girls alongside his parents, his mother in a green dress, a fanciful hat, and a fur stole.

Draped over a wall, one bedsheet banner read: GOOD LUCK COOZ.

Early in the ceremony, Rose Russell presented Missie with a bouquet of roses and a kiss on the cheek.

Dolph Schayes, in his Syracuse warmups, presented china to Cousy from the Nationals. As the only NBA player older than Cousy (by less than three months), Schayes began by saying, "Ladies and gentlemen, Bobby baby," and he finished a few moments later, saying, "To Bob O'Cousy from Dolph O'Schayes, Erin go bragh and Mazel tov!"

Frank Ramsey spoke next, representing the players. He presented Cousy with a cigar humidor from his teammates and said, in his Kentucky drawl, "You have been an inspiration to us as a leader, as a player and as a gentleman."

Little Martha Grady, representing cystic fibrosis children, gave the Cousy girls missals and reached up to kiss Cousy. He embraced her, holding her close.

A steady flow of speakers followed—Joe Looney, in his bow tie, speaking for Boston's basketball writers; Ned Irish, president of the New York Knicks ("Even when you beat us," Irish said, "it was always done the way nobody but Bob Cousy could do it"), and Boston's wheelchair-bound mayor, John Collins, who presented Cousy with a Paul Revere silver bowl and read a proclamation.

Podoloff, short, stubby, and white-haired, wore a carnation on his lapel. He put aside the labor relations sparring he had done with Cousy through the years and told the sellout crowd, "There has only been one Bob Cousy, there never will be another, and none can ever attain his heights of glory." Cousy listened to each speaker with head bowed. He accepted their praise and their gifts, posed when requested, and couldn't wait for his own speech to be finished.

Auerbach walked to the lectern. The Celtics coach carried a message, and a letter. He delivered his message with gruff humor.

"I know you people here are here to honor Bob and are sorry to see him go. Well," Auerbach said, his eyes imploring the crowd, *"how do you think I feel?"* On this day the coach's brusque exterior proved transparent. His devotion to Cousy was total. "All I've heard recently is, 'How are you going to replace Bob?'" Auerbach said. He lifted an open palm and gave an exaggerated shrug. *"That's* my answer," he said. "It can't be done."

He read from a brief letter written for the occasion: It began, "Dear Bob, Your record is an eloquent testimonial to your abilities as a basketball player and I will not attempt to improve upon it here. The game bears the indelible stamp of your rare skills and competitive daring, and it will serve as a living reminder of your long and illustrious career so long as it is played." Two short paragraphs later it ended: "It is a pleasure for me to join with the sports world in this tribute to you." Auerbach looked up and said, "Sincerely, John F. Kennedy, President of the United States."

The crowd cheered, and the organist tapped out a peppy tune.

Now Auerbach turned from Kennedy's letter. Standing at midcourt, he pointed to Cousy and said, "That's Mister Basketball." As the Garden filled with cheers, Auerbach stepped from the lectern, kissed Missie and the girls, and shook hands with Cousy's parents. Then he embraced Cousy, and as he tried to step away, Cousy pulled him tighter. Both men wept.

No one asked Russell to speak publicly on Bob Cousy Day. He sat with teammates on the Celtics' bench and heartily applauded Cousy. Russell's view of his retiring teammate would be heard not on this day but soon. To Cousy, Russell remained as enigmatic as any teammate he had ever known. A few opposing players told Cousy they had nightmares about Russell the defender, waking up in a sweat and seeing his big shot-blocking hand hanging over them. Cousy knew that some Boston sportswriters considered Russell aloof, and at times surly.

But McSweeny, the Boston sportswriter who knew him best, considered Russell a powerful, outsized presence, with much on his mind and much to say. He sensed that Russell was suspicious of the old breed of white sportswriters who came of age in Boston during the thirties and forties, some without college educations. Russell wondered if those sportswriters were sophisticated enough to correctly interpret his quotes about race and print them just as he said them.

To Cousy, Russ was his own man. He might have challenged Cousy's leadership as captain, and as the most senior man on the club, but didn't. Instead Russell let the team be Cousy's and made the game his. His many blocked shots, Wilson-brand basketballs swatted in every direction, became known as *Wilsonburgers*; after one such block Russell raised a brow and asked his victim, "Ketchup or mustard?" Cousy sensed Russell's mountainous pride even during pregame introductions. Cousy conformed to the accepted standard: He ran onto the court when his name was called during introductions, same as every other NBA player except Russell. Russ walked onto the court toward his teammates in the starting lineup slowly, theatrically, and seemingly with high self-regard. As his Celtics career was ending, Cousy believed Russell's slow entry delivered a statement: "I am black, I am proud, and I am independent." Cousy understood that. He *got* it.

On Bob Cousy Day, Russell heard and felt the fans' devotion to Cooz. For speaking his mind, some of these fans had taunted Russell through the years. In the privacy of his thoughts, Russell told himself, *I'm supposed to miss those folks? Hell, no! I won't miss them.* He turned to Auerbach and said, "When I retire, I will never do *this*!" Publicly, though, Russell played the good teammate on this day. In the locker room, he asked Auerbach, "Hey, Red, can I wear number fourteen next year?"

Walter Brown got the last word. He presented Cousy with a 1963 steel-gray Cadillac, though he apologized that he couldn't rip apart the Garden and drive the car onto the court since his Bruins had a game in about six hours. Brown admitted to a sinking feeling.

"I'm the guy that didn't want Bob Cousy," he said. "What a genius!"

The crowd erupted with laughter. Cousy appreciated Brown, not only for his self-deprecating humor and essential decency but for his unwavering commitment to professional basketball. Brown had suffered a heart attack three years earlier, and in eighteen months he would suffer another, this one fatal, at fifty-nine. His funeral procession would stretch for a mile. The *Globe*'s Arthur Siegel would praise Brown's racial fairness, writing, "His Celtics are living exponents of the theory that all men are created equal." Brown's widow, Marjorie, would loan Auerbach the good-luck piece her husband had always carried—his St. Christopher's medal—in advance of the 1965 NBA Finals, and the coach kept it in his pocket as his Celtics won their seventh consecutive championship, and eighth in nine years.

Now, looking out at a sellout, Walter Brown said, "Things always weren't so good with the Celtics." He reminded the crowd that once he needed to wait nearly a year to pay his players their postseason money: "Bob never said a word, neither did Ed Macauley, Bob Brannum or Bill Sharman or Chuck Cooper, all those great guys that we've had." Brown did not sugarcoat the Celtics' past. "They permitted the club by this action to exist. It was the greatest tribute ever paid to me, the greatest I ever hope to have paid to me. Bob, for that I'd like to thank you and the boys you represent," he said.

Brown turned from the lectern and faced Cousy. "For *thirteen* years you've been the Boston Celtics, and, boy, they have a lot to live up to. You certainly have done an awful lot for the National Basketball Association because, like Babe Ruth after the [Black Sox] mess in 1919, you came along in 1950 and we've been on the upbeat ever since."

As he built toward his conclusion, Brown said, "You've got a wonderful father and mother."

Sitting beside their son, Joe and Juliette Cousy listened impassively. Their marriage of nearly four decades was a French-American daily drama in which Joe knew his role. When a decision needed to be made, Joe would say, "If you'll see my wife, she'll tell you." In a few years Joe would take his most decisive action since boarding the *Mauretania*: He would announce to Juliette that he was going out for a loaf of bread, and when he left, he didn't come back, at least not for several years.

His daughter, Blanche, from his first marriage, had moved to New York, and Joe wanted to live with her. Blanche, recently divorced, had told Cooz of her eclectic past with the French underground during the war, as a champion bicyclist, and working at a hotel in Nice. To-gether father and daughter would live in a trailer on a farm in River-head, on Long Island. Newly separated, Juliette would go about her life alone at the house in St. Albans, taking care of her tenants, accept-ing a monthly check from her son, and filling her dining room aviary with twenty-five canaries and parakeets.

Joe and Juliette would reunite. After Blanche died from cancer, Joe lived for a time with Cooz. "He didn't say a word. Just a quiet little guy," Ticia Cousy, a high schooler at the time, says. "He would smile and we'd nod."

Cooz played Cupid between his separated parents. "That was Mom on the phone," he told his father. "All she does is ask about you."

"No she doesn't," his father replied.

His mother would ask, "How is he doing?" "Fine," Cooz would say. "He just asked about you."

Driving together to Boston from the Midwest, Cousy and his father stopped in St. Albans. Joe Cousy entered the house he had left for a loaf of bread several years before, saw his wife leaning over the stove, looked over her shoulder, and said, cheerfully, "What's for dinner?"

Hearing this entry line, Cooz stifled a laugh.

In short order, he saw his parents sitting together on the couch, holding hands, and when it was time to leave, Joe told his son, "Bring my bags in." He was staying with his wife.

Their honeymoon lasted about a week. Then, as best Cooz could tell, his mother started yelling at him: *"Sale Boche!"* In time he would move his parents to Worcester and rent them an apartment. Joe would die at eighty-one, in March 1972; on the night he died, Cousy spoke about his father with a sportswriter, and suddenly dropped his head on the sportswriter's shoulder and cried. Juliette lived eleven years longer. In a Worcester nursing home in 1983, rail thin and frail, her eighty-seven-year-old body failing, she whispered to her son, "Roby, come with the needle. I've had a good life. I want out." Juliette bemoaned how a nurse had to wipe her ass clean every day. She wanted to die—as she wanted all things—on her own terms.

"Mom, I can't do that," he said. "I'm sorry."

Willfully, she stopped eating and stopped taking her medications. Cooz received an early-morning call and raced with Missie to the nursing home. He took his mother by the hand. From her bed, she looked up at him, weakly, and smiled. He squeezed her hand just as she died.

"She had it," he says, "her own way."

To sportswriters on Bob Cousy Day, Juliette Cousy recalled how her son, at age six, had donned a top hat, brandished a cane, and announced to her, "Mama, I will be a big man someday." She told the sportswriters, "I knew he would come to a certain success, but this, never!" Then she said, "I know nothing about sports. But I knew my boy would be a big man because I saw in him this—what is the word in English?—the *passion* for this basketball."

Columnist Tim Horgan of the *Boston Herald* wrote that Juliette sat erect and proud, "attended by her quiet and dignified husband, Joseph." Writing on deadline, with little time to probe, the well-intentioned Horgan added, "So from his mother the son received the gentle quality that made a staid old city cry its heart out over his farewell."

"And now, ladies and gentlemen," Walter Brown said, "to wind up this wonderful occasion, I give you the greatest, Bob Cousy." The kneeling photographers suddenly stood. So did his teammates, and the crowd, the entire arena.

All eyes on Cousy. He moved to the lectern, picked up the microphone. The organist played a jaunty tune, and Cousy waved his left hand to the cheering fans. As the Garden at long last fell silent, Cousy began, speaking in a small voice and leaning forward, as if falling, his left hand holding the lectern for balance. The girls, in their matching green dresses, and Missie, in her form-fitting green wool dress, moved beside him.

He spoke extemporaneously at first. About ninety seconds in, he faltered with his words: "It seems difficult to find mere words that seem so inadequate to say the things . . ." He paused and rubbed his eyes. He choked with emotion. To fill the discomforting silence, fans cheered. The *Globe* would count thirty-one times during his speech that he broke into sobs or sniffles, and this was the first. The Cousy girls cried, and Missie tried her best not to look at them, to hold strong. In her thoughts, Missie remembered how thirteen years before, she had sat on Wives Row on her wedding day, and Dolph Schayes and the Syracuse Nationals were the opponents then, too.

The white towel around Cousy's neck came in handy to wipe his eyes and nose. He kept sniffling. He moved through his speech slowly. He thanked editors across the nation, the Syracuse Nationals, campers at Graylag, and the Cystic Fibrosis Foundation. He said, "I just couldn't imagine playing anywhere but Boston," and the fans, grateful for that, cheered. He kept reaching for the towel to wipe his eyes and nose until little Ticia handed him a tissue.

There wasn't a soul in the building unfamiliar with his voice—its smallness, the New York accent, and the way his *R*s became *L*s.

He thanked the local basketball writers: "I can honestly say that in thirteen years I don't have one single recollection of friction or difficulty of any kind with any member of the Boston radio, TV, or press."

He turned to his bond with teammates. "I have been asked many times this year what I will miss most about no longer playing." He paused again, wiped tears, and balanced himself with his left hand on the lectern. It was painful to watch, painful to hear—all of Boston Garden weeping, the *Herald*'s Horgan on press row biting deeply into a cigar stub to keep from crying.

From up in the cheap seats, Joe Dillon heard only snatches of what Cousy and the others had to say; the Garden's PA system wasn't great, and the arena was packed, creating a murmur. Now came the moment within the moment: From out of the stillness there came a mighty foghorn baritone blast from the upper reaches.

"WE LOVE YOU, COOZ!"

It was Dillon, a bachelor sitting with a longtime buddy, putting his lungs to use and insinuating himself into the moment. A water division worker and Korean War veteran, Dillon longed for spectacle in his life, and for years Cousy, as Celtics dramatist, had provided it. Basketball was a big part of Dillon's life. He had been enamored with Cousy since high school, and that feeling—a fan's devotion, really— exploded out of him. As many times as Cousy had thrilled him, here came Dillon rescuing Cousy when he most needed rescuing. With four words, Dillon became an emissary from all of New England. His booming voice shook the Garden from its reverie, like a train rumbling through an opera hall.

It took a moment for the crowd to react. Then it roared its approval. Missie stepped forward to make sure her husband was okay, whispering into his ear.

Cousy nodded, ready to press on, his voice stronger as he thanked the Boston fans. "You have written me congratulations when we've been successful. You have written letters of good cheer and sympathy when I've been hurt, and also letters of encouragement when I've been depressed or in a slump. I only hope that my playing has in a small way served to repay you for your many kindnesses."

Cousy's speech reached the nine-minute mark, nearly done. He said, "An affair like this takes only a few minutes to transpire, but please be assured that it will leave my family and me with a memory that will warm us throughout our lives." He closed by saying, "Thank you and may God bless you all." He put the microphone on the lectern, next to his speech.

The organist tapped out a fast-paced "Auld Lang Syne." The crowd gave him a standing ovation that lasted three minutes, twenty seconds. He kissed Missie and the girls, and his mother. His father stood behind, shuffling his feet.

Photographers knelt in front of Cousy, shooting up at him and his family, an angle reserved for heroes. Missie was crying, little Marie, too; Ticia, wide-eyed, clutched her tissues.

Cousy raised both arms overhead and waved to the crowd, proof that one god in Boston answered letters.

The ensuing game meant nothing, though the Celtics won, and Cousy threw a few fancy passes, and when K.C. Jones replaced him with about two minutes to play, the Celtics ahead by twelve, the crowd stood and cheered for him, on and on, until the game ended. Sportswriters surrounded Cousy after the game as he sat on LeRoux's training table. Exhausted, he called it "the greatest day of my life."

Auerbach playfully stormed in and blustered, "Okay, Cousy, turn in your uniform!"

Up early the next morning, Cousy drove his parents back to New York in his 1961 Cadillac with the license plate CELTIC14, a car he would give to them since now he had a new Cadillac of his own. He read the headline on the *Globe*'s front page: HUB'S TEARS STIR COUSY: GARDEN THRONG WEEPS—AND BOB WEEPS, TOO.

"A tear bath. It was raining outside and pouring inside," Nason wrote, calling the occasion "a deep and genuine tribute possibly unknown in sports since Lou Gehrig Day at Yankee Stadium."

Columnist Arthur Siegel, who first joined the *Boston Traveler* in 1924, about four years after the Red Sox sold Babe Ruth to the Yankees, wrote that in terms of great outbursts of devotion in Boston's sports farewells, "nothing comes close."

When Cousy chastised himself, saying, "I acted like a ten-year-old out there," the *Herald*'s Horgan clarified, "He acted like a very big man."

The *Globe* editorial page praised Cousy for his modesty and "fine human quality," adding, "He now ends his career on the court with the best wishes of everyone."

A few days later, the state's Knights of Columbus gave Cousy its Lantern Award as an "exemplar of American youth," an honor previously won by FBI director J. Edgar Hoover, U.S. attorney general Bobby Kennedy, AFL-CIO president George Meany, and Cardinal Richard Cushing.

Victor O. Jones, once a war correspondent and a former executive editor of the *Globe*, added his voice on the *Globe*'s op-ed page: "The retirement of Cousy and the emotions it evoked are quite extraordinary. . . . His particular influence has all been on the side of the virtues. If your boy imitated Cousy, he'd show off a touch of class, and you wouldn't have to worry about his becoming a showboat, a braggart, an alibi artist, or a rowdy."

A DREAMY SUNSET

He wanted to leave as a champion. Every ballplayer wants to ride off into a dreamy sunset, and for Cousy a sixth NBA championship would provide just that. His entire career he had creatively arranged for others to score, a consummate team man. He wanted to win this one for himself. He believed he had earned the right to a touch of self-indulgence.

Auerbach remained focused on the task at hand. Before Game 7 against Cincinnati in the division finals, he called a friend and said, "Let's take a ride." They drove fifty miles, whiling away the time as Auerbach drove (too fast), and talked (too much), and smoked his cigar all the way to Woonsocket, Rhode Island, before turning back. In his suite at the Hotel Lenox, where he lived alone with his bags of nuts and his hot plate for late-night Chinese food, Auerbach became restless during the playoffs. He washed dishes, sewed a couple of holes in his pockets, mended a few buttons. On off days he saw an afternoon movie alone and at night watched the late, late show on television. His

Celtics eliminated the Royals, 142–131, in a Game 7 seemingly played without defense, Oscar Robertson's forty-three points topped by Sam Jones's forty-seven-point magnificence. Cousy added twenty-one points and sixteen assists.

The Celtics advanced to play the Lakers in the Finals, naturally, and won three of the first four games. The Lakers had no answer for Russell, who averaged twenty points and twenty-six rebounds in the series.

Much was occurring on the periphery of this series. In Los Angeles, a sportswriter from the *Herald Examiner* confronted McSweeny and told him he was nothing but a homer rooting for the Celtics and always covering up for Russell and the blacks. McSweeny noticed this sportswriter had been drinking. Suddenly, he pushed McSweeny and started to throw a punch, at which point McSweeny shoved him into a chair. This was the second brief altercation McSweeny had with a sportswriter over race.

Before Game 3 in Los Angeles, the Boston sportswriter George Sullivan watched Cousy emerge from the motel gift shop, newspaper in hand, ashen-faced. "They just banned Hornung," Cousy said, tapping a finger against the headline. It looked as if Cousy had absorbed a sucker punch, Sullivan thought. Hornung, of the Green Bay Packers, and Detroit's Alex Karras had been suspended for a year by NFL commissioner Pete Rozelle for gambling on football games. Cousy had grown close to Hornung during their off-season photo shoots for Jantzen. In ten days, Cousy was to be honored by his hometown in a civic testimonial at the Worcester Memorial Auditorium, and Hornung was invited; now Cousy phoned him to affirm that his invitation stood, an act of friendship Hornung would not forget.

Friends in Worcester asked Cousy, *Wouldn't it be fitting if this year's Finals ended the same way as last year's, with Houdini dribbling out the clock and the Boston Garden crowd rushing to embrace him?* The Celtics had an opportunity to recreate that scenario and close out the Lakers at Boston Garden in Game 5, but Baylor and West combined for seventy-five points in a 126–119 Lakers victory. Auerbach sat on a bench in the dressing room after the defeat, his foot propped up on a rack of basketballs. He told sportswriters, "We'll still win it."

Before Game 6 in L.A., Cousy locked himself in his room at the Olympian Hotel. He took room-service meals, blocked all calls, soaked in the bathtub, and thought once again of his opposite number, Lakers guard Frank Selvy, his mortal enemy. In these intense imaginings, the game playing out in his mind, Cousy never did anything right, and Selvy always did.

Much later, in the Los Angeles Memorial Sports Arena dressing room, Cousy heard the laughter of singer Johnny Mathis, who stopped by to visit with Russell, his old friend from San Francisco. Auerbach gave players their assignments, while Russ dry-heaved into the toilet, his retching oddly reassuring to teammates, like an old favorite song.

Cousy told the Celtics, "We're a team that has to run. We're geared that way." Then Auerbach said, "This is for all the marbles."

As Cousy led the Celtics onto the court at the Sports Arena, he looked for actress Doris Day and spotted her in her usual seat, beside singer Pat Boone.

Cousy played a strong first half, scoring sixteen points. In the third quarter, he stole a pass, dribbled to his left, and pulled out a shot from the past, a slow, arcing left-handed hook from fifteen feet, and it banked in.

Early in the fourth quarter, West brought the ball upcourt as Cousy covered guard Dick Barnett, who suddenly cut sharply to the right. Cousy cut with him and fell at midcourt. For a moment, he sat alone on the floor, no one near him. An excruciating pain shot through the inside of his left ankle. He rolled over to his right side, and to his left, back and forth; no one on the Celtics had ever seen the captain this way. Helped off the court by LeRoux and Loscutoff, Cousy hobbled to the bench. LeRoux gave him a shot of Novocaine, and the anesthetic worked its magic, numbing his ankle.

This Game 6, Cousy decided, would not end with him on the bench. He missed more than five minutes of the fourth quarter. With 4:43 on the clock and the Celtics' lead down to a point, he walked slowly toward Auerbach. "I think I can go," Cousy said. They shared a mutual trust. "Go in for Havlicek," Auerbach said.

Heinsohn recovered a loose ball and passed to Cousy, who dribbled to the left side, then cut on a diagonal toward the middle, moving slower than before. Cousy threw a bounce pass to Sanders, who scored from the right side for a 104–99 lead with 3:32 to play.

Cousy thought Heinsohn the league's most underappreciated player. Heinsohn's game was shaped by intellect, ego, and a fighting spirit. When Cousy missed a soft one-hander with thirty-three seconds to play, the Celtics ahead by a point, Heinsohn bullied underneath for the rebound and was fouled. He converted two free throws for a 110–107 lead. He made two more free throws ten seconds later, and suddenly the Celtics led by five and Cousy felt goose bumps.

It was over: He would finish as a champion after all. When the ball came into his hands in the final seconds, feeling no pain in his ankle, floating on the gossamer wings of his sixth NBA championship in seven seasons, Cousy bent slightly and slung it as high as he could, toward the rafters of the arena.

The horn sounded; Cousy saw Russell and embraced him from behind. Russell had his eyes on the ball as it descended and bounced once, and then into his arms, a souvenir of glory. Auerbach ducked his head in between his two stars. Satch Sanders was there, too. The Celtics stormed into the visiting team's dressing room, where Russell and Cousy embraced again.

"You were a tiger tonight, baby," Russell said.

Called back onto the court as the crowd departed quietly, Cousy and Auerbach conducted a television interview together.

"It must have been old age creeping up," Cousy said, referring to his ankle sprain.

Auerbach, never an understated winner, crowed, "God, it was wonderful! . . . I hope that everybody that's been writing about those Lakers, and the fact that we were dead, I hope they know who won the world's championship. . . . Like I always say, a champ is a champ until he is beaten. And these guys are champs."

As their plane rose above Los Angeles later that night, Russell looked down, and Cousy heard him say, "And as the basketball capital of the world sinks slowly into the sunset, we can only say, 'Good-bye Los Angeles.'"

Cousy propped up his ankle and sipped champagne with his teammates. He couldn't help but consider the remarkable reversal of his own fortunes: It had seemed during his first six seasons that he would never win an NBA championship, and yet now, in the final accounting, he had won six, including in each of his final five seasons. As he closed his eyes at thirty thousand feet, riding east into his own dreamy sunset, he saw himself bending slightly and slinging the ball toward the rafters, and then reaching for Russ, a moment that would remain with him forever.

The Celtics held their annual Breakup Dinner the following night at the Hotel Lenox. Years earlier this dinner had started as an intimate affair for Auerbach, players, and beat writers, a chance to say a few words at season's end before each player went his own way into the off-season. In 1957, Celtics wives wanted to attend after the team had won its first championship, but Auerbach got wind of their intention to show up. He instructed one of his gatekeepers at Boston Garden to escort the wives to the bar downstairs. The wives were furious about being locked out and said so, even as the gatekeeper said, "But Red said you should stay here." The wives banded together, rushed upstairs, opened the doors to the dinner, and walked in. "Red," Diane

Heinsohn says, "was flabbergasted." The Celtics made room for the wives and now, six years later, it was a bigger affair. It offered players one more chance to say a few final words to Cousy.

Russell and Cousy had shared many conversations about basketball. But they'd never had a candid discussion about politics or civil rights or about their personal lives. Cousy was left to wonder what Russ truly thought of him.

Russell was developing into a compelling public speaker. What Cousy experienced in the locker room—Russ's intellectual depth, his comedic touch, his fire—emerged at times in his speaking. As startling images of the civil rights movement played out on America's television screens—fire hoses, snarling attack dogs—Russell increasingly engaged. He spoke out. He marched. Later in the sixties, when demonstrators in Boston protested the removal of black families to make way for an urban renewal project in Copley Square, Russell would feed them, sending over food from Slade's, his restaurant in Roxbury.

Beginning on this night, Russell became the main act at the Breakup Dinner. He loosened his tie, and his emotions. He spread his hands about an inch apart and said, "If Bob Cousy were this much less a man than he is, I would have resented him."

Then he said, "Here we are a bunch of grown men chasing a basketball, playing a boy's game. There is no depth to such accomplishments. You can get a cup of coffee for all your championships. But you can't get friendships like Cousy's . . . There is such a thing as professional jealousy. A fellow reads about Cousy, sees his picture often, but I can honestly say I never resented Cousy."

Russell became emotional: "I didn't want to come tonight. I knew what would happen. . . . I'm too big a man to cry. Cousy is outstanding. We see each other as brothers not as great athletes. Cousy, just by being himself, has given me so much. We never can find words to say what Cousy has done just by being himself. You never got the impression—'*This is Bob Cousy . . . [and] this is the rest of the team*' . . .

You meet a Cousy not once in a month but once in a lifetime. Bob Cousy has made playing with the Celtics one of the most gratifying things in my life."

He finished by saying, "Like the guy [at Bob Cousy Day] said, 'We all love you, Cooz,' and we really do."

Russell's words—his generosity of spirit—stunned Cousy. Missie and Rose Russell felt the power of the moment, too. They wept in each other's arms. Cooz had no idea that Russ felt this way about him—as a point guard and fellow basketball warrior, yes, but in terms of *friendship*, or as a *brother*, certainly not. This much he knew: Russ never said anything he didn't mean. Now, the big man walked away from the microphone with bowed head.

As the Cousy era drew to a close, Russell walked along Boylston Street with his friend McSweeny. In another year, McSweeny would be a war correspondent on an aircraft carrier in Vietnam. But now, a sportswriter still, he heard Russell say, "I've got to get something special for Cooz and Missie." Russell wanted to honor the seven years they had spent together and thank the Cousys for their friendship. He did not want to present his gift in public. He wanted this to be more personal and private.

They stepped into Shreve, Crump & Low, a historic jewelry store established in 1796 by watchmaker John McFarlane across from Paul Revere's silversmith shop. There, Russell purchased a desk clock, with bronze hour and minute hands set against a dark brown background.

The engraved inscription spoke warmly of friendship: *May The Next Seventy Be As Pleasant As The Last Seven. From The Russells To The Cousys.*

Missie loved the clock, especially what it symbolized. She put it in a prominent place at home.

That fall, a new season about to begin, a fan told Russell, "You better hustle now that you don't have Cousy to carry you." Russell wondered: *Does this fan not know that I have been the league MVP for the last three years?*

Cousy, Russell told a sportswriter that fall, was gone.

"He's not here. He's not going to be," Russell said. "He no longer exists as a basketball player so far as we're concerned. He's almost an opponent now, kind of a shadow that we're playing against. Our purpose is to erase that shadow."

Cousy read those comments and understood. The team needed to move on. Still, Russ's words stung a bit. Meanwhile, in that first season without Cousy, attendance at Boston Garden dropped by about 1,300 fans per game, roughly 15 percent.

Missie wasn't worried about the egos of alphas. When the Cousys soon moved to a grander house in Worcester, she placed the Russells' clock on the mahogany table in the dining room, opposite the piano, where it remained a favorite keepsake for more than a half century.

Cooz in Winter

SALISBURY STREET

The big house on Salisbury Street has become his refuge and fortress. Cousy is approaching ninety now, a solitary and mostly sedentary figure. His mind remains keen and alert, like a basketball Library of Congress. He lives alone, kept company by his memories, inside a house that feels as cavernous as Boston Garden, a house that he and Missie bought in 1963, when the girls were young and times were simpler. The girls grew up, and Missie died five years ago, a few months before their sixty-third anniversary, so now Cousy lives with his memories and his books. In the quiet you can hear his footfalls and the gentle thump of his cane as he walks from the kitchen into his bedroom, where he's got a crucifix on the wall above his bed. He attends Sunday Mass at Blessed Sacrament, his church for the past sixty years. He says he is more agnostic than believer. Still, being in church comforts him. He sits in the pew and thinks mostly about Missie.

His world grows smaller. Whereas once Worcester was his escape from Boston, now the house seems his escape from a dangerous world.

He has become, by his own term, reclusive. *The Howard Hughes of Sports*, he calls himself. In its time, the house was a palace, set on three lush acres with a swimming pool in back, a stone wall and circular driveway in front, and Old Glory flying from a flagpole. It is a two-story house made of stone and wood and built during the early 1950s, likened by one writer to an eastern version of Frank Lloyd Wright's prairie home. It includes six bedrooms, with four upstairs where the girls and Missie's mother once lived beside a sewing room, and a vacant servant's quarters. Designed for entertaining, it features an enormous sunken living room (thirty-one feet by twenty feet), an enclosed patio in back where he likes to read now in the warmth of summer, and a cellar so big they could never quite figure out how to fill it.

The house still gives him deep satisfaction, as it once did for Missie, as a sign of how far they rose from humble origins. "Only in America," Cousy says, "and for being involved with a child's game." Though there are stylish touches—a marble fireplace, a winding staircase—the decor feels as if it's from an earlier time, the 1970s, perhaps, a feeling heightened by Cousy, sitting in the living room, wearing a black sweat suit without a shirt beneath, his gray chest hair sprouting like crabgrass. Cousy has no time for modern gadgets. He doesn't own a computer, or want one. He has a cell phone but almost never uses it. He says he likes his house, and his life, just as they are.

He says he and Missie bought the house for $100,000, which in 1963 seemed a king's ransom. They were so discreet about the cost they asked writers not to mention it in their stories. "This is the first extravagance we've treated ourselves to," he told one writer. Missie told another, "I don't regard it as a particularly pretentious house. To me its beauty is in its simplicity." A sign of simpler times: In January 1964, when a sportswriter explained that his newspaper's photographer needed a few extra minutes to snap images of the house's interior, Cousy said no problem, explained that he needed to leave, and handed over his house keys, asking the sportswriter to leave them under the front door mat when the photographer was done.

Once the dynasty's center of gravity, Cousy has become its oldest surviving member. His raven hair has turned white and wispy, his angular facial features rounded into a cherub's. He's got a friendly, grandfatherly face, the kind Rockwell used to paint. At 228 pounds, he's puffed up more than forty pounds over his playing weight, though he wears the weight well. Only his voice remains, uniquely, as it was. When daughters Marie and Ticia visit, he'll call them by their child-hood nicknames, Ree-Ree and Tee-Tee, and in their chatter Missie becomes "Mommy," as if he's willing them all back to an earlier time. He says he has no interest in a new companion. He puts it simply: "One life, one wife."

In Worcester he's got friends aplenty. He takes dinner every Thurs-day up at the country club with his old friends, a weekly boys' night out for the past thirty years or so. These old friends and their kids, all grown up now, still look after him. Devotedly, they'll phone or drop off food.

On occasion he talks by phone with his former teammates—Ramsey, Sanders, Havlicek, or Heinsohn. In their presence, Cousy's pride kicks in: he stands a little taller and walks a little faster. One afternoon, answering an unexpected doorbell, he spots a big man out front wearing four or five days' beard growth and no socks. *A homeless guy*, he thinks. But he keeps staring, and, *Jesus, it's Heinsohn!* His old teammate, in the area for a Holy Cross luncheon, spends two hours in the living room with him and they talk mostly about (what else?) the Celtics.

When Havlicek, in Boston, calls him at his condominium in West Palm Beach, where both spend winters, Cousy becomes the captain again, his voice lifted, more animated, and stronger. He tells Havlicek that he feels fine—"temporarily"—and then he growls, "Get your ass down here. We'll have dinner."

He took several calls from obituary writers when Loscutoff died. Every day seems to bring another obit from his NBA years: Sharman, Lovellette, Guarilia. Dick Hemric. Bob Davies, Carl Braun, Harry

Gallatin. "How old?" Cousy asks of Gallatin, the former Knick. He was eighty-eight; Cousy thought he was a few years older than that. The wife of one former player called Cousy to say, her voice choked with emotion, that her husband had been diagnosed with Parkinson's disease. Another former player called Cousy to say that recently he had suffered a stroke.

Cousy blanched. His NBA generation was disappearing. "Don't look over your shoulder," he says, shaking his head. Funerals of NBA players from the Cousy years are so common now that Randy Auerbach, in Los Angeles, and her sister, Nancy Collins, in Washington, sometimes show up to represent their late father, Randy saying to Nancy, "I'll do the West Coast funerals, you do the East Coast funerals."

Mostly, Cousy feels vulnerable. Time does that to old men, even famous ones. It reduces them to scale, makes them cranky. He says he's paranoid about intruders and attributes that in part to reading too many espionage novels. He locks his doors, punches in the code for his alarm system. As a young man he led the league in self-analysis and intensity. That drove him, by career's end, to become like a tortured artist, with nightmares and nervous twitches. Now, his intensity moderated, he still leads the league in self-analysis. He knows he has many more yesterdays than tomorrows. He thinks about his life, its triumphs and its moments of sadness. He wants to close circles, button up important relationships while he still can.

Small noises in the house jangle his nerves: ice cubes falling from the icemaker in the freezer, a squirrel running across the roof. Even his magnificent peripheral vision—such a gift on the court—betrays him. Whereas once he maestroed the Celtics' fast break and saw Heinsohn out on the left periphery, and the bolt of Sam Jones running out on the right, sitting at his kitchen table now he sees shadows moving across the window, and his body tenses. He imagines a prowler coming, only to realize it's a reflection of cars passing on Salisbury Street.

Like all men of his vintage, he's got aches and pains, doctors and pills. He underwent hip replacement surgery in 2000 and later two lower back surgeries. That necessitated his giving up golf, a passion. He had brought his intensity even to the driving range, offering unsolicited advice to strangers: "It's shoulders—shoulders! Not hips." One woman in church recognized him, smiled, and said, "Shoulders, not hips, right?" He has atrial fibrillation. He has been treated about a half dozen times for skin cancer; after the most recent scraping of cancer cells from his face, he announced to his mirror, "You look like Rocky Balboa." When the temperature drops, it causes his knee to lock up, and in the morning he can barely walk.

Among other maladies, he has suffered from middle-of-the-night panic attacks that leave him momentarily in a frenzy and imagining he's one short breath from joining his bride in the hereafter; diminished hearing in his right ear; and "dropped toe," which twice caused his big toe to catch in the rug and prompted him to fall. Fortunately, the last time he fell on the living room rug and not on the hardscape of the nearby patio. "If I fall the other way on the pavement," he says, "then I'd bleed out."

Time passes. It's as if he built a career—a life—that became a monument and then time chipped away at it, breaking off pieces: age, infirmity, Missie's death, and vandals.

Two vandals broke into the house during the early 1980s; actually they walked through an open back door in mid-afternoon. From the living room they grabbed the sterling silver sets from the Syracuse Nationals and the Celtics—Bob Cousy Day gifts—and when Missie's mother, then in her eighties, walked in and saw the young thieves, she said, "Boys, I'm sorry but Mr. Cousy is not here. You'll have to come back." She thought they came for his autograph. *Thank God they didn't hurt her,* Cousy thought upon his return that night, but they had done their damage. He had a trip planned and had withdrawn seven hundred dollars in cash from the bank and hidden it with his handkerchiefs in his bedroom bureau. He looked: The cash was gone, pilfered.

He contacted Worcester police and said he wanted the sterling silver returned, if possible. Too late, a policeman told him: "Those kids probably have their truck down on Jamesbury [Drive]. They've already smelt that silver down to a ball."

He spends most of his time sitting in his favorite chair in the den, the smallest room in the house. With a couch, a TV, and his comfy chair, the den has become his cocoon, safe, secure. There he reads his latest book for up to four hours a day, taking breaks for lunch, a short walk, and to respond to autograph requests that show up in the mail. He rips through novels by Michael Connelly, James Patterson, and David Baldacci (he calls him "Balducci"). In the quiet you can hear pages turning. He's read books that his daughter Marie recommended, including *The Underground Railroad* by Colson Whitehead and *Angle of Repose* by Wallace Stegner. She sent him thirty-two books from Amazon over a six-month period. "Amazon is amazing," he says. "Two days and it's at my door!" He read Condoleezza Rice's *Democracy*, a collection of short stories edited by Garrison Keillor, and *Just Mercy*, by Bryan Stevenson, a nonfiction work about the inequities of America's criminal justice system.

At four o'clock each afternoon, he puts aside his reading and turns to Fox News to watch business journalist Neil Cavuto, or, as he says, "my hero Cavuto." Cousy is addicted to Fox News, a source of embarrassment for his liberal-minded daughters. Sometimes he turns to MSNBC to hear the views of Chris Matthews and Al Sharpton. A registered Independent, Cousy, in recent presidential elections, voted for Barack Obama in 2008, home-state acquaintance Mitt Romney, a Republican, in 2012, and Libertarian Gary Johnson in 2016. He says he empathizes with his daughters' politics more than he lets on.

He inhabits only a few rooms of his house; he says he hasn't been upstairs in about six months, and then only to retrieve some old papers from a cedar closet. He can't remember the last time he made it down to the cellar. When he feels up to exercising in the summer, he might go to the pool out back for his "nudie swim," hoping the neighbors won't peek (he walks in the water more than he swims). More regularly, he walks around the circular driveway in front, holding his wooden cane, given to him years ago by a fan who made it and burned COOZ into the wood, just below the handle; a dozen laps take him about ten minutes.

Moving slowly through his house, Cousy seems a period piece from a bygone era. He's lived long enough to become a historical figure. He was a stylized original emulated by stars of later generations. As the Celtics' team captain with an air of cool, he was Jeter before Jeter. As the dynamic passer and dribbler, he was Maravich before Maravich, Magic before Magic, Stockton before Stockton, Westbrook before Westbrook.

There's a basketball statue of him at his alma mater across town at Holy Cross, and a twenty-three-foot vinyl banner featuring him in his Crusaders uniform that decorates the side of a building visible from Interstate 290. He still drives around Worcester in a 2013 Toyota Avalon. At one local service station where attendants handle the pump for customers, an attendant recently paid for Cousy's tank of gas. "Don't be silly," Cousy said. But the attendant, an African-American man, perhaps in his fifties, insisted, saying, "You're a good guy." Later, Cousy figured this had cost the man about forty dollars. *I mean, who buys anybody a tank of gas?*

In the old days, tourists drove to his house just to get a look at him because that's what people did when they visited Worcester. Now, when he walks his laps around his driveway, a friend driving past might see him and honk a horn in acknowledgment, and sometimes pull in to say a quick hello.

"As much as I like my privacy, when the friggin' phone doesn't ring, it's like *Everybody in the world is ignoring me!*" Cousy says. "Now my ego kicks in. Then when it rings twice in a row, I say, 'Leave me alone.'" He shrugs. "Who the hell can explain the human psyche?" He gets regular visits from wild rabbits and raccoons, and he likes that since it reminds him of Missie, who adored animals.

The house has become a Missie museum. Her expansive spirit fills the rooms. On the dining room wall hangs the pastel painting of her smiling demurely, a Bob Cousy Day gift from the Knicks. He talks aloud to the portrait as if Missie is really there: "I'm going to run some errands this morning, sweetheart, back by ten-thirty. Then I'm here for you all afternoon." Such conversations keep her in his life, a source of comfort.

Her 1996 Mercury Sable station wagon is still parked in the garage. In the cellar, Missie's notes, handwritten with a Sharpie, remain on a water heater, the walls, and also in the kitchen pantry, reminders to herself about how things work ("Once a month push control button"). Missie ran the house, she ran the family, and she ran Wives Row at Boston Garden—she ran everything, really.

Daughter Ticia describes her in a single word: "Powerhouse."

When she died in 2013, Cousy thought to sell. He didn't do it. "I don't think I'd survive a move elsewhere," he says, before his voice trails off. "God forbid it's assisted living. . . ."

But the old house had its mysteries. He didn't even know how to operate its many valves and dials. When a plumber showed up and asked him where the shutoff valve was, he looked up from his chair and asked, "How do you expect me to know? I've only been here fifty-one years."

Later he was heard to mutter, "You have to be a goddamned MIT engineer to run this place."

Ofttimes, he meditates. In his chair in the den, he fatigues from reading and closes his eyes, and he lets his mind drift.

Now he sees himself and Heinsohn sitting in a bar at Los Angeles's tony Beverly Wilshire Hotel with actress Lauren Bacall. They're waiting for her husband, actor Jason Robards, because, after all, it's not every day that ballplayers get to meet multiple movie stars. Robards arrives wearing a cape. He twirls around, his cape flowing, until his back is to the Celtics, at which point, completing his big-movie-star grand entrance, Robards cuts loose a fart, loudly. Thus introduced to Hollywood manners, the Celtics and the actors have a few pops. Then Bacall sees the ballplayers' gear bags on the floor and asks, "What do you keep in those bags?" Stuff you don't want to see, Cousy tells her. Too late to stop the frisky Bacall, who rummages inside the bag until she pulls out the jockstrap Cousy wore that night against the Lakers. She flings it at him and laughs. He throws it back at her, and this game of jockstrap catch goes on awhile. It provides the answer to a trivia question never before asked: Who was the first NBA star to throw his dirty jockstrap to a beautiful movie star in the lobby of the Beverly Wilshire?

Now there's Auerbach in the Celtics' locker room, master of his universe. What's that word he uses? *Shwatz?* Or is it *Shwatzkas?* *Shvartzes*, that's it, Yiddish derogation for blacks. He says, "You *shvartzes*, get over here!" and nobody gets mad. Black guys outside the locker room probably would take him on for saying it, but inside it is accepted, and the black Celtics let it go, just Auerbach being Auerbach.

Now, in his reverie, eyes closed, Cooz is on the court again, taking an outlet pass from Russell and seeing Russ's head tilt downward slightly, a telling sign that the big man is a-comin'. When he sees Russell run the floor, Cousy will not give the ball to Heinsohn or Sharman, dependable finishers both. Instead he will reward the big man for running all ninety-four feet. On the fly and into the frontcourt, Cousy delays slightly, veers gently to the right, and pulls back the throttle. Here comes the onrushing Russ in long loping strides, a magnificent sight. Opposing centers can't keep up, not when Russell accelerates. Cousy sees the middle of the court clearing and passes to Russell—high and accurate, on a parabola—rewarding his center with an easy layup from the left, Russ's natural side.

Now Cousy sees himself in the Los Angeles Sports Arena in Game 6 of the 1963 NBA Finals, his last moment with the Celtics, and as the clock ticks down in the final seconds ("Six . . . five . . . four"), he slings the ball toward the rafters even before the horn sounds. He slings it hard, as if hoping it never comes down, because now it is over and he will retire a champion. With the ball in the air, Cousy looks for someone to embrace. He spots the long, lean Russell and reaches out to him, and the reverie fades. . . .

Cousy opens his eyes. What does that moment in '63 mean? It seems fraught with significance and camaraderie, but now it has been six years and more since he last was with Russell. He always asks teammates if they've seen or talked with Russ lately. Heinsohn says he would get occasional calls from him. "Russ says to me, *You are one of the few people I still like,*'" Heinsohn says with a laugh. Ramsey says he has talked with Russell every so often, too. Once, he bought one of Russell's books, sent it to him, and asked him to inscribe it. Two months passed without a reply, so Ramsey wrote Russell another note, saying if he wasn't going to sign it, could he at least return the book since it was difficult to obtain in Kentucky. Now Ramsey proudly reads aloud the inscriptions Russell wrote to him in two of his books:

Frank, There are no chasms of time or distance that cannot be bridged by friendship. William Felton Russell.

To Frank Jr., One of the finest persons I have ever had the pleasure to know and call my friend. William Felton Russell.

Cousy hears that Russell and Sam Jones paid a visit to Hartford, where K.C. Jones, now eighty-five, struggles with health issues. "That's nice that they did that," Cousy says. "That's good."

Cousy never was adept at hiding his feelings. Learning of his teammates' interactions with Russell stirs discomfort decades old. He regrets that there's not much to his relationship with Russell anymore, and that there hasn't been for many years. The whole truth is that he regrets much about his time with Russell. Is it still possible to close that circle? He does not harbor such regrets about his relationships with other teammates; to him, those circles were never broken. But he wonders about the man who was his greatest teammate. *As an old man, in his eighties, too, does Russ have regrets? In his reveries, what images does Russ see? What story does he tell himself?*

RUSS

On his television screen, Cousy senses the second coming of Russell, at least as a shot blocker. "This kid Whiteside," he says, TV remote control in hand and pointed toward Miami Heat center Hassan Whiteside, "prepares himself the same way as Russ. He looks to go after any penetrator." Whiteside is seven feet tall and spidery. He led the NBA in blocked shots in 2016; his nickname Count Blockula.

It is winter, which means Cousy is at his condo in West Palm Beach, sitting in his favorite white leather recliner. He's wearing a tan sweat suit and slipper-like shoes, his modern-day uniform. Out front, the lovely interconnected canals of the Bear Lakes Country Club community shimmer in the moonlight.

He is remembering Russell's formidable presence under the basket and how it allowed him to take risks in defending opposing guards.

"I don't have to worry," he says, shrugging. "My old buddy Russell is there waiting to save my ass!"

—————

Maybe it was all predictable the way it played out for Cooz, Russ, Auerbach, and the Celtics. After Cousy retired, the Boston Celtics dynasty captured five more NBA championships over the next six years. That made for an unprecedented eleven in the thirteen seasons between 1957 and 1969.

"In history now, it's *Russell's* team," Cousy says, "not *Cousy's* team."

He knows what happened.

"Reality happened."

That wasn't a handoff Cousy willingly made. It was made for him, and he accepts it grudgingly.

He is thinking about Auerbach when he says, "Let's face it, if he doesn't acquire Russell, *none* of this happens."

In December 1964, Heinsohn suffered a foot injury, and Auerbach replaced him in the starting lineup with veteran Willie Naulls. That meant the Celtics had the first all-black starting lineup in NBA history. Earlier in that era, the joke among NBA writers, aware of the arbitrary quota among owners that limited the number of black players, had been, "You can start only one black player at home, two on the road and three if you need to win."

But now at Boston Garden, moments before tip-off, the *Globe*'s Clif Keane, an inveterate needler sitting courtside, looked up at the caged press area in the balcony and called to his colleague Jack Barry, "Hey, Barry! Barry!!!! Count them! FIVE of them! *FIIIIIVE!*"

That season, about half of the league's players were African American; by the later sixties, seven of the NBA's top ten scorers were black. As a player, Cousy recognized the increasing numbers and influence of black players. But, he says, "I don't remember saying to Heinsohn or Sharman, 'Jesus, we are going to be in the minority pretty soon.' . . . If someone had said in twenty years the league will be eighty percent black, I would've thought about it and discussed it. But you are so freakin' wrapped up [day to day] in getting the job done."

A few white fans told Heinsohn in 1964 that the black Celtics were freezing him out by not passing the ball to him. "Listen, we should all be so lucky to play with people like these guys," Heinsohn replied. "They are all great competitors; they want to win. What you are saying is bullshit."

The Celtics were achieving such highs that, after they won the 1966 NBA championship, the *Globe*'s Bud Collins wrote, "Who needs LSD?"

Auerbach once said that only two things could make him quit coaching—"My wife," he said, "and Russell's laugh." But now, approaching fifty, he stepped down as coach to become the Celtics' general manager. Cousy, Ramsey, and Heinsohn all turned down his offer to replace him as coach; Cousy liked his arrangement at Boston College, Ramsey had business obligations in Kentucky, and Heinsohn said, "Red, I can't coach this team. . . . Nobody can handle Russell like you." For that task, Auerbach hired just the right person: Russell, as player-coach. Now the franchise could lay claim to having drafted the NBA's first black player (Cooper), put forth the league's first all-black starting lineup, and hired the first black head coach in any American major league sport.

"I have fought a problem the only way I know how," Russell wrote in his first book, *Go Up for Glory*, coauthored with McSweeny in 1966, as tensions percolated in Boston over charges of racial inequity in public schools. "Maybe it was right or wrong in the approach, but a man can only ultimately be counted if he thinks he is doing right. Then, at least, he is a man."

Cousy understands those words today. "If I were black," he says, a half century later, "I would have been a bomb thrower."

Russell's pronouncements on race became bolder over time. He told *The Saturday Evening Post* in January 1964 he believed there was a quota among NBA teams that limited roster spots for black players. Leonard Shecter of the *New York Post* agreed, pointing out that five NBA teams at the time had four black players, and four teams had five black players. "There should, one would think, be one team that has seven Negroes, another with only two," Shecter wrote. "While this isn't evidence of a quota system, it makes a logical man wonder."

"You owe the public the same thing it owes you. Nothing!" Russell told *The Saturday Evening Post*, his views on this topic the antithesis of Cousy's. "I refuse to misrepresent myself. I refuse to smile and be nice to the kiddies. I don't think it is incumbent upon me to set a good example to anybody's kids but my own."

He said black Americans needed to continue to push for equality: "It's like the story of the old man who starts every day by hitting his mule over the head with a club to 'get his attention.' We have got to make the white population uncomfortable and keep it uncomfortable, because that is the only way to get their attention."

Russell believed a racial showdown loomed: "We will reach a breaking point and either there will be a really integrated society or we will understand, absolutely and finally, that we will never become a part of society. And then it will be a question, you know, of will we go the way of the American Indian.

"What's better, to live as a subservient minority or 'die like men'?"

Russell lent his voice, and activism, to the civil rights movement in ways few other professional athletes did. His comments in *The Saturday Evening Post* prompted the *New York Post*'s Milton Gross, a liberal thinker, to compare him to boxer Cassius Clay. Russell had exceeded Clay, Gross wrote on January 29, 1964, as "an articulate grown man who happens to be a great basketball player. Cassius is a loud-mouthed kid, whose charm has worn thin. If I were forced to choose between one or the other, I'd have to go with Russell, whom I know longer, admire more and deeply respect as a man of sincere convictions." Then Gross added, "I agree completely with Russell that there is a quota in the N.B.A., just as there is in baseball, but I disagree with him just as thoroughly when he says that in the sports pages whites are praised only for their strong points, Negroes damned only for their weaknesses. If the sports pages have been guilty of anything it has been an over-emotional kind of antiseptic writing in which we have gone out of our way to avoid writing anything derogatory about a Negro athlete. . . . Russell has no more right to pigeonhole all whites as anybody else has to contrive a stereotype of all Negroes."

The crisis over public schools intensified in Boston. The Reverend Martin Luther King Jr., in a January 1965 speech, charged Boston with de facto segregation, and said he would return to the city because "there is a need for a strong and vigorous movement against slumlordism." Three months later, the Massachusetts Department of Education's blue ribbon committee studying racially imbalanced schools recommended that five thousand black and white students in Boston be transferred through busing. Louise Day Hicks of Southie howled, her carefully coded language suddenly melting away, replaced by terms such as "racial agitators," "un-American," and "undemocratic." A Brandeis professor compared Hicks to Adolf Hitler and Alabama's George Wallace. But that fall, voters reelected Hicks to a third term on the Boston School Committee, her campaign focused on "Defending the Neighborhood School."

In such tense times, few professional athletes joined the conversation about race, politics, and society. Too risky, Oscar Robertson later said: "No [NBA] owner was going to have on his team an outspoken black man making political statements. . . . If you stepped forward and spoke out, your livelihood was cancelled."

But Russell defied such accepted wisdom. He stepped forward and spoke out, even as Auerbach cautioned him that, as the team's new head coach, he mustn't.

In June 1966, Russell served as graduation speaker at a predominantly black junior high school in Roxbury. At the school's formal graduation a week before, a black minister had leaped onto the stage and denounced the presence of Hicks, who was escorted from the room for her own protection; the ceremony ended before some students received diplomas. On the morning of Russell's speech at the school's makeup graduation ceremony, Auerbach told him, "Since you're committed, go and do it. But when you start getting involved in political things—stop real quick. . . . You no longer speak as Bill Russell, athlete. You're now part of the [Celtics] administration."

Russell took the stage and said that "certain members" of the city government had ignored the best interests of the black community—he meant Louise Day Hicks—"but we are not expected to respond." He said, "There's a fire here in Roxbury that the school committee refuses to acknowledge, and the fire that consumes Roxbury will also consume Boston. . . . Because of a lack of real communication, a polluted atmosphere hangs over our cities, an atmosphere of hate, distrust, ignorance, a complete lack of knowledge of each other. . . . I do not say we have to love each other, but we must try to understand and respect each other."

In the Celtics dressing room after one practice, Russell told sportswriter George Sullivan of the *Herald Traveler*, "Boston is the most prejudiced city in the United States." Sullivan replied, "Don't talk like that," but Russell continued. Sullivan said maybe he would write a story about Russell's comments.

"Your paper won't have the guts to print it," Russell said.

"Give me more," Sullivan said, his newshound instincts kicking in, "because you are off to a hell of a start."

Russell called out Boston as a racist hotbed.

Sullivan rushed to his newsroom, told his sports editor, "Russell says Boston is the most prejudiced city in America." His editor told him to start writing. Sullivan wrote feverishly, certain his story was bound for the front page, but only until his sports editor returned and told him to stop because the higher-ranking editors thought his story would further inflame Boston.

The next day in the dressing room, Russell feigned thumbing through the *Herald Traveler* and called out to Sullivan, "I can't find it. I've read it inside out. Can you tell me which page your story is on?" Other players, in on Russell's dare, laughed, and Russell, not holding back, erupted with his great big squeal-laugh and said, "What did I tell you? I knew your paper wouldn't have the guts to run that thing." Sullivan received a small bonus for his story that never appeared, but now he swallowed hard and told Russell, "You were right."

Cousy saw the nation fraying. He watched on television after Senator Robert Kennedy, Democratic candidate for the presidency, was murdered in a Los Angeles hotel on June 6, 1968. In another week Cousy was scheduled to introduce RFK at a fund-raising dinner in Rochester; he already had his plane tickets. Four months later, Cousy watched the televised protest at the Olympics in Mexico City as American sprinters John Carlos and Tommie Smith stood on the medal stand with bowed heads and raised fists in protest of discrimination and poverty in America. To Cousy their protest seemed a powerful extension of the way Russell slowly walked onto the court during pregame introductions, a demonstration in its own right, he thought. Russell was asked if he *had a problem* with the Olympic protest, and he replied, "Yeah, I have a problem with it: I didn't think of it first."

As the civil rights movement inexorably rolled on, Russell inexorably rolled on, too. One night in 1968, after playing the Pistons, he brought Celtics guard Mal Graham to a Detroit neighborhood without telling him where they were going. He knocked on the front door of a house, and the tall, young African-American woman who opened it and smiled was sprinter Wilma Rudolph, a U.S. Olympian in 1956 with Russell; her three gold medals in the 1960 Olympics had launched her to international stardom. They shared a few hours that night reminiscing. Graham considered this conversation between two of America's finest athletes a great moment in his young life.

The Celtics, meanwhile, kept winning. It was as if Cousy had retired and his team barely noticed. They won NBA championships in 1964, 1965, and 1966, and then, after Chamberlain finally won one in 1967, the Celtics, with Russell as head coach, won two more in 1968 and 1969. That made six titles for Cousy, eleven for Russell.

"In all the slow processes of history, defense always conquers in the end. Bill Russell is The End," Jim Murray wrote in the *Los Angeles Times*. "He owns the game of basketball as no one ever has before and as no one ever will again."

In May 1969, though, Russell resigned as coach and retired as a player. He moved out to Hollywood to be with his friend, football-star-turned-actor Jim Brown. Russell tried his hand as an actor even as Auerbach wisecracked, "Russ, how many parts do you think there are for a six-nine *shvartze*?" Russell also lectured on the college circuit, and told students at the University of Nevada, Reno, that they made up "the greatest generation the world has ever known. White and black are going to make it together, or destroy it together."

Soon after Jackie Robinson died in 1972, his widow, Rachel, phoned Russell. "I want you to be a pallbearer at Jackie's funeral," she said. Russell was only thirteen in 1947 when Robinson broke Major League Baseball's color barrier. To Russell, Jackie Robinson had taken black athletes from Point A to Point B, and he hoped that, as the first black head coach in American professional sports, he had carried the cause from Point B to Point C. He learned that he would be the only pallbearer who had not been Robinson's teammate. Though honored, Russell asked, "Why me?" Once, Ty Cobb had called Russell the greatest money player he'd ever known, other than himself. Now, Rachel Robinson told him, "You were Jackie's favorite athlete."

When Russell told Auerbach in March 1972 that he didn't want to participate in a public ceremony at Boston Garden to retire his jersey number, Cousy didn't understand. Already jersey numbers had been retired for Cousy, Heinsohn, Sam Jones, K.C. Jones, Sharman, and Ramsey. So how could Russell, of all Celtics, not want to join them?

Auerbach turned creative: He held an informal ceremony before a game, five minutes before fans were allowed inside the Garden, per Russ's wishes. Russell showed up, but only as an ABC television commentator at courtside preparing to work. Up to the rafters went No. 6, stitched in green and placed in the eighth and final spot in the bottom right square of the white banner, and only a few players, sportswriters, ABC colleagues, vendors, and ushers saw it ascend. During the game that followed, some in the sellout crowd awarded Russell a standing ovation, but he did not acknowledge it, much as Ted Williams in his final at-bat at Fenway Park had not acknowledged his cheering fans.

Russell unloaded on Boston again a year later. At a press conference announcing him as the Seattle SuperSonics' new general manager and head coach, Russell described his Boston years as "a very traumatic experience, and there are some scars left." Boston, he said, "is probably the most rigidly segregated city in the country." (Hearing this, sportswriter George Sullivan, recalling his unpublished story, told himself, "Hey, I had that scoop years ago!") Russell criticized Boston's sportswriters, saying, "I felt they had a code of conduct—first for athletes and another for black athletes." Later he said, "I tried to do things to change it, but I couldn't." Then he said, "I tried to be a man."

Return fire came from Boston's press row, the *Herald*'s Tim Horgan suggesting that Russell "segregated himself" in Boston. "He was the most surly, selfish, boorish and uncooperative athlete I've met in twenty-three years as a Boston sportswriter," Horgan wrote. In the *Globe*, Leigh Montville wrote, "[Russell] built a cover of aloofness and called it 'dignity.' . . . If it was a bad day, he would look up at you slowly. Menacingly. 'What is this insect that has flown into my room?' he would seem to think." Montville believed Russell left Boston carrying only the worst memories: "I think it is sad that he never chose to look for the best ones. I think they were there if he wanted them."

On the day Russell was inducted into the Naismith Memorial Basketball Hall of Fame in May 1975, Cousy was there, but Russell was not. Russell had made it clear he wasn't coming, though he did not explain why. He had long said that he thought personal honors didn't matter in a team game. Some sportswriters theorized that he was reacting to what he perceived as the Hall's racial bias—he was, after all, the first black player ever inducted. Robert Douglas, coach of the bygone New York Renaissance (aka the Rens), was the only other African American among the Hall of Fame's ninety-seven inductees; Douglas's Rens, an all-black barnstorming team from 1923 to 1949, had been inducted collectively in 1963. Russell was the first black star player of the modern era to become eligible for induction. Cousy, a member of the Hall's 1971 class, spoke with Russell by telephone a few weeks before the ceremony. He told the press only that his old teammate "just wishes the whole matter would go away."

Satch Sanders didn't understand the commotion. At a speaking engagement with Russell, Sanders heard a man from the crowd angrily ask why Russell had skipped out of the Hall ceremony. With cool precision, Sanders eviscerated the questioner: "Excuse me, sir, but did something happen to your mortgage when Russell decided not to show up? Or does it still come every month? Do you still get hunger pains? Do you still look at attractive young ladies when they pass? How important can it be that Russell wouldn't stand? Did you get that disturbed over Watergate? Do you get that angry over politicians on the take, tearing down a system that perhaps you fought for in Korea? Who is Bill Russell to you? He's an entertainer. That's all. He's that small in your life, and I just can't see how his refusal to enter the Hall of Fame can possibly irk you this much."

There was another view of Russell: "A black bigot is still a bigot," Ed Macauley, the former Celtic, would say. "And that's where Russell struck out with me. He'd condemn white people for the same kind of attitude he had. In that way he always reminded me of the peace demonstrators who'd protest violence by burning down a city."

Russell had seen, heard, and felt racism in Boston from the first, from white sportswriters and white fans, and also at home in suburban Reading, where white police eyed him suspiciously as a black man driving a fine car, and white real estate agents and neighbors made clear they didn't want his black family in their midst, and thieves wrote racist graffiti ("NIGGA") on the walls of his home, tore up his pool table, smashed his trophy case, and topped it all off by shitting in his bed.

There came a flash point in Boston's busing crisis in April 1976 that perhaps validated Russell as a truth teller. A group of white students boycotting South Boston and Charlestown high schools visited City Hall at the invitation of Louise Day Hicks, now city council president. In the council's chambers, the white teenagers read a list of antibusing demands, recited the Pledge of Allegiance, and then went outside and attacked Ted Landsmark, a twenty-nine-year-old black attorney in a three-piece suit. Two whites pinned back Landsmark's arms, while another lunged at him with the sharp point of a flagpole carrying an American flag, which they had taken from council chambers. The white hooligans broke Landsmark's nose, and he needed eight stitches for facial lacerations.

A *Boston Herald American* photographer, Stanley Forman, captured the raw image, rife with symbolism, of whites attacking a black man in Boston with an American flag. Published far and wide, the photo won a Pulitzer Prize.

"The chickens have come home to roost," said Vernon Jordan, executive director of the National Urban League. "This great state of the abolitionists must get its house in order. . . . If blacks are not safe, then neither will whites be safe, and that would be a lawless society. We must live together as people or die together as fools."

Boston's liberal reputation burned, even in casual talk during a free throw at Boston Garden, reported by Celtics center Dave Cowens, that went like this:

Lakers center Kareem Abdul-Jabbar: "Boston has a bunch of racist people."

Cowens: "You are right. But they are everywhere, man."

That's where the discussion ended, Cowens says, because "I wasn't going to get in a conversation with him when I'm about to get a rebound." In 1979, the Knicks traded Bob McAdoo, an African-American forward and three-time league scoring champion, to the Celtics; to him Boston carried a reputation as "a graveyard where black players went to die."

Russell continued to scald Boston with his words. He characterized Boston as a "flea market of racism" in a second memoir, *Second Wind*, published in 1979. "If Paul Revere were riding today," Russell wrote, "it would be for racism: 'The niggers are coming! The niggers are coming!' he'd yell as he galloped through town to warn neighborhoods of busing and black homeowners."

Russell also wrote in the book of his relationship with Cousy. In sixteen years, his perspective and tone seemingly had changed. At the Breakup Dinner in 1963, Russell, with teary eyes, had said, "Cousy is outstanding. We see each other as brothers not as great athletes. Cousy, just by being himself, has given me so much." Three years later, in his first book, Russell portrayed their relationship much differently: "Cousy was captain of the 1957 team. He went his way and I went mine. There was no personality conflict involved. Later, as the years passed, Cooz and I would occasionally play in the same card game and occasionally say a few words. It was a remote relationship, although I had deep respect for him and believe he returned it for me. In fact, Cousy could do some things which were very pleasant surprises."

Now, in 1979, Russell explained the parameters of friendship between teammates:

> I have always believed . . . that there are limitations to the kind of friendship teammates can have. We were special friends but limited ones. I used to joke with Bob Cousy, and I admired what he stood for and the way he conducted himself. I thought he was the smartest man I'd ever played with, and I had too much respect for him to ever get sucked into the jealousy others tried to promote between us. Still, I can't say that I was ever close to Cousy; we never sat down and had a talk the way real friends would. The same was true with most of the other Celtics while we were playing. There is simply too much competitive pressure in professional sports to share your hopes and fears with somebody in the same business. You cultivate your strengths, keep merry and stay on your guard. . . . Our kidding helped us to have fun and to win, but it didn't make us the closest of friends. That changes after retirement; then you had a better chance of becoming an ex-teammate's friend.

Nearly forty years later, Cousy says he did not read Russell's 1979 book: "Maybe I don't want to read anything about the past that interferes with my memory of it, you know? Maybe it's a selfish thing. I just want to remember the past the way I choose to. If I let other people's interpretation of it interfere then it raises other questions. It might be just a defense mechanism."

But when he heard Russell's views about their relationship as teammates read aloud, he said they were essentially true. As Celtics, they were not close. "In this case I would agree with Russ—that it was my personality that created this."

That assessment is not what Russell wrote; it is what Cousy heard. "I'd break it down more to individuals and our own particular idiosyncrasies—my shyness, his maybe with a chip on his shoulder," Cousy says. "I never read that in [Chuck] Cooper from the beginning. He and I were close and had exactly the kind of relationship that Russell says here is difficult in sports. I would agree that we are all competitive animals and so there are jealousy factors. . . . In a team sport a certain amount of togetherness is required for the ultimate success. You've got to subjugate even if you think the guy is a racist from down South. Well, okay, but the sonovabitch scores twenty-four a game so you've got to learn to get along. A lot of things come into play here. But I would agree with Russ. I've been accused of being a loner, very private, and all of that is true. I think it stems from this initial insecurity of the ghetto, learning the [English] language in the street, speaking funny, whatever creates our personality later.

"But personality-wise, in terms of individuals, we should get a shrink in on this conversation. Perhaps being an only child works into that. I didn't have siblings to interact with. I had a terrible, dysfunctional home atmosphere. How did this affect how I responded to other people or teammates later on? Someone better trained than me would have to explain that to me. I know that I was a little bizarre."

Cousy defends Boston, but self-doubt creeps in. "I didn't share his opinion then, and I still don't, that Boston was the most racist city in the world, or in the United States," he says. "I didn't *not* think there was racism in Boston. I knew what Southie was like. Now I certainly know the extremes of racism. . . . Maybe I was being naïve about some segments of the city."

About Russell: "He must've been having constant mixed emotions. . . . Jesus, I can't imagine living in a community that would break into my home and defecate in my bed."

Then, typically hard on himself, Cousy says with regret: "I might have been able to neutralize some of this, if I had been more outspoken."

THURSDAY NIGHTS

On Thursdays, his favorite night of the week now, Cousy heads to Worcester Country Club, where he has been a member since 1967. He drives along a tree-lined entry road to the red-roofed clubhouse perched atop a hill. In his slacks and loose-fitting Tommy Bahama shirt, and using his cane, Cousy walks through the lobby with its chandelier and smooth, polished wood floors and into the dining room where his old buddies await.

They started gathering for a Guys Night Out dinner on Thursdays about thirty years ago. Usually a half dozen or maybe a dozen show up. No invitations, no RSVPs: They come if they can. They start at six o'clock and typically return home by seven-forty-five or eight. Some of the group's younger men are in their seventies, and the oldest, like Cousy, are in their late eighties or early nineties.

They talk about politics, sports, the latest happenings in Worcester, the weather, and whatever ails them. "Don't ask an eighty-seven-year-old how he's feeling," Cousy says, "because you'll get a long boring soliloquy." They are retired from business, law enforcement, dentistry, accounting. Their heritage runs from Irish to Italian to Syrian to French, the last being Cousy, who is sure to clarify that he isn't French-Canadian but the real deal. Most are Republicans, though longtime group members aren't sure anymore to which party Cousy belongs: Democrat? Republican? Independent?

"They are all Republicans," Hank Lusardi, a ninety-three-year-old retired accountant, says later. Lusardi says he's neither Republican nor Democrat. "I'm a *bullshitter*," he says, with a laugh. "I take all sides. I love to argue. All my life I've done nothing but argue." Lusardi roomed for a time, stateside, during World War II with Henry Kissinger, the future U.S. secretary of state, and later fought in Europe, where he was captured by the Germans and held as a prisoner of war.

"If somebody said it's raining out, Hank would disagree with him," Tony Stevens, another longtime Thursday night group member, says playfully. "We all agreed the only reason we won the war was so the Germans could get rid of Hank."

Mostly Cousy blends into the Thursday night conversations. Some-times he'll tell a story about a celebrity he met long ago or a faraway land he visited, and his old friends offer their rapt attention. Like the time in 1966, at President Lyndon Johnson's White House for a photo op as a representative of the Big Brothers mentoring program, when Cousy listened to evangelist Billy Graham brag about how close he and his wife were to LBJ and Lady Bird Johnson. "He never makes a decision without consulting me," Cousy heard Graham say. He watched LBJ arrive and hug Graham, but once photos were taken, the president turned on his heel and left without even saying good-bye. Cousy almost felt sorry for Graham. Or the time he and Auerbach rode in a U.S. State Department car in Morocco and the sky suddenly went dark, and a black cloud of locusts struck their windshield. Later, free from locusts, they came upon a shepherd wailing in the street af-ter a speeding truck had killed some of his goats. Cousy spoke to the man in French, and it was heartrending.

His old friends in Worcester know Cousy as few do. Their friendship with him goes back thirty years for some, fifty or sixty years for others. They know who he is, what he has done, and where he has been. In some cases, their kids know his kids. These men convey their familiarity with easy nods and smiles. They know. They remember.

They remember when Cousy coached six seasons at Boston College between 1964 and 1969, and his players wanted to be just like him. At practice, one player threw a behind-the-back pass, Cooz-like. "We don't do that!" Cousy snapped. He participated in practices, running the break, whipping no-look passes, his intensity off the charts. Cousy produced an impressive 114-38 overall record at BC, reached the Elite Eight once, and captured New England Coach of the Year honors twice.

His old friends grew accustomed to his unusual voice decades ago and remember when he provided color commentary for NBA games for ABC Sports during the mid-sixties, Chris Schenkel handling play-by-play. Cousy learned that Roone Arledge, the ABC executive, was telling snide jokes on the banquet circuit about his speech impediment, and that Arledge said he had hired Cousy without first putting him through an audition and how that was a big mistake because he was *unintelligible*.

They remember how losing always was untenable to him. Cousy once described the effects of losing by asking a physician friend, "Do you know how you feel when you lose a patient on the table?" Almost instantly he wanted to take back those words; his analogy embarrassed him. Still, the point could not be missed: A part of Cousy really did die with every defeat.

They remember how Cousy wept during a press conference at BC in September 1967 while defending himself against *Life* magazine. In an investigative series about mob influence in America, especially in illegal sports gambling, *Life* identified a friend of Cousy's, Andrew Pradella, as a partner in a gambling syndicate with ties to the Genovese family of La Cosa Nostra. Pradella owned a lounge in Springfield, and his sons attended Cousy's summer camp. An FBI man had warned Cousy to stay clear of Pradella five years earlier. *Life* quoted Cousy saying, "I don't see why I should stop seeing my friends just because they are gamblers. How can I tell [Pradella] when he calls and asks about a team that I won't talk to him about that?" At the press conference, Cousy said, "I am not guilty of anything and therefore I do not sneak around with Mr. Pradella." He said he might have broken off the friendship but "I couldn't bring myself to do that."

In the days that followed, Cousy resourcefully leveraged his friendships with leading sports columnists to build a beachhead. In New York, Red Smith of the *Herald-Tribune* wrote, much like the *New York Post*'s Milton Gross and Jim Murray of the *Los Angeles Times*, in supportive fashion: "Dragging Cousy into this was cruel, but his reputation can survive it. When time has eased the hurt, he will find everybody on his side." In the *Boston Globe*, Nason, the sports editor, took his devotion a step further: "For those of us who've known him for twenty-one years, Cousy was still clad in shining armor . . . a man far above the shady implications." The *Globe*'s editorial page took a more nuanced, less chummy position. Like Caesar's wife, the *Globe* editorialized, Cousy needed to be above suspicion: "Cousy, by his own choice, has not fulfilled this obligation nearly as well as he might have. And this is tragic for all concerned." For Cousy, the controversy quickly passed; Pradella later died, and today, a half century later, Cousy still counts his son Andy Pradella as a friend.

On Thursday nights, Cousy is at ease in the company of these old friends. His devotion to them runs deep. "Pure companionship," he says of his Thursday night gang. "These are lifelong friends. Without getting maudlin, how often at our age do we say, 'Life is about family and friends'? The distrust we feel about society around us, [together] we feel safe and loved. It's a positive experience that all of us look forward to for a couple hours every week. You don't have to worry about your back. You are among people you love."

They all recall a more restrictive time at the club, which was dedicated in 1914; former president William Howard Taft, on hand for the occasion, hooked the honorary first drive. Lusardi says, "This was a golf course started by old Yankees. In the old days, they had signs that said NO IRISH NEED APPLY."

Stevens recalls, "Bob would bring blacks to Worcester Country Club which didn't have black members [at the time]. He would bring Jewish people to the club and there were no Jewish members." In 2010, Cousy cosponsored the club's first African-American member, Milan Brown, then Holy Cross's new basketball coach.

His friends also remember when Cousy volunteered for the Big Brothers program, first mentoring a white teen and later, during the eighties, two black teens. He took the second, Kevin Murphy, to Celtics games, where Auerbach, in his office, always made a fuss over him. He also took Murphy to Mass at Blessed Sacrament Church, where once, after hearing a priest deliver a sermon endorsing integration and intermarriage, Cousy watched several angry parishioners walk out.

One night, Cousy took Murphy to a movie with Missie and her mother. He drove to the low-income housing development in Worcester where Murphy lived. Missie's mother, Mary O'Hanlon Ritterbusch, looked forward to meeting young Kevin Murphy for the first time. Out he came, six-foot-two and black, not what she was expecting from a boy with a nice Irish name, and as he ran toward the car, she frantically fumbled with her door lock, fearful of the approaching young black teen. Cousy calmed her and introduced his embarrassed mother-in-law to Kevin Murphy.

At Worcester Country Club, a club official invariably stopped at their table to say to Murphy in a voice Cousy thought patronizing, "And who is this nice young man?" The official patted Murphy atop his Afro. "Well, isn't this nice! Welcome to Worcester Country Club!"

"To me," Cousy says, recalling those times, "bringing my black 'Little Brother' to Mass was making a soft statement. At the time, I was Bob Cousy and that was meaningful because what I did would get a reaction. It was not like walking across the bridge with Dr. King and getting beaten by the dogs or hosed down, but it was a soft declaration about how I feel about racism."

Many years after Cousy joined Worcester Country Club, he learned that the club's membership committee had worried in 1967 about his candidacy for membership: "If we let him in, do you think he will bring Russell here?"

AUERBACH

In his living room, Cousy holds a visitor's iPhone. He is watching a video of the Bob Cousy Day ceremony for the first time since it happened. He positions the iPhone screen horizontally to take in more of the scene of Johnny Most as master of ceremonies. Once again he sees Dolph Schayes, Missie, and the others. Cousy is wide-eyed, amazed, emotional.

"I was such a crybaby," he says. "Look at Ticia! She's looking kind of embarrassed by the whole thing."

He watches in silence, transported back in time. "There's my parents!" He says he never asked what they thought of the ceremony. "It would have been interesting to know how they felt."

He watches the video again, this time with his daughter Marie. She sees Auerbach and says wistfully, "It's fun to hear him again," and Cousy nods, knowing his coach was, in every regard, unforgettable.

McSweeny always remembered the last night of Auerbach's coaching career, a 95–93 victory over the Lakers in Game 7 of the NBA Finals on April 28, 1966. At game's end, Auerbach leaped and punched his fist into the air and Russell drenched him, fully clothed, in the postgame shower. Auerbach had his arm draped over Russell's shoulder when a sportswriter asked if he had any coaching advice for his replacement. He looked at Russell, smiled, and shouted, "WIN!!" Like Cousy, Sharman, Ramsey, and Heinsohn, Auerbach wanted to go out a winner, and now he had.

It wasn't so much the thunderous ovations at Boston Garden after the Celtics' eighth consecutive NBA championship that McSweeny remembered; it was what happened later that night.

His colleague Murray Kramer, a Boston sportswriter for more than thirty years, took McSweeny to Auerbach's suite at the Hotel Lenox. It was nearly midnight when they arrived, the tumult and shouting over. There came no congratulatory telephone calls, no well-wishers dropping by. It was only Auerbach and two sportswriters eating out of cardboard cartons from Anita Chou's Chinese restaurant.

Auerbach had been coaching professional basketball for nearly 1,600 games across twenty years without suffering a losing season, and here was his final stop.

Ninety minutes after the pandemonium, McSweeny was struck by the loneliness of it.

In the years that followed, other NBA teams, and the Celtics, too, looked to players who had been touched by Auerbach's wand. It's no surprise then that Russell, Sharman, Heinsohn, K.C. Jones, Sanders, and Cousy all became NBA head coaches.

Cousy had gotten queries from about a half dozen NBA teams while at BC and brushed them aside. He told Missie he would accept only if some NBA franchise owner offered him crazy money, and that's what Max Jacobs of the Cincinnati Royals did.

Publicly, Cousy said he returned to the NBA in June 1969, just as Russell was leaving, because, like Vince Lombardi in the NFL, he missed the pro game and felt compelled to return. But it wasn't that. It was the money, and only the money. Cousy would earn in excess of $100,000 per season over three years to become head coach of the Royals at a time when some NBA coaches made about a third that much. With his hiring, ticket sales spiked in Cincinnati, and the team secured a new local radio deal after appearing on local radio for only eight games the previous season.

The Royals even put the forty-one-year-old Cousy on the active roster as player-coach, but only after Auerbach squeezed them into a trade for his playing rights, infuriating Cousy and Royals officials. (Auerbach got reserve forward Bill Dinwiddie, who played for one year in Boston and was traded.) The Royals had guard Oscar Robertson and all-star forward Jerry Lucas on an otherwise modestly talented, young team, and no fan base to speak of. Robertson had supplanted Cousy as the league's best guard even before Cousy retired. Now the two men eyed each other warily; others sensed outright hostility between them.

Activating Cousy was purely a marketing tool to generate bigger crowds. He played only seven games for the Royals, thirty-four minutes in all. When he entered a game against the Knicks, opposing guard Walt Frazier noticed how Cousy "walked onto the court in such an arrogant way, like he was still the king of basketball." Robertson, no fan of Cousy's, later would say, "One month into the season, Bob Cousy, age forty-one, completed our youth movement."

Offense wasn't the problem for Cousy; he took only three shots and racked up ten assists in those thirty-four minutes. The problem was defense: Opposing guards—younger, stronger, faster, and taller—

annihilated him. They were all six-foot-four now, or so it seemed, and took Cousy into the lane and easily jumped over him.

"I knew immediately," Cousy says. "It was like a boy trying to guard a man." He pulled himself off the active roster.

The Royals' losses built up, a fifth-place 36-46 record that first season, 33-49 the next season, and after that it didn't get much better. Sportswriter Tom Callahan of the *Cincinnati Enquirer* sensed that Cousy became frustrated because, like Ted Williams as manager of baseball's Washington Senators, Cousy realized that his players, apart from Robertson, could not perform as he once had. His relationship with Robertson, great player though he was, foundered. The Big O tired of hearing Cousy call everyone *Babe*. Of their rapport, Cousy says, "We just kind of ignored each other." In time Lucas was traded, and Robertson, too. Cousy thought motivation and dedication among NBA players was gone, eroded by bigger paychecks.

During games, he stood by the bench wearing a sport coat and long sideburns and holding a rolled-up program, just as Auerbach once had. Sitting courtside beside the Royals' bench, Callahan once heard a fan jeering Cousy, at which point Cousy half turned to Callahan and growled, *"If he would just touch me . . ."*

Cousy dealt with race in his own way, mostly beneath the radar. The Royals' roster was roughly half white, half black, and when Cousy arrived to practices, the black players often shot at one basket, the whites at the other. Cousy pulled aside guard Tom Van Arsdale, his blond team captain, pointed to the far end of the court, and said, "Tommy, go down there and integrate that basket."

In the 1970 *Pro Basketball Guide*, published by Cord Communications, Cousy sought to dispel some racial stereotypes in the NBA. "As a man with deep liberal convictions, I have always been concerned about the ugly situation that plagues our community," he wrote in a story carrying the headline BLACK IS BEAUTIFUL IN THE NBA. To old stereotypes that suggested blacks were lazy, lacked competitive drive, and did not make strong leaders, Cousy wrote, "I hear these words and

I cringe at the thought of men I have played with and against, such as Bill Russell, the Jones boys—Sam and K.C.—Oscar Robertson, Elgin Baylor, Maurice Stokes and countless others, men who had shown unusual dedication, ability and courage in all outlets of their existence."

By building a racial pride, Cousy wrote, "Negroes stand as equal to white men, and if they have the ability to do something and then complement it with the dedication, they will be successful. If each black man, or black athlete, or black boy can believe this, I think this is how they are going to attain a just equality. I feel this is what the Black Is Beautiful concept is all about and I stand behind it all the way."

For a time, Cousy's daughter Marie dated one of his black players, guard Norm Van Lier. A twenty-year-old college student in Boston, four years younger than Van Lier, Marie visited her parents in Cincinnati during winter break. Van Lier phoned her at her parents' house, and Missie, who adored Van Lier, chatted with him for some time, keeping Marie waiting.

"C'mon, Mom," Marie said, finally, "he's calling for *me*."

Marie and Van Lier grew close. He talked honestly with her about how difficult it was to be a black man in America. He had been an all-star quarterback in high school in Pennsylvania, and when a University of Alabama recruiter showed up at his school, he was startled to find that Van Lier was black, and told him, "Boy . . . if I had known you was colored, I would have never come here." One night at his apartment, past team curfew, Van Lier told Marie she would need to drive one of his cars home. His curfew with the Royals was earlier than the one Marie had established with her parents. The next morning when Cooz awoke, he asked, "Why is Norm's car in our driveway?" and Marie explained about the curfew.

He admired Van Lier's playing style. He played with a fighter's spirit, diving for loose balls. "Van Lier and I were very close," Cousy says. "Of all the guys I had, he was a warrior. . . . He was a great kid."

In November 1971, the struggling Royals traded Van Lier to

Chicago. Rumors spread through the league that Cousy had traded him because he was dating Marie. Van Lier didn't believe that even as his relationship with her soon ended. Decades later, he remembered a private moment when Cousy had told him, "I'd be proud to have you as a son-in-law," and Van Lier said he respected his coach for saying that.

In November 1973, Cousy, at forty-five and in his fifth season as an NBA coach, stared into his hotel room mirror and didn't see Auerbach staring back. Nor did he see Auerbach-quality results in the standings, his Royals having won just six of twenty games, stuck in last place. He resigned as head coach with a four-seasons-plus record of 141-207, hardly Auerbach-like.

He returned with Missie to the house on Salisbury Street in Worcester, told Auerbach he needed a job, and got one, as a TV analyst for Celtics games, a job he would keep for the next thirty-four years, a sage truth teller through Havlicek and Bird and the 2008 NBA championship won by Kevin Garnett, Paul Pierce, and Ray Allen. Several months later, Comcast SportsNet summarily told Cooz he wasn't needed anymore. Cousy replied with an eighty-year-old's wounded pride, saying, "Thank you very much, have a good year," and then hung up.

At a flower shop in Brookline during the early seventies, two young women were talking about flowers when Randy Auerbach, the coach's younger daughter and manager of the shop, noticed the medallion her customer wore on a necklace. A tad larger than a nickel, she recognized it at once. At its center was an enameled green shamrock with a diamond, surrounded along the circular edge by these words: "Boston Celtics 1961 World Champions." She recognized it because she was wearing a similar medallion on her necklace, commemorating the team's 1959 championship; it had been part of the tie clip and cufflinks awarded to her father and his players after they won their second NBA title. Randy Auerbach and her sister remade the cufflinks into medallions. She had been wearing hers for nearly fifteen years, hardly ever took it off.

As they chatted amiably about flowers, Randy Auerbach suddenly felt a special connection to this woman. *I know who you are. I know your background. I know your history.* It was similar to the kindred feeling she experienced when she met someone Jewish.

This customer, she knew, could be one of only a dozen or so people, but which one? She studied the young woman's face and finally asked, "Are you Bob's daughter?"

The question startled Marie Cousy. "Yes," she said. "How did you know?"

Their conversation took on heightened meaning. They talked about their fathers, and their medallions, and their childhood memories of the Celtics dynasty years, when their fathers were often away from home. Randy had always felt lucky to grow up in Washington, D.C., and not in Boston where she would have had to deal with press coverage critical of her father. That would have been uncomfortable, so *in your face*, she thought. Maybe Marie Cousy did not have to deal with that because her father was so beloved by Boston's sportswriters. Their fathers had been through the basketball wars together and had traveled the world together.

This chance meeting affirmed to both women that they shared membership in a special club.

The city of Boston honored Auerbach with a statue near Faneuil Hall in 1985, the coach sitting alone on a bench and smoking his cigar, with plenty of room for passersby to sit next to him. Auerbach had won nine NBA championships as Celtics coach, and through the subsequent years he would win seven more as a Celtics executive.

Shrewdly, he had accumulated multifaceted athletes, especially during those earlier years: Havlicek and K.C. Jones had spent time in NFL training camps as a wide receiver and defensive back, respectively; Sharman had been in the Brooklyn Dodgers' dugout as a reserve outfielder in 1951 when the New York Giants' Bobby Thomson hit the Shot Heard 'Round the World; and Conley ("Probably the best fighter I ever had," Auerbach said) pitched eleven seasons in the majors and won a World Series in 1957 with the Milwaukee Braves.

Sitting in his chair now, Cousy says, "We always used to say, 'Arnold was put in this world to live by himself.' He is a loner, focused and dedicated to what he wants to do." Cousy liked to tease Dorothy Auerbach about how her husband spent eight months a year alone at the Hotel Lenox, eating Chinese food late at night, and then Cousy took him overseas for six weeks. "So can you put up with him," Cousy asked, "for two and a half months a year?" Dorothy howled with laughter; Arnold Auerbach called his captain an SOB.

But then, to Cousy's surprise, Auerbach seemed to change once he became a grandfather. Auerbach's family could tell how deeply moved he was at the birth of his granddaughter, Julie. At the hospital Auerbach held her, smiled, and spoke the same words he had spoken upon his daughter Nancy's birth: "Well, she's OK, but she'll need a nose job."

Cousy and Missie noticed at Celtics games during the mid-seventies how little Julie sat on Auerbach's lap, and how he became a doting grandfather known to her as *Goomp*. "Neither one of us had ever seen Arnold act that way toward another human being," Cousy says. "He doted over that little girl and gave her more love than anyone thought him capable of."

Through these years, Auerbach spent more time at home in Washington and had a regular gin rummy game at Woodmont Country Club in suburban Maryland. At Boston Garden, his small office, crammed with photos from the dynasty years, drew celebrities of all sorts. There Auerbach held court and waited to be adored.

Before one playoff game during the 1980s, a crowd packed into his office, wedging Cousy and Missie into a corner. Suddenly, there was a murmur down the hall, and Cousy heard someone say, "Look who's here!" In strode Senator Ted Kennedy with his entourage, shaking hands, working his way to the desk, at which point Kennedy playfully genuflected before Auerbach. Cousy got the sense that Kennedy's staff had phoned Auerbach about twenty minutes beforehand to get tickets to this big game. By genuflecting, Kennedy tried to be gracious and funny, but Auerbach, ever the grump, said, "You know how much trouble it was getting you those tickets?" To Cousy, "that kind of killed the moment."

Auerbach stormed into old age a curious curmudgeon. He was quieter and more relaxed at home than at Boston Garden. As his daughter Randy, in Los Angeles, put it, "I'd go to Washington to see my dad. I'd go to Boston to see Red Auerbach." To entertain his granddaughter, Auerbach brought home live lobsters from Boston and put them on the floor to terrorize the family dog. At the store, he bought whatever he was in the mood for. At Costco once, daughter Nancy told him, "Dad, you don't need *ten pounds* of steak!" "It's a good deal!" he replied, loading up their shopping cart; when his wife, Dorothy, saw what he'd bought, she gasped: "Oh my God!"

From his car window, he threw out his cigar wrappers, Randy saying, "How can you do this? It's not biodegradable!" He replied, "Aw, cut the crap. It'll dissolve."

He stored Celtics knickknacks in his car trunk to use as tips for parking attendants, nurses, and janitors. "Tip this guy a T-shirt," he'd tell his daughter. Or: "Give the guy a cap." Or: "Give him one of those little pens."

When Dorothy died after a lengthy illness in 2000, Auerbach asked Randy to phone Mel at the deli to see if he would deliver cold cuts to the house. "People will be coming by," he said. Randy phoned the deli, and also called comedian Mel Brooks, whose film production company she worked for in Los Angeles. When Brooks heard that Dorothy Auerbach had died, he phoned the old coach, saying only,

"It's Mel," and asking how he was. Auerbach thought it was Mel from the deli and said, "Well, the corned beef is kind of fatty." (Randy later told her father that he was speaking *to the other Mel.*)

Even as he walked his granddaughter, Julie Auerbach Flieger, down the aisle on her wedding day in 1991, he had to have his way. "Slow down!" he told her. "Speed up!" she answered. "SLOW DOWN!" he said again, as guests noticed. "This is my wedding," she told him. "SPEED UP!"

Near the end of his life, kidneys failing, Auerbach called Nancy to ask about the Celtics game on TV. "What's the score?" he said. She replied, "Are you watching?" He said, "Nah, it makes me too nervous. Tell me what's happening," and she provided details.

Auerbach made his last public appearance on October 25, 2006, when the U.S. Navy Memorial Foundation gave him the Lone Sailor Award for navy veterans with distinguished careers in the service or civilian life. Cousy flew to Washington in a private plane with the Celtics' owners. It was a glitzy event. Auerbach wore a tuxedo, a white scarf around his neck. His eyes were red-rimmed, and he had oxygen tubes in his nostrils.

A family member brought him into the room in a wheelchair and placed him next to Cousy.

At one moment, Cousy's eye caught Nancy's, and both became emotional, Cousy because he knew the end was near for his eighty-seven-year-old coach, and Nancy because Cousy was like an uncle and this was a special moment she would never forget.

Seeing the Celtics' coach and captain together one last time, Nancy says, "It wasn't an act, not for a camera, just because his friend was ill: There was real love there."

The evening ran with military precision, every moment scripted, until Auerbach spoke. From his wheelchair, he talked on and on. Cousy noticed the master of ceremonies nervously pacing. Auerbach, still feisty, told old stories—without notes, naturally, and Cousy had heard them all a hundred times.

The night grew late, and Nancy saw military aides waiting for their opportunity to intercede. She heard the master of ceremonies say more than once, "Okay, Red," until finally Auerbach suffered a coughing fit, and military aides swept in and wheeled him away.

"They practically had to drag him off," Nancy says.

Three days later, Auerbach died from a heart attack and renal failure.

Of all the players her father had coached through the years, Nancy phoned only two to personally break the news—Cousy and Russell.

MISSIE

In 2003, Cousy turned seventy-five and began to think about closing circles in his life with the people who mattered most to him. Over lunch with his daughter Marie and her husband, Bruce Brand, at the country club in West Palm Beach, he explained that he had been approached to sell his basketball memorabilia, and that he and Missie had decided to do it. They would give all of the proceeds to their two daughters, in part to help pay for their grandchildren's college education. He was proud that his daughters (and Brand) became schoolteachers. He knew they could use financial help. The sports memorabilia business had grown exponentially, and Cousy and others from the Celtics dynasty were like royalty to Baby Boomers, defining sports figures from their formative years.

Besides, hardly anyone even goes into the cellar anymore, he told Marie. A pipe could burst or thieves might break in again.

He said he would sell all of his basketball mementos—the trophies, plaques, scrapbooks, and rings, and whatever else was down there. He said, "What the hell do I need that stuff for, anyway?" Grateful, Marie became emotional.

Representatives from SportsCards Plus of Laguna Niguel, California, spent a few days at Cousy's house canvassing his material. Missie made lunch, and at the kitchen table Cousy regaled his visitors with stories about trophies and magazine covers. Dan Imler, vice president of auctions for SportsCards Plus, who grew up in a family of Celtics fans near Springfield, realized that Cousy's was "a monster collection."

"It was a very deep collection in terms of content," Imler says, "combined with his legacy and his popularity and his stature within the history of the game."

Cousy had kept nearly everything, dating back to Andrew Jackson High School. He had old family photos, including one of the infant Cooz sitting beside a ball. The cataloguing process was especially hard on Missie. Each item represented a precious memory to her. She pulled back some items too personal to give up—a few old photographs and the clock from Rose and Bill Russell.

He would sell his framed black-and-white photograph of the Celtics posing with John Kennedy in the Oval Office, signed by JFK with a black fountain pen, "To Bob Cousy, With esteem and very best regards, John F. Kennedy." From Bob Cousy Day, they boxed up the cigar humidor from his teammates; the laminated cherrywood plaques from Podoloff; and his four-page typed speech, with an attached envelope on which Lou Pieri, Celtics part owner, wrote, "Bob Cousy, Picked this off table Sunday. Thought you might want it. It was a great day for the Cousys and the Celtics. Lou Pieri."

The Cousy Collection totaled 150 items and was joined in auction by collections once owned by baseball stars Honus Wagner and Tony Lazzeri. Conducted by Internet and telephone on November 20, 2003, the auction of Cousy's memorabilia raised more than $450,000. The top-grossing items were his signed lithograph of the NBA's fifty greatest players, which sold for $86,940, and his 1957 NBA MVP Award, which went for $51,673. His 1957 Celtics championship ring brought

$27,180; the original framed Oval Office photo signed by JFK went for $25,300. (The value of this item mattered greatly to Frank Ramsey when, in 2005, his house in Kentucky was destroyed by a tornado; a few of his possessions later were found about a hundred miles away in Indiana. Ramsey never recovered the same Oval Office photo that JFK had personally inscribed to him and says his insurer paid him the value established by Cousy's $25,300 auction sale.)

In the end, Cousy says, his daughters netted about $160,000 apiece, and that pleased him.

But he had other worries.

Missie was not right, and hadn't been for quite some time.

Forgetfulness was all that it was, Missie said. He knew better.

It had started slowly, Missie repeating herself, asking the same question two or three times. She began putting items in the refrigerator that belonged in the pantry. She read the Worcester newspaper daily and underlined only the important news to better remember it. But then she underlined every sentence in the paper. She became frustrated and at times lashed out.

"At our age, that puts you on notice, 'So-and-So is slipping, she asked the same question three times,'" says Tony Stevens, Cousy's close friend. "Over the years it just continued to get more pronounced. You'd respond to it very carefully."

"Ticia," Missie said, "do you think I repeat a lot?"

"Well, Mom," Ticia began, careful to say it the right way. "Ask your friends if you do. Maybe you do. I think you do a little bit."

Cousy told his daughters not to get angry with Missie and to remember that she had special needs.

Bob and Missie befriended Clyde Phillips, a younger man who lived in the condo next door in West Palm Beach. Phillips is African American, a career Palm Beach County firefighter, tall and handsome, with broad, sloping shoulders and a shaved head. They gave him a key to their condo and invited him each Thanksgiving for dinner at the Bear Lakes Country Club, where Missie, ever attuned to race, whispered, "Clyde, if anybody is looking at you strange and if you feel uncomfortable, let me know. I'll straighten them out."

Missie sometimes made breakfast for Phillips, or if he sat shirtless with Cooz outside on the patio on a cool evening, she would bring him a blanket and drape it over his shoulders. In return, Phillips occasionally took her to shop for groceries at Publix, where Missie once sensed a white woman staring at them.

"What are you looking at?" Missie asked the woman, then nodded at Phillips and said, "This is my son."

Privately she confessed to Phillips that she was losing her memory and sometimes got lost. "Don't tell anybody," Missie pleaded.

Cooz took her to a neurologist. The diagnosis was what he feared, dementia. Missie wouldn't accept it. "I don't have dementia," she said. He suggested, "Doc, tell her that she just has a forgetfulness problem," but the neurologist wouldn't go along with that.

Twice a year, the neurologist tested Missie by asking a few simple questions, including, "Where do you live? Who is the governor? What's your phone number?" Missie fought hard to disprove the diagnosis. En route to the neurologist, she asked her husband, "What questions is he going to ask?" and he went through the usual list, knowing that she would forget the answers as soon as he spoke them. The neurologist's questions came, and if Missie didn't know the answer, she looked to her husband.

"Can't help you, sweetheart," he would say. "You are on your own."

The neurologist told him later that Missie was an unusual case. She scored roughly the same on his list of questions year after year. Her cognitive decline wasn't precipitous; its progression, over a dozen years and more, was slower than in most cases. He didn't have an explanation for it.

Life often shapes an athlete's performance. But Cousy offers a less common example of how an athlete's performance shapes his later life. Just as in his role as the Celtics' point guard, Cousy, as Missie's caretaker, proved resourceful and a little cunning. He created a home atmosphere that played into Missie's denial about her dementia, making it seem as if her problem were nothing more than a little forgetfulness and a slight loss of hearing.

Each morning he got up before she did and placed her pills on the kitchen table with her fiber bar, banana, and newspaper. Sometimes she wouldn't get up until ten or eleven, and he'd gently wake her to take her medicine. In her beloved garden, Cousy and his daughters planted perennials, knowing that Missie believed the bright colors the result of her own handiwork.

They drove together each winter from Worcester to their Florida condo, and he shipped Missie's car even though she didn't use it. She *believed* that she did, and so he parked her car in the space in front of their condo, and there it sat for four months each winter. Missie also thought she had done chores around the house, but he had. For the most part, he thought, she seemed happy.

Golf became his escape. Four or five days a week, he left home by seven thirty to play his round. Afterward, he would skip the sandwich and beer with his friends and rush home to Missie in time for lunch; sometimes, she was still reading the paper. Her balance was failing, but as she told him, "I fall a lot but I know how to fall."

Once, in Worcester, he came home from a golf round and she told him, "I went to the butcher shop." He knew it wasn't so, but nodded as if she really had.

Then the butcher on Pleasant Street phoned. "Cooz, when do you want to pick up this stuff?" he asked.

"What stuff?"

The butcher replied, "Your wife was in this morning."

Cousy said, "You're kidding me."

"No," the butcher said, "she ordered all this stuff."

He gasped in disbelief. The butcher shop was on a busy intersection in Worcester where it was difficult to park, and Missie had navigated her car through it safely—at least this time.

His daughters wanted him to take the car keys from her, but he wouldn't do that. He thought that would injure her sense of pride and independence. Instead, he chauffeured her all about, to her doctors' appointments, her hair salon, and to get her manicures. He hoped she wouldn't sneak out again. She wanted to drive herself. "I'll run you up," he would say, and nearly always she would let him.

On many afternoons, they watched *General Hospital* together. They went to see movies together, sometimes twice a week. He picked up their dinners. On Thursday nights, his one night out, he made her a cup of soup and a half sandwich before leaving to join his friends.

Cousy never sought outside help or sympathy. The captain handled this himself, closing another circle.

Slowly, Missie's dementia worsened. Brand, her son-in-law, arrived in Worcester on a visit and had the distinct feeling that Missie, with panic in her eyes, didn't know who he was. Cooz took her to Celtics games, where she seemed happy even if she could scarcely identify old friends there.

Cooz remained her safe harbor. On Saturday nights he took her up to the country club. Sometimes, a friend stopped by their table, and Missie would say, "This is *Bob Cousy*, you know?" It was embarrassing and out of character—it was the dementia speaking, not Missie—but it pleased him to think that through the years Missie took great pleasure in being his wife.

Her dementia became more apparent. Her old friend Diane Heinsohn talked by phone with Missie every month or so. She and Tom had divorced in 1994 after thirty-seven years of marriage. Missie still wanted to talk about their divorce more than fifteen years later. "I tried to change the subject," Diane Heinsohn says, "and she went back to it."

Cooz had often said that he married Missie and then went on the road for thirty years. He determined to make that up to her, and if that meant hearing her ask the same question six times in ten minutes, then he would answer it six times. This was no sacrifice, he believed. Missie would have done the same for him. Still, there were times he wanted to scream, and when he did, he made sure Missie was out of earshot.

This was Cousy's life at eighty, and he was okay with it. He held Missie's hand wherever they went, even from the living room to the kitchen. They were pals, and lovers. Friends marveled at his patience, not knowing he had it in him. He decided that the intensity of most marriages happened at the beginning, but he and Missie had saved their romance for the end. "I love you, honey," he said at the end of each night, and Missie answered, "I love you, too."

Marie says, "We saw a very tender side of Dad that you didn't necessarily see when he was young. I think it enhanced who he is. It helped him to grow as a person."

Honors came to him. The Naismith Memorial Basketball Hall of Fame in 2004 created the Bob Cousy Award, presented annually to the NCAA's top male point guard. His excitement over the award related more to love of sport than vanity. Cousy worried the game was losing some of its basic principles, that dunking was becoming the exclamation point in basketball at the expense of the role of the point guard.

Time was passing. His old friend Bill Sharman and his second wife, Joyce, visited Worcester. Sharman was eighty-six, Cousy eighty-four. Once they were both six-foot-one, but now Sharman stooped. "I'm growing in my old age," Cousy joked, noting that he was taller than Sharman now. "I'll be big enough to be a center soon." He and Missie took the Sharmans to lunch; a local sportswriter came to write a feature on the storied guard tandem. Cousy noticed that when asked a question, Sharman looked to Joyce, and she often answered for him. He seemed so uncertain, and Bill Sharman had always been so confident and self-assured. It was their last visit; Sharman died about a year later.

On a Saturday night in September 2013, after dinner at the club, Missie fastened her seat belt as Cooz pulled out of the club's driveway. He asked a question she didn't answer. Her hearing was poor, so he asked again, this time louder. She still didn't answer, and when he half turned, he saw her slumped in the passenger seat. He sped directly to the hospital.

Missie had suffered a massive stroke. Marie took a red-eye from Seattle and arrived the next morning. Doctors discovered that Missie could not swallow. They were pessimistic about a recovery. Missie had written instructions that she did not want to be kept alive on tubes.

Cooz did not want hospice care; he wanted to be alone with his wife, and so he brought her to a facility up the street.

There, in a coma, Missie hung on for thirteen days. He and his daughters visited each day in shifts. Cooz admitted to his daughters that he always thought he would die first. His lower back tightened from tension until he could barely walk. Each day Ticia sang to Missie. When she stirred in bed, Cooz put his face close to hers, cheek to cheek, and said, "Yes, sweetheart, we are here! We love you!" He hoped she could hear him. Ginny Sanders, Satch's wife, phoned. She updated other wives from the Celtics dynasty years about Missie's dire condition.

The funeral at Blessed Sacrament brought a nice turnout. Cousy, held up by his daughters, looked broken. It was mostly a local affair: old friends from Worcester and Holy Cross. Members of the Thursday night dinner gang were there in force. So were John and Beth Havlicek, Tom and Diane Heinsohn, Lynn Loscutoff, Celtics co-owner Wyc Grousbeck, and former Celtics Togo Palazzi, Jo Jo White, and Mal Graham. Jim Nelson, one of Cousy's BC players, showed up. Clyde Phillips drove twenty-two hours from Florida to be there. Ticia performed a reading, looked up, and saw Uncle Tommy Heinsohn with a huge grin, giving her two thumbs-up. "I think everyone knew that I was [once] the shy, quiet little Ticia," she says. Missie was buried beside her mother at St. John's Cemetery, not far from the gravesites of

Joe and Juliette Cousy, who were aboard the *Mauretania*, en route to Ellis Island, eighty-five years before, in December 1927, when Missie was born.

During the ensuing months, friends worried about Cousy. He seemed more fragile, quiet, and lonely than before. He had stopped going to Celtics games. He barely left Worcester—Boston might as well have been as far away as Egypt. He read and reread the several hundred cards and letters of condolence he received. He turned to reading books, lots of them, a solitary pursuit.

He read in the newspaper that LeBron James had apologized to his wife for his single-minded chase of basketball greatness because, James said, that journey carried a personal cost for his family. Cousy knew that feeling. He never apologized to Missie for the costs of his single-minded basketball journey, but he believes the last thirty years of their sixty-three years together closed that circle.

Marie says her parents were a celebrity couple and they made it through the marital ups and downs; some of her father's teammates' marriages had not survived.

Inside the big house, his daughters heard Cooz speaking aloud to Missie, to the card from her funeral Mass atop his bedroom bureau and to the pastel painting of her on the dining room wall.

"Well, Miss, the kids are here. . . ."

They saw him gently touch her picture and kiss it. Nearly five years later, stronger and more resilient, he is still doing that.

LEGACY

Here comes a man with firsthand memories of battling against Cousy in his glory. Walking into the Bear Lakes Country Club restaurant is Richie Guerin, once an all-star guard and team captain of the New York Knicks. Cousy sits quietly, wearing a Hawaiian shirt and slacks. Guerin, in his soft blue knit shirt and shorts, is four years younger than his old friend. He vibrates energy, always did. Guerin seems to know everyone in the room, kissing one woman on the cheek, saying, "Hi, Mare, how-ah-ya?"

He arrives at Cousy's table with a smile, sticks out his hand, and says, "Hi, Cooz Man."

They reminisce.

"I used to use our friendship during games," Cousy says. "I said, 'I'll give you whatever you want, Richie. Just get your ass out of the paint.' He was big and strong and a bully."

Guerin nods. "I guess I was gritty. I didn't have natural beauty type of stuff," he says. He jerks his thumb toward Cousy. "This guy was a showman, and an architect. I worked hard. I went to the basket strong. The old two-handed set shot from my era was what we learned how to shoot, not one-handed. He's a one-handed shooter, which back in that era was an exception."

"I was accused," Cousy answers, "of never leaving the ground on my shot."

It is lunchtime, and the Hall of Famers no longer eat as they did in their playing days: Cousy orders a cup of Italian soup; Guerin a half order of Asian chicken salad, light fare for a former Marine and six-time all-star once known as "The Leatherneck." His Knicks teammate Donnie Butcher admired Guerin's moxie, thought Guerin's personality as big and luminous as New York. Richie knew everybody, Butcher would say, Richie liked a good party, and Richie could dance. Guerin played golf with the Yankees' Whitey Ford and Billy Martin, and knew New York football Giants like Chuck Conerly and Rosey Grier. A crowd favorite in New York, Guerin was a star.

The New York media hyperbolists needed stars and created them on the tabloids' back pages. Had the local boy Cousy played nightly for the Knicks at Madison Square Garden, he might've been basketball's Mickey Mantle. His style invited hyperbole.

Greatness begets imitators. Guerin and Cousy call out names of those whose playing style resembled all or part of Cooz's—Guy Rodgers, Ernie DiGregorio, Magic Johnson, John Stockton, and the point guard who most closely approximated Cousy's style, Pete Maravich. *Cousy never saw the day he had moves like Pete,* Press Maravich, the Louisiana State University coach, once boasted about his son. But while Pete Maravich sold tickets and won endorsements through his showmanship, he did not win a championship during his NBA decade; a former teammate, Rich Kelley, called Maravich "an American phenomenon, a stepchild of the human imagination."

Guerin was Maravich's coach on the Atlanta Hawks from 1970 to 1972, Pistol Pete's first two NBA seasons.

"He was an entertainer," Guerin says. "That was the way his dad raised him at LSU, and he did entertain. He was a heck of a ball handler and a heck of a player. But sometimes he did things when it wasn't necessary to do that to get the guy the ball. When you've got guys running down the wing and somebody gives you a behind-the-back pass that goes into the side of the arena, they are not the happiest campers. Neither is the coach. I got a few more gray hairs coaching him."

"If you could do it the orthodox way," Cousy says, "you are better off than the unorthodox. But when the unorthodox is called for, and you can do it, then it's justified. But don't do it for the sake of doing it. I watch some of these guys now, and they slap it behind their back coming up the floor without any reason. There is no need for it. Thank God, I had the physical skills to do some of this stuff but at the time I was the only one doing it so I got all of the attention for it. These days, every twelve-year-old in every schoolyard is doing more and with more panache than I was."

Guerin remembers Auerbach lighting his cigar on the bench. "It was frustrating," he says. "Disrespectful in my opinion."

"Remember what [Syracuse coach] Paul Seymour said?" Cousy says. "They asked him once what his ambition in sports was: 'To be ten behind and come back after Auerbach has lit up and beat them.' Psychologically that hurt the Celtics on the road because it would piss off people."

The topic shifts to Cousy's legacy.

"A big showoff," Cousy says.

Guerin shakes his head. "He saved the league. He gave credence to newspaper people to write about basketball. They had great people out in Minneapolis—Mikan, [Jim] Pollard, and [Vern] Mikkelsen—dominating, but . . . nothing. But when Bob got in, it's excitement. I guess people like entertainers. We are all entertainers to a degree. But when you can compete at a high level, and be one of the best players playing, and be able to do the other aspect of it, *that* was unusual. Nobody else could do that. Nobody had ever seen anybody do that. He was unique. Nobody played like that before. Because we couldn't do it. That was the reason."

Today's pro game, they agree, is so much faster, the big men so much more athletic, the shooting so much better. Cousy shot 37.5 percent from the field during his career, and Guerin 41.6. By comparison, the Golden State Warriors' Stephen Curry shoots nearly 44 percent on three-point shots alone. "Curry is sensational," Guerin says.

"Their shot selection: So often, I say, 'Oh, God!'" Cousy says. "But they make it. Their confidence in their shooting is so much greater than ours."

"They aren't even worried about centers anymore," Guerin says. "They are taking guards who can dominate and control the game. You know what I am saying? Think about that for a minute. This is what's controlling the game today—half a dozen guards that are out there. The Westbrooks, the Hardens, Pauls, and Currys. I would've loved to play in this type of an environment. I mean, that would be another story, how many times we traveled on trains together and—"

"Buses!" Cousy interjects.

Guerin laughs. "—and buses together. I mean I would love to get my own plane after a game and fly someplace where they have everything on there for us, and get off and play in these arenas, and with endorsements, and television, and stuff like that." He looks at Cousy. "I mean, be honest: You'd like to be a part of something like that! At least I would."

The old man of the Celtics shakes his head. "I would like getting behind the gates in Worcester," he says, "and . . . leave me alone."

A charity event in Carlsbad, California, in 2007 created an unforgettable feel-good scene: Cousy, Russell, Sam Jones, and Havlicek brought in front of the crowd as the master of ceremonies enthusiastically posed a question to each.

"Bob, how many?" (NBA championships, he meant.)

"Six," Cousy said.

"Bill, how many?"

Russell answered, "Eleven."

"Sam, how many?"

"Ten," Sam Jones said.

"John, how many?"

Havlicek said, "Eight."

The audience cheered; some held up cell phones to record the moment. The old Celtics posed for photos and let the warm affection wash over them.

"People can wax poetic about those years," Satch Sanders is saying now. "I recognize that it comes down to, like where you were when the Celtics won in '65: You graduated from school, or you were having your first kid. That's how I think people romanticize their relationships with the teams they root for, by what was going on in their own life at the time. We were just like clocks. We happened to be happening during that time."

They were not alone. There was a confluence of overlapping sports dynasties. The Montreal Canadiens qualified for ten consecutive Stanley Cup Finals between 1951 and 1960, winning five in a row between 1956 and 1960; the Canadiens won four more Stanley Cups from 1965 to 1969. The New York Yankees, after winning six World Series during the fifties, made it to five World Series in a row between 1960 and 1964. UCLA's basketball dynasty, coached by John Wooden, began in 1964, the year after Cousy retired; the Bruins won ten NCAA titles over the next twelve seasons.

Among Boston's players only Russell was a part of all eleven titles. A Celtics constellation of eight star players from the dynasty—Russell, Cousy, Havlicek, Heinsohn, Ramsey, K.C. Jones, Sam Jones, and Sharman—glitters in the Hall of Fame today, along with Auerbach, Brown, and Sanders as a "contributor" for his lifelong contributions to the game, including his later work in the league office creating programs to help NBA players develop life skills. Six times the Lakers played the Celtics in the NBA Finals during the sixties, and six times they lost. "The same team, over and over?" Jerry West would say. "It haunts me still." He added, "I dislike the color green."

It took some doing, but the Celtics finally caught on in Boston. Two years after Cousy retired, Havlicek made a last-second steal to secure Boston's victory over Philadelphia in the 1965 Eastern Division Finals. Radioman Johnny Most screamed a blue streak ("Havlicek stole the ball! It's all over! It's all over!"), and fans stormed the court at Boston Garden. In their mad celebration they tore off Havlicek's jersey. At a party a few years later, a woman approached Havlicek, and he couldn't believe what he saw. Pinned to her blouse like a brooch, about half the size of a dollar bill, was a piece torn from his jersey. "You are one of those people," Havlicek told her, "that I was trying to hold off." The fans had also tried to rip off Havlicek's shorts, but he says, "That's when I really started whacking them."

No other NBA team could emulate the Celtics, not without Russell. It wasn't that these Celtics reinvented the game; they just played it better than anyone else. Among NBA dynasties, they were the first to merge stars, black and white, in multiples. They created the league's first true "Showtime" fast break; Cousy remains the gold standard of the middle man in the transition game. Auerbach coined the "sixth man" concept, an ego-balancing act that ennobled stars such as Ramsey and Havlicek by convincing them that it didn't matter who started a game, only who finished it. Auerbach also convinced his team that personal statistics didn't matter; Lenny Wilkens, who would win 1,332 games as an NBA coach (nearly four hundred more than Auerbach), would say decades later that it's one thing to say that to your players, another to get them to buy in. The Celtics bought in. With K.C. Jones replacing Cousy as point guard, the Celtics evolved over time, improving their halfcourt offense and, with Russell still in the middle, becoming an even better defensive team. Nowadays, much is made of a "three-peat," a term created by the Lakers in the late

1980s. As one measure of the Celtics' dominance, in the fall of 1966, they chased after a *nine-peat*.

As the decades keep passing, the Celtics dynasty grows more distant, seemingly visible now only by telescope. "It's been a while," Sanders is saying as he tries to recall the last time he gathered with his teammates. "A few of us got together for the Havlicek Stole the Ball anniversary [in 2015]. I think it was just—was it fifty years?" Sanders shakes his head. "I was going to say it was the twenty-fifth anniversary."

Inevitably the flesh and bone of that Celtics empire withers, but the statistical achievement endures, the gleaming skyscraper of eleven titles in thirteen seasons.

"Like twenty years ago," Cousy says, "when Michael [Jordan] was doing his thing in Chicago with [Scottie] Pippen, [sportswriters] were calling me and saying, 'Hey, isn't this the greatest team ever?' I used to take offense and say, 'Hey, guys, give me a freakin' break, will you? They've won twice in a row and you are asking me if this is the greatest team?' It was tough to handle. I didn't want to tell them but at the end of the day I was saying to myself, 'We won eleven out of thirteen freakin' years! You are asking me *now*? Wait seven or eight years and if they win six or seven times in a row, then we can make comparisons.'" The Bulls, with Jordan and Pippen, won six titles in eight seasons during the 1990s. Cousy says, "Now, of course, we don't hear that much about it. What we did will never be done again. It's a legacy that will live forever in American professional sports. . . . And that's what I take great pride in—that I played a role in that, you know?"

Heinsohn had a similar response about comparisons to the San Antonio Spurs, who, beginning in 1999, won four titles in nine seasons, saying, "They talk about the Spurs. 'What a wonderful team.' Shit! We were a ten times better team. We beat people because we were a team. We picked on people. It was your night tonight because you had the best matchup. I mean, that's what we did. We were a true basketball team."

Now the comparison is with the Golden State Warriors of Stephen Curry and Kevin Durant. "I think the Celtics were *light-years* ahead of anybody at that time," says Steve Kerr, the Warriors' coach, who won five NBA titles as a reserve player with the Bulls and Spurs, and three more as a head coach. Winning eleven championships in thirteen seasons in the modern NBA, Kerr says, would be, in a word, "impossible." He says, "For one thing, it's a thirty-team league. The playoffs go forever. . . . [There] is an emotional toll that I think is different today [than in the 1960s] from a combination of a two-month-long playoff journey—four rounds and twenty-five playoff games—combined with the never-ending judgment and twenty-four-hour criticism that the players face the entire season. . . . What these guys deal with now on social media and sports talk radio, it's exhausting spiritually, and emotionally." Kerr believes Russell would "thrive in today's game because he was so active and versatile," whereas Kareem Abdul-Jabbar might struggle defensively. Kerr makes his point: Stephen Curry would slide off a high screen-and-roll, and, he says, "How is Kareem going to get out there? Bill Russell could do it." As for Cousy playing in today's NBA, Kerr says, "I think he'd be great. But if he were playing today, my guess is he would have shot five hundred three-point shots every day in the summer to become a three-point shooter." Cousy has his own view about how the Russell-Cousy Celtics might fare against today's Warriors. "I'd like to think we'd get their attention," Cousy says with a smile, "and make them shower after every game." As proof that he is mightily impressed with these Warriors, Cousy projects, "Maybe we'd win two out of six."

Artists in various forms have tried for decades to capture the essence of Cousy, an artist in his own right. A photographer for *Collier's* magazine in 1953 used a multiflash sequence that took less than two seconds, sophisticated and high style for its time, to feature Cooz in a two-page black-and-white photo spread dribbling behind his back and shooting a layup—"graphically showing," *Collier's* marveled, "why he's known as the flashiest basketball player in the world."

The writer Herbert Warren Wind authored three magazine profiles of Cousy, a two-part series in *Sports Illustrated* in 1956 and one seven years later in *The New Yorker*. He didn't suffer fools. To Wind, Cousy was "an absolute gentleman." Years later, with admiration that bordered on reverence, Wind pantomimed Cousy's passing style for friends—even stopping traffic in the middle of a street once to do it. At the cocktail hour, Wind, a former basketball player at Yale, once mimicked Cousy throwing a no-look pass and forgot he had a drink in hand—vodka splashed the face of his young nephew, Bill Scheft. Sometimes before dinner, Wind would encourage Scheft, saying, "Give us a little Cousy." Scheft, who years later wrote comedy for David Letterman, would mimic Cousy's speech impediment, saying, "The vet-lan tulned to the lookie," and Wind would laugh. Wind wrote in 1963 that Cousy was "the commanding figure: a bravura individual star who was first and foremost a team man; a person of modest nature whose flair and fire nevertheless made him a majestic showman . . . all in all, an unusual sports hero, who grew with his fame and, even at closest range, was always a man to admire."

As a sculptor, Brian Hanlon is an artist of a different sort. His bronze statue of Cousy, cast with a green patina and, with its impressive stand, weighing about ten thousand pounds, was dedicated in 2008 at the entrance to the Hart Center at Holy Cross. At the statue's base, panels define his legacy ("The Cooz, An Athlete With Flair" and "Robert J. Cousy, The Humanitarian"). In his speech on a sweltering dedication day, Cousy rolled out his best self-deprecating humor: "I don't know what this means but I'm told that the statue looks better with the cloth on than off." Most statues are created to honor figures already deceased, he said, which made him feel lucky. "You may be looking up in Rome at some old church figure or in Paris and it's some warrior on a horse and you look at the guy standing next to you—*and it's the guy!*" College teams visiting Holy Cross often line up and snap photos and selfies in front of the Cousy statue. Hanlon studied hundreds of photographs of Cousy. He carefully noted the lean upper body, long arms, and big hands and came to a startling realization: "Cousy had no muscle on his body whatsoever." But, Hanlon noted, "His legs were enormous. Monster thighs." Hanlon envisioned a sculpture that would depict Cousy across the full spectrum of his basketball life: yes, Holy Cross in the postwar years, but also his storied seasons with the Celtics.

So he cast Cousy dribbling a ball with his right hand, in Holy Cross jersey No. 17, and used an older, more mature face that everyone would instantly recognize, taken from a 1955 photograph of the Celtics Cousy. Hanlon portrayed him in an upright stance, head up, the personification of the point guard as floor general. He imagined Cousy looking upcourt, but to whom?

Russell!

It had to be Russell.

That much seemed obvious to Hanlon.

To those who saw Houdini play, he will always be heroic, and in their own ways they've reached out to him.

Bob Cohen is in his early eighties, retired from a forty-year career in pathology and nuclear medicine in the San Francisco Bay Area. As a young pathologist at Boston City Hospital, Cohen attended a few Celtics practices in 1959–60 wearing his white coat and carrying a stethoscope. He'd heard it said on a radio broadcast—it might've been Johnny Most talking—that fans could watch the Celtics practice at the Garden; all they needed to do was show up. On a lark one afternoon he took the train to North Station. Cohen knew the team at least as well as any other twenty-three-year-old Jewish fan raised in Dorchester, and Cousy was his man. He studied Cooz closely as he sat courtside in the cavernous Garden, no one else at the practice except Auerbach and his players. Cohen noticed small details—the patter between Cousy and Sharman, the way they called for the ball with a simple "Now" or "I'll have it." Russell spoke barely a word, and Auerbach seldom smiled. If Auerbach saw something he didn't like, he stamped his foot in anger, as if he were trying to punish the parquet floor, and then gathered his men around him and told them the way it had to be. At some games Cohen had seen Cousy expend every last ounce of energy and collapse from exhaustion on the team bench. It was enough to make Cohen wonder if Cousy might have an arrhythmia. To sit in the arena virtually alone and watch Cousy dribble in his characteristic way, Cohen imagined that he could almost hear a smooth melody playing. Battling cancer in more recent years, Cohen climbed inside an MRI tube and felt anxious and claustrophobic. To calm himself, he closed his eyes and imagined a beautiful sight—not a beach at sunset, but Cousy dribbling up the middle of the court, leading the Celtics' fast break at a medium-fast lope, with Sharman trailing. That image, Cohen says, "was like my Valium." Each sequence of imaging in the MRI tube brought the same triumphant image in Cohen's mind, Cousy leading the Celtics' break, on an endless loop.

Joe Dillon never got over Cousy's retirement. After he shouted "We love you, Cooz!" on Bob Cousy Day, Dillon became famous in Southie, at least for fifteen minutes. Friends say his call to Cousy from the Boston Garden balcony might've been the pinnacle of Dillon's life. Basketball meant everything to Dillon, and to be associated with Cousy was more than he could have ever hoped for. For years, Dillon became a regular at the local horse track and dog track, and often hung out at Jim Harvey's corner store on F Street in Southie, drinking coffee, eating doughnuts, and calling to a passing friend, "Hey, how many did Havlicek get last night?" Of course, he already knew the answer.

Always stout, he ate himself into a mini-zeppelin, with broad shoulders, a big belly, and a steel-grip handshake. Dillon died from a coronary attack in 1997. He was sixty-five years old. In his final moments, alone in bed, he was watching the Celtics pregame show on TV. His funeral drew a sizable crowd in Southie. Brian Dillon, his nephew, sent a letter to Cousy notifying him of the death, and Cooz wrote back to say that Joe Dillon was a part of Celtics history and a part of his own history.

After Cousy retired, Joe Dillon never attended another Celtics game because, he said, there would never be another Cooz. Brian Dillon only wishes that Uncle Joe had saved his ticket stub from Bob Cousy Day. That he'd love to have.

The thought of Cousy brings Boston's former mayor, Ray Flynn, nearly eighty, back to 1950, when he was an eleven-year-old Celtics ball boy. That's when Flynn picked up towels in the locker room and stared with wide-eyed wonder at Cousy, who seemed a born leader and such an inspiration. Later, at Providence College, Flynn became a star basketball player (he would become the Celtics' last cut in fall 1963). On April 27, 1963, just three days after Cousy's final game with the Celtics in the NBA Finals, Flynn played against him in a benefit exhibition honoring Cousy at Worcester Auditorium. A photo appeared in the Worcester newspaper the next morning of the young Flynn guarding Cousy.

To Flynn the photo was priceless, though his copy, autographed later by Cousy, was stolen. He would become mayor in 1984 and President Bill Clinton's U.S. ambassador to the Holy See in 1993, but as a young man what he most wanted to be was Bob Cousy.

Flynn had seen Boston in good times and bad. Known in Southie as Radar Ray for his bull's-eye shooting touch, Flynn thought the crisis over court-ordered busing in the seventies brought out the worst in Boston. If he had been mayor at the time, instead of a Democratic legislator representing Southie, Flynn says he might have placed Cousy and Russell on the buses with the schoolkids bound for new districts.

"Because people liked them," Flynn says, "and respected them, and they would have felt comfortable with them instead of a faceless bureaucracy telling them what to do with their kids and where they could go to school and where they couldn't go to school."

Flynn got another copy of the newspaper photograph of him guarding Cousy, and Cooz autographed it for him. The former Boston mayor told his wife that when he is being waked at O'Brien Funeral Home in Southie, he wants the Cousy photograph on display, and it's the only photo he wants at his wake.

The modern NBA's style and substance, its startling growth, and its far-flung global popularity attach to Cousy. His theatricality and free-form improvisation live in the soul of today's NBA. His artful dribbling and no-look passes rate among the NBA's historic signature images with, among others, Abdul-Jabbar's sky hook, Russell's shot block, Jordan's midair levitations, and Julius Erving's swooping dunks. Cousy founded the NBA players union at a time when he was among the game's highest-paid players, seeking to improve playing conditions and professionalize the league's operations even as owners brushed him aside. One sign of increased player affluence: Since Cousy's time, the decimal point has moved three places. Whereas Cousy earned $35,000 in 1963, Stephen Curry earns about $35 million today.

With Auerbach, and sponsored by the U.S. State Department, Cousy traveled the continents—Europe, Asia, and Africa—to spread the American game of basketball through clinics and demonstrations. Those trips, and ones made by other players, bore fruit: 108 players from 42 nations and territories made opening-night NBA rosters for the 2017–18 season. Cousy also served as an NBA coach, a longtime Celtics broadcaster, and for two years as president of the Naismith Memorial Basketball Hall of Fame, which curates the game's history.

You cannot understand today's NBA without dealing with Cousy. With his style and determination, he did more than change the game:

He adrenalized and popularized it. He was the league's star attraction as the game began to shift from feet-on-the-floor to above-the-rim and, in a more seismic way, with the coming of the black superstar. Few star players have cared so deeply about the welfare of the game that made them famous.

His influence has been far-reaching and long-lasting, emulated across the decades by every ball handler who ever imagined making the perfect unpredictable pass.

He also influenced generations of others who did not play in the NBA.

Shoveling snow in his backyard in 1951 and pretending to be Cousy, Rollie Massimino, a high school guard in Hillside, New Jersey, near Newark, would do "that little jitterbug move Cousy used to do. *Boom-boom-boom*." Massimino recalled, "Cousy was running the corporation to perfection, know what I mean?" As a coach, Massimino later led Villanova to the 1985 NCAA title.

In the middle 1960s, near Savannah, Georgia, Clarence Thomas took his high school basketball seriously, and the future U.S. Supreme Court justice was known to friends by his hero's nickname, Cooz.

Cousy's playing style drew the attention of athletic girls, too. In the early sixties, Tara VanDerveer, a grade schooler, watched the NBA's Game of the Week on television with her father in Schenectady, New York. To VanDerveer it seemed like the Celtics were always on TV, and the way they ran the fast break thrilled her. It mirrored the pace of hockey, she thought. Cousy was "a very clever passer, a leader, and high-energy player," she says. "He would penetrate-and-pitch before that was even talked about." VanDerveer would become Stanford University's women's basketball coach, one of only five coaches, male or female, to win more than one thousand NCAA games.

Maura Healey saw a film of Cousy's exploits and heard all about him growing up during the 1980s in Hampton Falls, New Hampshire. Her father told her stories about Cousy and the Celtics, and her grandmother told her that "growing up, the girls used to swoon: They were all in love with Bob Cousy." Healey played on the Harvard women's basketball team, and then professionally in Austria, and she wore No. 14 on both teams to honor Cousy. Today Healey is the attorney general of Massachusetts.

At his 1963 retirement, Cousy rated as the league's second all-time leading scorer. He was named one of the NBA's fifty greatest players upon the league's twenty-fifth anniversary in 1971, its thirty-fifth in 1981, and its fiftieth in 1996.

Ever since, he's been slipping down the steady flow of lists, replaced by modern-day players. CBS Sports named its top fifty all-time greatest NBA players in February 2017, and though it acknowledged Cousy as "one of the most influential guards ever," he ranked as only the league's thirty-sixth greatest player; Russell ranked sixth best.

"I'll walk off with my tail between my legs to number thirty-six," Cousy says. "Obviously as time goes by you keep going further down the list."

The captain's pride surges over his rightful place in basketball's pantheon: "At this point in my life I'm not going to aggravate myself because obviously the individual always thinks that he should be higher up on the list than he is. But I refuse to give it that kind of an emotional reaction. Suffice to say, 'Okay, I'll let basketball historians put me in the place that I belong.' . . . I wouldn't argue the point. I wouldn't give anyone the satisfaction of saying, 'TEN? I should be seven!'"

Cousy adds, "Nor can I believe that Russell wouldn't be completely competitive today or that Oscar or West or myself would not be playing some sort of leading role."

Off the top, Cousy starts to list his five greatest players of all time. He begins with Russell, and then Robertson. "Michael Jordan, absolutely, and LeBron [James]." He pauses, and says he needs more time before naming the fifth player. He thinks about the subject that night.

The next morning he pulls out a pen, as is his way. He dashes off a full-page handwritten letter.

"Let me improvise," he writes. He lists the names of the top fifteen NBA players "all 15 within 1950–2000 window," and puts an asterisk (*) next to his Top Five during that period. He explains that his list is still evolving and that he hasn't seen enough of today's players to include them:

CENTERS—WILT, RUSSELL*, KAREEM

POWER FORWARD—BIRD*, PETTIT, K. MALONE

SMALL FORWARD—M. JORDAN*, DR. J, HAVLICEK

'2' GUARD —WEST, OSCAR R*

POINT GUARD—MAGIC*, NASH, I. THOMAS (DETROIT)

He adds a notation: "E. Baylor deserves mention to one of these positions."

Then he lists his five greatest point guards between 1950 and 2000, adding two names to his above three: John Stockton and "RJC"—the latter, his own initials. "In making a case for '*Moi*,'" he writes, "I would say (in all modesty) that I would put my creativeness, imagination and innovativeness (all abstracts) as they relate to basketball up with anyone who has played the game so far." In a postscript, he writes that he is prepared to add LeBron James, Russell Westbrook, and Curry. If he forgot anyone, Cousy writes, "blame it on 'early senility.'"

He jokes about senility perhaps because he is familiar with it.

"Why don't I remember that?" he says.

The topic is Lexington, Kentucky, October 17, 1961. Cousy says he cannot recall that night, cannot remember any of it, and that bothers him. He saw what dementia did to Missie. For an instant, he carries a look of panic.

Two of his black teammates were denied service in the hotel coffee shop, and that night Russell, Sanders, Sam Jones, and K.C. Jones, in a show of protest, refused to play in an exhibition against St. Louis. They flew back to Boston; only the white Celtics played.

Now, thinking about it, Cousy says, "Why wouldn't I remember that? Jesus, that's such a traumatic incident. Where the hell was I?"

He recalls small details from the night he joined Chuck Cooper in the Raleigh train station; side by side, in defiance of segregated men's rooms, they peed off the platform in the postmidnight darkness. That happened in February 1952, nearly a decade *before* Lexington.

He phones Frank Ramsey in Kentucky and asks, "Do you remember the night in Lexington?"

Yes, Ramsey replies, though he tells Cousy that some of the details have grown fuzzy. Ramsey recalls that he and Cliff Hagan were honored that night by their alma mater. He remembers the game occurred at the end of a long road trip of exhibitions for the Celtics. It wasn't that the hotel wouldn't let Satch and Sam stay there, Ramsey says, it was that the hotel coffee shop would not serve them. There was a big crowd expected at the game, maybe the biggest ever in the arena for a professional game, about ten thousand. That's the extent of his memory.

At the time, Auerbach told reporters the exhibition in Lexington was under contract so the entire Celtics squad could not leave; they would meet their contractual obligation. The next day's *Boston Herald* confirmed: "The Celtics who played were Carl Braun, Bob Cousy, Gene Guarilia, Tom Heinsohn, Jim Loscutoff, Gary Phillips and Frank Ramsey."

Cousy reads photocopies of the coverage in Boston's newspapers from that night in Lexington. He expresses disappointment he didn't do more.

"I mean, Arnold was a warrior up to a point," he says, "but he wouldn't have turned his back, or reneged on a situation like that [in Lexington] out of principle if it was a big payday. . . . Today, I would've gone to Arnold and said, 'I'm going with the black players. I'm out of here, too,' but I didn't do that. If I had a better recall, I could be more specific. I did not respond. I went along."

Memory often functions in a self-defining, or self-serving, way. In Raleigh with Cooper, Cousy was the man he wishes now that he had always been, the Celtics captain taking action and demonstrating fair-mindedness and cross-race camaraderie. In Lexington, he did nothing, just went with the white crowd. He wishes now he had not played. *Who was I in 1961? Why can't I remember that night?* Maybe Cousy unconsciously forgot about Lexington as he has so many other game nights, or maybe he simply willed it out of his mind. *What would have compelled me to play? And in only an exhibition!* The mistreatment of his black teammates went over Cousy's head.

"Now, in retrospect," he says, "I'm ashamed of myself."

RUSS REDUX

As teammates, the Lakers' Shaquille O'Neal and Kobe Bryant had their falling-out, and, after winning three NBA championships, Shaq was traded. More recently, guard Kyrie Irving needed to separate from LeBron James in Cleveland.

Auerbach was asked once how he handled two stars, Cousy and Russell, on the same team. "No problem," he said. "Both have pride; both love to win and both know that it takes a team to win championships, not one man. Men such as these need no handling. They took care of themselves."

What brings a group of men from disparate backgrounds closest together, Satch Sanders says, is winning: "Winning helps. It's the glue. It's a good glue. A lot of people talk about *chemistry*. The chemistry they should be talking about is the chemistry people have on the court. That's where the guys get along. That's all that really counts. People have a habit of thinking of 'chemistry' as off the court. But [players'] families don't get together. That's not going to happen. We're talking professional leagues. It's whether or not you play well together. A better word is *work* well together."

Cousy has plenty of time to think, and reflect and reminisce and reconsider. The Celtics dynasty was more than special; it was unprecedented, and historic, with one foot in pro basketball's old world, one foot in the new. His teammates, in some ways, mean more to him now than before. He says, "Heinsohn, I talk to. Ramsey, I talk to. Satch Sanders, I talk to. Sam Jones and K.C.—when he was better—not frequently but we have a relationship." He pauses and says, "I wish I had a better relationship with Russell."

Russell lives in Mercer Island, Washington, near Seattle, three thousand miles from Cousy, and about as far from Boston as a man can travel and still live in the continental United States.

In May 1999, sportswriter Frank Deford, in a *Sports Illustrated* profile, recalled how thirty years earlier he had told Russell that he considered him a friend. Russell told Deford, "No, I'd like to be your friend, and we can be friendly, but friendship takes a lot of effort if it's going to work, and we're going off in different directions in our lives, so, no, we really can't be friends." At the time of Deford's profile, Russell had been out of the public eye for nearly a dozen years, since he coached the Sacramento Kings to a 17-41 record in 1987–88 and was quoted saying, "I'd rather be in jail in Sacramento than be mayor of Boston."

Deford's profile was part of Russell's renaissance, a coming-out of sorts choreographed by Karen Russell, his daughter, and Alan Hilburg, his business adviser. They convinced Russell that at century's end there would be stories told about the greatest athletes of the last hundred years—Thorpe, Ali, Ruth, Russell—and that he had an important story to tell, his own.

"Russell Redux is, in essence, a product relaunch," Richard Sandomir wrote in *The New York Times*, "designed to emphasize Russell's championship pedigree, not to deal with his image, ingrained with the public as enigmatic and aloof."

This multipronged plan amounted to legacy-conscious business savvy. For Russell at sixty-six, there was money to be made. The plan was executed shrewdly: Three weeks after Deford's poignant profile, the Celtics re-retired Russell's No. 6 in a ceremony at the Fleet Center, this time not before an empty arena, as in 1972, but to a standing ovation that stirred Russell to tears. A gala dinner was held in Russell's honor to benefit his favorite charity, with comedian Bill Cosby as master of ceremonies. Cousy and Auerbach attended, as did Chamberlain, and Schayes, who called the gala "a forgiveness episode," though it wasn't clear if Russell was forgiving Boston, Boston was forgiving Russell, or both.

Cooz was happy for Russ. "Despite what he meant to Boston sports lore, he wasn't beloved, and most of that had to do with race, I would guess," he says.

For all those years that Madison Avenue advertising agencies looked away from African-American sports stars, Russell had lived long enough to see a new day, and he would cash in on it. The *Times* reported that Russell landed a $400,000 deal to coauthor a book on leadership, that he was suddenly in demand as a motivational speaker at $25,000 per speech (his overarching message to corporations: team effort), that he still didn't sign autographs for fans but did for collectors in return for a handsome fee, and that HBO was at work on a documentary about Russell that he and Hilburg had pitched. All told, Russell figured to earn enough to secure his retirement.

Time had enhanced, not diminished, him. He was seen in a new context, more courageous and principled than before. A confluence of factors—the brevity of public memory, broad cultural shifts on matters of race, and an appreciation of Russell's herculean run of championships by a new generation of young fans—had softened and burnished his reputation and made him, suddenly and belatedly, a more appreciated legend of the game.

During this period, ESPN's *SportsCentury* selected Russell as one of the twentieth century's greatest athletes, but he became the only living choice not to participate in the project; at least part of Russell's decision to forgo an interview, Deford wrote, was that Russell had heard an ESPN announcer praise the 1964 Celtics as "Bob Cousy's last team"—a mistake, since Cousy had already retired.

As research for its Russell segment, ESPN's camera crew came to Salisbury Street to interview Cousy. In his office at home, surrounded by old Celtics photographs, including a few featuring Russ and Rose, Cousy felt at ease talking about Russell's athletic greatness and about how Russ had transformed the pro game. Nearly four decades had passed since they were teammates.

Now the interview subject shifted to race.

"We could've done more to ease his pain and make him feel more comfortable," Cousy said on camera. "I should've been much more sensitive to Russell's anguish in those days. We'd talk—uh . . ."

Cousy hesitated. It was as if an emotion buried deep inside of him dislodged and surged to the surface. On camera, Cousy paused in an attempt to assert control over his emotion. His face trembled, then shattered. He broke down weeping, his hands covering his face, the camera holding this powerful scene for several seconds.

His reaction surprised even Cousy. Later he tried to identify its source and understand it: subconscious guilt, he decided. His thinking took him back to Chuck Cooper and Don Barksdale, his first black teammates in Boston.

"Then I run into literally my first angry black man. And Russ to this day is angry," Cousy says. "It's obvious from the get-go, and now in my Psych 101 analysis, I think this simply scared me off. I still think it was my fault. I'm six years older, I'm the Man. I'm in charge. I'm the captain. It was my responsibility to reach out, but it intimidates me for whatever reason. I don't know how to deal with this. Like so many times in life, when we are unsure, or stumbling, and doing the wrong thing in establishing a relationship, I do nothing. Obviously nothing is not good enough. At the end of the day, Russ doesn't know how to take me, and I don't know how to take him. We don't have any confrontation. We get along, but it's like a couple that decides to stay together for the sake of the kids, you know?"

He laughs. "You live in one room and she lives in the other. In this case we are thrown together for obvious reasons. So we not only function, we function effectively, and, thank God, we have the common goal of both being extremely competitive. That binds us together, at least during working hours. But it doesn't affect the relationship—and I walk away.

"This is my final analysis: So I do nothing about it. Somehow, despite my general feelings about social justice, civil rights, et cetera, I walk away from that. I don't make any move to establish or solidify a relationship.

"So thirty years later when it comes up in that interview, I have an emotional reaction because in my mind I must've had this subconscious guilt going on where I knew, even though I didn't articulate or think about it until now, I knew in my heart that I was the one that should've reached out."

At another moment, Cousy says: "I think it was immaturity and some intimidation. I'll tell you—[Russell] would've scared you. He would glare, you know? You see the Black Panthers in front of those voting booths, standing and just glaring at whitey? So I wasn't physically afraid of Russ but that was enough to hold me at arm's length, [and] to not reach out and say, 'Russ, let's go have a beer.' So that's on me."

As Russell's teammate from 1957 through 1963, Cousy decided, "I went along with the status quo. And I ended up with a lot of guilt, which manifested itself years later."

For a time, Cousy and Russell, both avid golfers, saw each other once a year, in October, at the American Airlines/Susan G. Komen celebrity golf tournament in southern California. A few months after the ESPN segment aired in 2001, Russell spotted Cousy eating breakfast alone before his round. Russell smiled, threw his arm around his old teammate, and joined him at the table. Russell mentioned Cousy's recent ESPN interview.

Now, Cooz heard Russ say there was nothing more that Cousy could have done as a teammate to make life easier for him in Boston.

Russell talked for some time. Cousy had much that he wanted to say and wished later that he had said it, like, "Russ, we should have the same relationship that I've had with Satch, where I feel free to call him and say, 'C'mon, let's go have dinner together.'"

But Cousy said none of that.

Instead, he listened.

He knew Russ was trying to make him feel better. He accepted it as a great gift, and felt his guilt diminish. To Cousy, at seventy-three, this was the most heartfelt and meaningful conversation he had ever shared with Russell. Certainly they had shared soaring emotions as teammates, but this breakfast table conversation was different; it was higher ground, a merging of the head and heart. Cousy hoped this conversation might improve their relationship, and maybe it did for a short time, or maybe it didn't.

Guilt, less repressed than before, ate at Cousy's conscience still.

Russell's personal odyssey, with its majestic narrative arc, took him in February 2011 to the White House, where Barack Obama presented him with the Presidential Medal of Freedom, the nation's highest civilian honor, sometimes likened to American knighthood. By design, it honors those who contribute with distinction to the security or national interests of the country, world peace, significant public and private endeavors, and to American culture; past winners include authors, politicians, astronauts, entertainers, business leaders, and athletes. By the time he left office in 2017, Obama would present more of these awards than any other president—114.

At the White House ceremony, Russell sat with other honorees, including former president George H. W. Bush, poet Maya Angelou, investor Warren Buffett, and cellist Yo-Yo Ma. Russell would say later that it was the second-highest honor he had ever received, behind his father telling him, "I'm very proud of you as my son. I'm also proud that I am your father." Russell said, "You can't top that, not coming from the hero." Privately Obama told Russell that he had helped make it possible for him to become president. "I don't see that," Russell replied, "but thanks anyway."

About Russell, Obama said, "He marched with King; he stood by Ali. When a restaurant refused to serve the black Celtics, he refused to play in the scheduled game. He endured insults and vandalism, but he kept on focusing on making the teammates who he loved better players, and made possible the success of so many who would follow. I hope that one day, in the streets of Boston children will look up at a statue built not only to Bill Russell the player, but Bill Russell the man." Then Russell leaned backward to lower himself so that the six-foot-one Obama could place the medal around his neck.

Diminished by racial prejudice in his playing days, Russell, in a new century, had won the historical narrative of the Celtics dynasty.

The president's words kick-started a campaign to create a Russell statue in Boston, and two years later it was unveiled at City Hall. Cousy didn't attend the ceremony ("I wasn't invited," he says), but Randy Auerbach did. *How far Bill Russell has traveled*, she thought. "From when people are breaking into your home and doing these horrible things to having a statue at City Hall," she says, "that's as full circle as you can get." She also flashed back to 1976, when a white teen from Southie lunged at a black man with a pole that carried an American flag. *And all over busing*, she thought. Russell's statue was placed near that spot.

Satch Sanders smiled over the great honors that flowed to Russell. He heard people recounting Russ's activism, the way he stood up for causes. "To them, it's huge," Sanders says. "To us, who have lived with him, it was what was expected of Russell. That's the way he was."

With his eleven world championships (Sam Jones won ten, and so did the Yankees' Yogi Berra), Russell assumed the moniker of *the greatest teammate* in all of American sports.

"Well, he was," Heinsohn says. "Was he the greatest human being?" He shrugs. "He's like all of us."

Cousy knew Obama spoke truth about Russell. Russ had achieved greatness while absorbing more racial insults than any hundred men.

In September 2017, a verified Twitter account opened in Russell's name. The first tweet included a photo of Russell on bended knee in support of NFL players protesting racial injustice during the playing of the national anthem. From Russell's neck dangled the Presidential Medal of Freedom.

The posted tweet read: "Proud to take a knee, and to stand tall against social injustice. *#takeaknee #medaloffreedom #NFL #BillRussell* #MSNBC."

"Russell is doing what Russell does," Cousy says, upon learning of the tweet. "I'm not surprised that he would take this opportunity to be part of what's going on."

Behind the scenes, a movement had taken flight to get Cousy a Presidential Medal of Freedom, too. Friends in Worcester and at Holy Cross spearheaded it. They believed that Cooz, as a basketball innovator, champion, and goodwill ambassador, fit the bill. Politicians sent supportive letters to Obama and then Donald Trump. Cousy thought the award would be the capstone of a life well lived. It also would raise the eternally competitive Cousy to a place in American history alongside Russell. That matters to him, even at this late hour.

VERSAILLES, BOOKS

Such was Cousy's enduring fame that he was pulled over for speeding on the roads between Worcester and Boston, by his own estimate, about twenty-five times over the decades, and not once did he get a ticket. This infuriated Missie. She wanted him to slow down and thought a speeding ticket might do the trick. He got pulled over once in later years. A young Chinese-American state trooper stepped beside his car and asked for his license. Sitting in the passenger seat, Missie beamed: after all these years, finally, his comeuppance! But when the officer read the name on the driver's license, he reached over to shake Cousy's hand and drove off without issuing a ticket.

Missie stewed in silence.

His living room has become like a basketball Versailles, a grand meeting place for those who seek a few moments with Houdini.

Maura Healey, vying to become the first gay woman to serve as Massachusetts's attorney general, came for a visit in 2014. A point guard at Harvard, Healey idolized Cousy. In his living room, they talked basketball and politics for hours and held hands, and she earned his public endorsement in what became a winning campaign. (On another occasion, Healey, with a scheduled appearance at Holy Cross, asked Cousy if he had any message to pass on to students. "Yeah," he told her, "tell them when they walk by the statue to wipe the pigeon poo off my nose.")

Chinese basketball representatives—in Springfield in September 2016 for Yao Ming's Hall of Fame induction—came to Cousy's living room to hear him talk about basketball.

A couple weeks later, the Holy Cross men's and women's basketball teams came for a visit.

The current Celtics coach, Brad Stevens, came to see him, too. Cousy had written a few letters to Stevens, including one that said he deserved the NBA's Coach of the Year award for getting the Celtics into the playoffs. Stevens, an Indianan, was born in 1976, thirteen years after Cousy retired. Stevens knows Celtics history. When he got hired as head coach, he received cigars from fans paying their respects to Auerbach.

"I've never smoked a cigar in my life," Stevens says. "My wife always jokes that if we are ever able to win [the NBA title], I think her favorite part is going to be me smoking a cigar and puking at center court."

With Cousy, Stevens discussed family, Holy Cross, the role of the point guard, and the current Celtics, the last topic at great depth. Stevens says today's Celtics "know how many banners are on the wall and they know the major figures in them." He spent seventy-five minutes in Cousy's living room and says, "He has a great vision of both playing and coaching. It was just fun to hear him." Cousy admitted he still watched Celtics games on television but usually turned them off at halftime—his bedtime.

Cousy's review of his life, a personal reckoning of sorts, plays out as an inner narrative that isn't just about nostalgia and regret. It's about mortality. He is attempting to get his life in order, to understand its meaning, to assure himself that he was alive, and *is* alive. Reading helps provide context.

Just Mercy, the book Marie sent him about racial bias and injustice in America's criminal justice system, written by Bryan Stevenson, an African-American lawyer and human rights activist, landed particularly hard. Moved by what he read, Cousy wrote a three-page letter to Stevenson at the Equal Justice Initiative, a nonprofit in Montgomery, Alabama, founded in part to end mass incarceration and excessive punishment in the nation.

Stevenson saw a stack of letters on his desk, including one with a handwritten return address.

"Bob Cousy," it read, and he laughed. *Same name as the famous basketball player*, he thought. Stevenson opened the letter and was astonished to discover that it was *that* Bob Cousy.

In scrawled cursive, Cousy praised *Just Mercy* ("Bravo, Bravo") and Stevenson for his life's work at EJI to "'walk the walk' as well as fight the 'good fight' against a hopelessly corrupt judicial system as it deals with minorities in the U.S." In his "end-of-life to-do list note," Cousy introduced himself as the onetime MVP of the world-champion Celtics and cited his friendship with Chuck Cooper and decades as a volunteer mentor with Big Brothers.

About American race relations, Cousy wrote, "I'm hoping that this 'conversation' the country is having @ the moment could possibly be helpful in moving us forward but I'm not hopeful. It could change some minds but hearts I don't think so. *Someone is different so they're going to take something away from us.* A great oversimplification I'm sure, but that's the best I can come up with. Racism is alive and, I'm afraid, well in our country."

At his advanced age, Cousy told Stevenson, "I'm not very mobile, so [it's] difficult to offer my physical presence, but if you need to add my name & voice to your efforts please feel free."

Stevenson thought the letter remarkable. It led to an exchange of letters and a phone conversation between them. "Even if it wasn't Bob Cousy I would've still remembered that letter," Stevenson says. "It was just so genuine." Stevenson knew all about Cousy and Russell and their great Celtics teams, and about racism in Boston. In 1981, walking on a downtown street in Boston, Stevenson saw a car pull beside him, a white man inside asking, "Where is Roxbury?" "What?" Stevenson asked, taking a step closer to the car. "Go back to Roxbury, nigger," the white man said, and the car sped off.

Cousy's letter, Stevenson says, "seemed to be from a soul that appreciated what it's like to witness mistreatment and abuse and unfairness and not have it just brush off your back, that it does something to you. . . . So when he talked about 'my end of life,' it resonates with me because I think an honest person who has seen what he has seen, and heard what he has heard, wants the ability to give voice to the truth of the ugliness of it so that they can reconcile themselves to that past. We don't do that very much in the United States. . . . We are all implicated. We haven't made it very easy for people in this country to recover. If you are genuine and you are reflective, that burden starts to weigh on you.

"My big critique of the American psyche when it comes to racial history," Stevenson says, "is that there is not enough shame. We don't actually give voice to shame. We do a lot of things great in America. We do victory in sports great. We do pride great. We do winning great. We do power great. We do creativity great. But we do not do shame very well. We don't apologize very well. We think that shame and apology makes you weak. A lot of athletes embody that approach. What Bob Cousy represents to me is recognition that shame and apology are what make you strong. That's how you get where you are trying to go."

MEA CULPA

For Cousy, the panic attacks were new, and terrified him. They struck at night, when the old man, alone in the darkness, felt most vulnerable. Nightmares, he had known forever. He suffered them as a boy and as Celtics captain. The stories of Cousy's nightmares were legendary in the locker room. Poor Sharman. One night at the Paramount Hotel in New York, Sharman awoke to hear Cousy, his longtime roommate, screaming in the darkness: "I CAN SEE YOU, YOU SONOVABITCH! DON'T MOVE!" Sharman saw Cousy, in silhouette, take a swing at an imagined intruder. The standup lamp between their beds took the brunt of his blow, crashing down on Sharman's head. Cousy came out of his trance and turned on a different light, and there was Sharman, wide-eyed but okay. It happened again the next night, only this time Cousy shouted in French, his first language, then turned on a light and saw Sharman, wary of falling lamps, hiding beneath his covers.

He had a handful of panic attacks. They all occurred at roughly 11:30 P.M. and lasted a minute or two. Unlike nightmares, the stark fear began when he awoke. Each time it happened the same way: Cousy anxious and disoriented, feeling a physical distress he could not pinpoint. It was not chest pain, and he didn't lose consciousness. He suffered fear more powerful than any he had ever known. His heart and his mind raced, and he wasn't sure why. He knew only this: *This is it. This is the end of my life.* He sat at the edge of his bed and waited for death to come. He spun in an emotional vortex of pure fright. The first two panic attacks, after a minute or so, passed. The third didn't end so quickly. His life about to expire, or so he thought, Cousy pushed a button on the lanyard he wore around his neck, and it triggered a call to 911. And then . . . the panic attack passed.

With a sudden burst of clarity, his heart rate slowing, Cousy wished he hadn't pressed the button.

He hoped paramedics had not received his call for help. He waited at his desk, near the front of the house, Missie's favorite photo on a nearby bookshelf—Cooz and Missie sitting together like two movie stars, a glamorous shot, Cooz in a white turtleneck, his hair combed back, Missie's right arm curled around his neck in a loving pose, her eyes, big and luminous, looking straight at the camera. He waited several minutes until he saw flashing lights. He trembled with embarrassment. Thankfully, the flashing lights whizzed by on Salisbury Street. Maybe it wasn't the paramedics after all. But then the flashing lights reappeared, and the paramedics pulled into his driveway. They knocked on his front door. Sheepishly, Cousy let them in.

One EMT recognized the most famous man in Worcester and said, "Hey, you're Bob Cousy!"

"Yeah," he replied, and then softly said, "I want you guys to go home." He insisted he was okay, just embarrassed.

"Don't be embarrassed," a paramedic said.

Cousy apologized several times. They insisted on taking his vitals.

The young paramedics were as nice as could be, and when they left, the old man shook their hands, thanked them, and said, "The next time you come here you'll be taking me out in a box."

This was his humor, his way. It was past midnight, though you couldn't tell from the desk clock in the dining room. Its batteries had died some time ago. It was the clock Bill and Rose Russell gave to Cooz and Missie in 1963 when he retired from the Celtics. Missie adored Rose, and when she heard that the Russells were divorcing in 1973, it pained her. Atop the clock, the smooth bronze surface carries that engraved inscription: *May The Next Seventy Be As Pleasant As The Last Seven. From The Russells To The Cousys.* He had forgotten about the inscription. Seventy years must've seemed like an eternity to Russ. Fifty-five years have gone by. As best Cousy can remember, no other teammate gave him a retirement gift. Just Russ. Now Rose was gone, and Missie, too. It made him wonder again about Russ, and the passing of so many years, and what had become of their relationship.

Generally, Cousy does his best thinking in bed in the dark of night, thoughts and ideas flying at him as if he's on the defensive in a five-on-one fast break. In February 2016, he was thinking about race in America. It was hard not to—because of the continuing conflict between white police and young black men across the nation, because of the burgeoning Black Lives Matter movement, and because he had just finished reading *Between the World and Me* by Ta-Nehisi Coates. The book stirred him greatly; it allowed him to peer inside the black experience today. As homage to James Baldwin and his 1963 book, *The Fire Next Time*, Coates addresses his book to his African-American son, saying he fears for the teenager's physical safety. He writes,

> There is nothing uniquely evil in these destroyers or even in this moment. The destroyers are merely men enforcing the

whims of our country, correctly interpreting its heritage and legacy. It is hard to face this. But all our phrasing—race relations, racial chasm, racial justice, racial profiling, white privilege, even white supremacy—serves to obscure that racism is a visceral experience, that it dislodges brains, blocks airways, rips muscle, extracts organs, cracks bones, breaks teeth. You must never look away from this. You must always remember that the sociology, the history, the economics, the graphs, the charts, the regressions all land, with great violence, upon the body.

To Cousy, the book contextualized the high-profile deaths of Trayvon Martin, Eric Garner, Tamir Rice, and other black youths and black men who were tragically cut down, stories that played across his television screen. And, as often happens when the old man of the Celtics ponders race, his thoughts returned to Russell.

It's rare in America for a white man approaching ninety to reconsider race and how it played out in his life.

Cousy thinks about how race shaped Russell's career, and his.

If Cousy had been black, he says, "I would not have been perceived as *innovative*." More likely, he says, the league's response to his Houdini style in the early 1950s would have been, "That fancy black shit will never work at this level."

If Russell had been white, Cousy says, "He certainly would've been remembered, then and now, more fondly. [Vandals] wouldn't have broken into his house and defecated in his bed.

"Maybe they would've named a bridge after him like they did [a tunnel] for Ted Williams.

"It's a distinction," Cousy says, "where the difference in his life would've been extreme."

His conversation with Russell in 2001, after his emotional ESPN interview, became only a moment, not a bridge that led to a more meaningful relationship.

In the darkness, he filled with regret. As captain, Cousy wishes he had pulled Russell aside and said, privately, man to man, *I've got your back. We all do.* He wishes he had been more outspoken in public, too, telling the Boston sportswriters who adored him, "I understand Russ's feelings. If I were black, I'd be a bomb thrower." No, Cousy says, reconsidering the tone of that statement: He would not say it that way. He would be more careful. He would say it more like this: "If I were black, I'd feel every bit as intense about whitey as Russ feels."

A question begs: What if Cousy, between 1957 and 1963, had publicly defended Russell against the prejudice and racism that he faced across the league and in Boston?

Gene Conley and Heinsohn think it might have helped Russell, at least a little. "[Cousy] could've bragged on him a little more," Conley said, "about how talented he was and what he meant to our team." Heinsohn: "Whatever Cousy said would've gone. By that time he was the MVP of the league. He had created the image; he was the Houdini of the Hardwood. He was carrying the prestige of the league."

Sanders, on the other hand, doubts it would've made much difference: "Cousy would just be seen as a nice man, a respectful guy: *He knows some black guys*, and that's it."

Others in Boston view it differently. Mel King, a black community organizer and politician in Boston who ran for mayor in 1983, says, "Of course it would have made a difference given his stature. Every little piece that comes from people who care and challenge the negativity, it's always good. If he had done more of that, it would have been very important and impactful."

Ray Flynn, the Boston mayor from Southie, says, "I couldn't say that Cousy could have done more. He did as well as he could do. He was a basketball player. He wasn't a politician. He wasn't a philosopher. He wasn't a priest. He was a basketball player and led by example."

Cousy believes that if he had spoken out in defense of Russell during those years, the Boston sports pages would have printed what he said, and he would have received hate mail and angry phone calls for it. "Race is a very emotional issue," Cousy says. Some white Bostonians, he adds, "would not have liked old number fourteen making any excuses for that black guy playing center."

For several nights, Cousy thought about Russell and his own misgivings. He wrestled with what to do about it. He tossed and turned. He considered phoning Russ. But what would he say? "Russ, whatever I did I'm sorry for. I should've been more sensitive. I should've reached out. I'm sorry."

No, a phone call might bring rejection. He would do it in a different way.

He would write a letter. Maybe a letter was a cop-out, but it was a better icebreaker. In a letter there would be no fumbling for the right words. Cousy, an old-fashioned letter writer, knew that letters were less spontaneous, more deeply considered, like Cousy himself. He handwrote letters, usually signing off, as if still in the sixties, "Peace, Bob."

In a letter he would say it right, from the heart.

If Russell wrote him such a letter it would mean merely everything to Cousy, and, given the distant nature of their relationship, it would mean even more than if Sharman reached out to him with a letter from the grave.

Cousy made his decision: *This might be the right time to make my last stand with Russ, make my mea culpa. I want that box crossed off.*

In the light of morning, he pulled out a pen and his stationery and wrote a letter to Russell in his best cursive. It covered a page and a half. He wrote that his letter must come as a surprise since they had hardly been pen pals. Cousy said this mea culpa letter was on his end-of-life to-do list. He said he was sorry they hadn't shared a more meaningful relationship through the years, and he accepted full responsibility for that. As senior member of the Celtics, and team captain, Cousy wrote, he should have reached out more to Russell during their seven seasons as teammates. That was his responsibility, even if it wasn't his nature; he wasn't a *reach out* kind of guy. It was important to him that Russ understand this.

Then he wrote that he wasn't sure if Russell was reading much anymore, but in case he was, he enclosed *Between the World and Me*, which he greatly admired. The author Coates, he wrote, might just be the next James Baldwin. Cousy also recommended Stevenson's *Just Mercy*.

And that was it. Cousy had said what he needed to say.

He contacted the Celtics to make certain he had Russell's correct home address. That's when he was told that Russell's namesake son, William Jr., always known as Buddha, had died in Utah only a few weeks earlier from cancer, at fifty-eight. Cousy remembered Buddha as a boy; Russ and Rose used to host Christmas parties at their house for Celtics players and their families, and all of the kids played together. Cousy spoke with Sam Jones and Sanders about Buddha's passing. Before mailing his letter, he added a postscript, expressing condolences to Russ, saying that no one should have to bury a son or daughter and that he would include Buddha in his long list of prayers.

This letter was part of Cousy's late-in-life journey to deeper enlightenment. He was trying to draw closer to someone he had never completely understood. He hoped to get a reply, but he wasn't sure that he would.

This was his last pass to Russ. The ball was in the air.

Six months went by without a response, and then a year, and then a year and a half, and then two years. Every now and then he spotted Russ on television. There he was at Shaq's Hall of Fame induction ceremony and on a new commercial with Russell Westbrook. He saw him hand out the Bill Russell Award to the Most Valuable Player of the NBA Finals, one year to LeBron James, and to Kevin Durant the next two. ("It's almost scary to meet him," Kerr, the Warriors coach, says about Russell. "He's just like this NBA god, and he's just got that intimidating presence. I feel very deferential when I meet him. He is royalty.") When the Lakers retired Kobe Bryant's jersey numbers in L.A., Russ was there, too.

Cousy spoke with former teammates and opponents, who told him that Russ was experiencing troubles with his hearing and his heart, that he had suffered a small stroke, and that his mind wasn't as sharp as it once was. Russ kept making public appearances, so Cousy surmised he couldn't be that bad off.

The months kept passing, with no reply. There might be a simple explanation for that, Cousy thought. Maybe Russ wasn't getting his mail. Or: "If I'm getting five [fan] letters a day, he's probably getting twenty-five. It might be overload and he's not dealing with it." Or maybe Russ figures he said what he needed to say in their breakfast conversation fifteen years earlier.

Cousy's memory is imperfect. He does not recall Russell's warm remarks about him at the Celtics' Breakup Dinner in 1963. "You can get a cup of coffee for all your championships. But you can't get friendships like Cousy's. . . . You meet a Cousy not once in a month but once in a lifetime. Bob Cousy has made playing with the Celtics one of the most gratifying things in my life."

Hearing those words now, Cousy says, "I wish I'd gotten up from the table and gone up and given him a big hug knowing that he even thought of me in that way.

"Maybe that's an indictment of my sensitivities in those days."

Cousy has regrets and doubts now that didn't cross his mind then because he was too busy being Bob Cousy, Celtics hero. Now he looks back and wishes he had been a slightly different person and done more. He enjoyed friendships with his first two black teammates, Cooper, his roommate, and Barksdale, who once played a full quarter with the Baltimore Bullets in 1953 without receiving a pass from his white teammates. Barksdale later described Cousy as "a gentleman from the word go. . . . The Cooz, to me, was a guy that just opened his arms up." (At the invitation of Barksdale's sons, Cousy presented their father at his posthumous induction into the Hall of Fame in 2012.) Publicly endorsing Ted Kennedy in 1962 and campaigning with him was more than most athletes did politically at that time. Taking two African-American boys in the Big Brothers program in Worcester perhaps seems relatively insignificant judged against the times today, but judged in those earlier times was more meaningful. How many star white athletes, after all, were reaching out to help black children then?

Now, though, Cousy wishes he had marched with Dr. King. He wishes he had become Russell's public shield and been more publicly supportive of his other black teammates. In 1966, the writer Gay Talese wrote in *Esquire* magazine of Joe DiMaggio in retirement, "The baseball hero must always act the part, must preserve the myth, and none does it better than DiMaggio." But Cousy isn't like DiMaggio in that way. Cousy recognizes his flaws. He's admitting them, even drawing attention to them. He is not gilding any lilies or embellishing any truths. He is trying to set the record straight: *This is who I was.* This is his dying declaration: *I wish I had done more.*

Cousy is not alone among white NBA players of his generation to harbor racial regrets. In his favorite chair, he interrogates himself. "If I had perceived a threat to myself, to my family or my livelihood as a result of being outspoken, I'll be honest with you, I probably would have pulled back," he says. "I would have considered my well-being and the well-being of my family. I wouldn't have been a hero, I don't think. I would've taken that into consideration. I'm guessing. Who knows?"

Dating back to his mother's anti-German cry of *sale Boche,* Cousy says he has never understood racism. "I always just felt, 'Hey, this is stupid. How can there be mass discrimination or mass hatred?' My bride went with me [to church] but she didn't need God to tell her that the Ten Commandments make sense: 'Treat everybody the way you want to be treated.' . . . She just went by her conscience. She was nice to everybody, and reached out. And that was basically my feeling about anti-Semitism, or anti-any-group. It didn't make sense."

Harry Edwards, the African-American sociologist who organized the protest at the 1968 Olympics in Mexico City and a longtime friend of Russell's, says, "Cousy probably saw more than some [white NBA players], but was about as naïve as most in terms of what Russell, Satch Sanders, Sam Jones, and K.C. Jones were really going through. . . . That doesn't diminish Cousy. The fact that he comes back all of these years later and makes that statement publicly and sincerely and heart-felt: You know what? To me, that's more than enough. I think Cousy is an eminently decent man and with a tremendous amount of empathy and compassion, and more than that he has the courage to stand up and say, 'I wish I could've seen more clearly and done more.' Most people settle for, 'Well, there was nothing that I could do,' and that's the end of it."

His letter sent, Cousy wasn't consumed by thoughts of Russell, though they bubbled up every now and then. Thinking about Russell in the darkness one night, Cousy had an epiphany: Maybe their distant relationship wasn't about race at all but simple misunderstandings in the decades since their time as teammates. Once, before a Celtics game during the early eighties, he had approached Russell and Rick Barry, CBS Sports colleagues, at courtside to say hello, and Russ had ignored him. Even worse, Cousy thought he saw Russ step in front of him to keep him from their little huddle. Then there was the time Russ in-vited him to his basketball fantasy camp in Las Vegas—"The only time he's ever called me since we retired." Cousy had had only one previous fantasy camp experience and hated it; he had sweltered in a little dor-mitory room at Fordham University with a small fan that Missie had sent, and vowed never to appear at another. He declined Russ's invita-tion. *Maybe that set him off?* And then—*was it twenty years ago?*—a promoter in California phoned to invite Cousy to a charity dinner hon-oring Russell and Magic Johnson and others, and asked if he would like to sit on the dais to honor his old friend Russ. Cousy didn't want to fly six thousand miles round-trip to sit on a dais, so he begged off.

Now he played this out in his mind: *Putting myself in Russ's position— my not showing up after being asked didn't build any brownie points in*

terms of our relationship. Maybe it's my fault. I turned down his represen-
tative.

Frank Deford understood Cousy's uncertainty about Russell. Deford's relationship with Russell might not have measured up to full friendship by Russell's definition, but they shared a mutual respect. In the years following Deford's profile of Russell in *Sports Illustrated* in 1999, Russell phoned Deford a couple times, including once on Thanksgiving just to say, "On Thanksgiving, I make it a habit to call a few people that I really like just to say hello."

"I was sort of touched: Wow!" Deford said.

Deford wrote Russell a letter after Auerbach's death in 2006, but Russell did not reply. He wrote Russell another letter. No reply. He phoned Russell a couple times, too. No replies. They had no contact for a decade, Deford said.

"I couldn't have done anything wrong because I haven't written anything else about him," Deford said later. "As sensitive as he is, I may have done something wrong which would never in a million years occur to me, but he found it wrong. I mean, that's it. Bye-bye. He may have the fondest memories of me but just doesn't want to see me or talk to me."

Deford envisioned a complicating factor in Cousy's wait for a reply: "Old age is factored into this as well so that you are not just dealing with the usual difficult Russell. You are dealing with a difficult old man."

All these years later, Cousy says he has never really understood how Russ's mind works: "One day he throws his arms around me, the next day he glares at me. I can't get into his head." Like Deford, Cousy feels nearly certain that Russell is upset with him, though why, and to what depth, he does not know.

He hopes to hear from him at some point. But, he says, "I didn't do it for Russ. I did it for *moi.*"

IN THE HOUSE OF RUSSELL

His letter carried heightened importance and urgency to Cousy. But when it landed at Russell's home near Seattle, his old teammate had much else consuming him. There was turmoil in Russell's personal life—legal and familial—that played out in King County Superior Court in Seattle. It was vastly more disruptive, painful, and problematic for him, and no doubt preoccupying, than anything Cousy might have imagined.

Questions were being raised about Russell's cognitive well-being. Friends, family, and doctors were suggesting that, after he suffered a stroke in March 2015, which initially left him with facial drooping and an inability to speak coherently, Russell, at eighty-one, might have lost some of his cognitive powers; questions were being asked, too, about Russell's competence to make important decisions in his life.

Russell had long drawn strength from his family. His closeness with his children and grandchildren helped fill the void after his third wife, Marilyn Nault, died in 2009. They stopped by his home, dropped off food, shared family dinners. He gave generously to them: cars, homes. But now Russell's family safety net tore.

On one side was his caregiver and romantic partner, Jeannine Fiorito.

On the other were Russell's two surviving grown children, Jacob and Karen.

The most pressing legal question to be answered: Was Russell now vulnerable to undue influence from Fiorito?

Nearly thirty-three years younger than Russell (and younger than even his children), Fiorito, according to court documents, was a former professional golfer. She ran a bedbug detection business that employed a trained canine to identify homes and businesses with infestation. Beginning as golfing friends, Fiorito and Russell had a long-term relationship that intensified after his stroke when she slept in a chair at the hospital for a week, and later moved into his home to provide full-time care. For some time, Russell had been paying some of Fiorito's expenses, according to court documents.

In June 2015, Jacob and Karen, an attorney by profession, filed a Vulnerable Adult Protection Action, alleging that Russell was being isolated from long-standing friends, employees, advisers, and family, and that his finances had been taken over.

For the next sixteen months, those who loved Russell and were closest to him fought an internecine legal battle about who, and what, was best for him. One old friend noted that Russell, as an alleged vulnerable adult, had been placed in the middle of a storm and had reacted, as was his way, by "shrugging his shoulders and just wanting everyone to stop yelling."

The court assigned a guardian *ad litem*, Janet Somers, to work in Russell's best interests by investigating the allegations and Russell's capacity to participate in the proceeding and then to make recommendations to the court. Somers reviewed extensive medical and financial records, contacted Russell's physicians and caregivers, interviewed twenty people (including Russell three times), and produced a detailed report.

A court-appointed geriatric care manager, whose findings were considered by Somers and included in Somers's report, stated that Fiorito had been doing "a good job of providing Mr. Russell's care and overseeing his medical care." However, she was concerned about "the level of mutual dependency" that had developed because Fiorito had given up her home and job to care for Russell full time. The care manager was particularly concerned about Russell's social isolation since his stroke. She noted that Russell had changed physicians, attorneys, bookkeepers, and his dentist, and had fired his longtime housekeeper, in addition to cutting out many long-term friends and family. This seemed antithetical to Russell's history of deep loyalty to friends, family, and advisers. "It seems unusual to suddenly want to cut out so many significant people," the geriatric care manager wrote. "To suddenly have ill feelings and mistrust of so many different people that he had previously trusted for decades is abnormal and troubling."

Somers understood that Russell was in fragile physical health and had been diagnosed with "cognitive decline, memory loss, and altered mental status." Based on her own interviews with Russell, Somers wrote that Russell had "variable memory and cognitive issues." At some moments he was "sharp as a tack," at others much less so. From Somers's perspective, "Despite sixteen months, multiple court hearings, seven lawyers, one guardian *ad litem*, three full days of mediation, and one arbitration, the case never fully resolved—to Mr. Russell's physical and financial detriment and the further deterioration of his relationship with his children. . . . The rather tortuous path this case has taken has been extremely frustrating. Cases involving allegations of undue influence are often extremely complex and nuanced."

Russell declined to undergo a neuropsychological examination, a test Somers considered essential to determine whether he was acting of his own volition or subject to undue influence.

"[He] is adamant he wants to be left alone to make his own choices," Somers wrote, "and that he is content with his life."

Among her recommendations for resolution, Somers advised that Fiorito return to live in her own home and provide care for Russell only three days per week, the other four provided by outside caregivers; paying a romantic partner for caregiving, Somers wrote, "is generally considered inadvisable and a blurring of important boundaries."

Somers also recommended that all parties not criticize each other in Russell's presence and "commit to providing as calm and positive an atmosphere for Mr. Russell as possible."

In October 2016, court records available to the public show, the two sides finally reached agreement.

Then, in early December 2016, ten months after Cousy mailed his letter, and only about six weeks after the court case formally was dismissed, Russell and Fiorito took out a marriage license. She became his fourth wife.

Cousy was left to wonder if Russell ever saw or read his letter. If he did, was he distracted or preoccupied? Was he even capable of responding? Had Cousy sent his letter *too late*?

Two and a half years later, in Worcester, Cousy answered the phone and heard the diminished voice of the man who has been in his thoughts for years: "It's Bill Russell." Cooz knew that others in the Celtics inner circle had learned of his letter, and urged Russ to call. Cooz did nearly all the talking—about Frank Ramsey's recent death at eighty-six, about Russell's continuing travels to NBA games and events—in part to fill long, uncomfortable pauses. He asked about the letter: "Did you receive it?" Russ said he had. Nothing more was said about it. Cooz had hoped their conversation would rise to a more substantive level. Still, he had made his last pass to Russ. He felt at peace.

SERENADED

Cousy stays away from big crowds and makes precious few appearances.

An organization calling itself the South Florida Basketball Fraternity called to ask him to appear in Boca Raton at its thirty-eighth annual luncheon to honor Dolph Schayes, the old Syracuse National. As best Cousy could tell, it was a loosely organized group of old high school and college basketball players, coaches, referees, and broadcasters from the New York area who had resettled in south Florida, most of them Jewish, and more than a few in their seventies and eighties. They met informally for breakfast every Tuesday, talked hoops for a couple hours, recalled their days in the Catskills, and then chipped in two bucks apiece to tip the waitresses.

Ossie Schectman, credited in 1946 with scoring the first basket in the history of the Basketball Association of America (the precursor to the NBA) as a member of the New York Knicks, had been a regular for years, and so had the longtime NBA referee Norm Drucker. The group used to have an annual dinner, but most of the men couldn't stay up that late, so it was changed to a luncheon. The organizers of the Schayes event told Cousy that more than five hundred guests had registered and that Schayes specifically asked for Cousy to be there.

He didn't want to go.

Cousy had done enough of these luncheons and Man of the Year fund-raiser dinners to last ten lifetimes. He knew how it worked: Organizers told you five hundred people were coming and maybe sixty showed up. Kids would swarm him for autographs; the speakers would prattle on. No doubt Schayes would tell his favorite Cousy story from the podium, the same story he always told, about Bob Cousy Day. "We are sitting there before the game," Schayes would say, "and Cooz is crying for twenty minutes, his daughters are crying, his wife is crying, his parents, fourteen thousand people are bawling. I didn't think that we were in trouble until I looked up"—here, Schayes would pause for comic effect—"and I saw the two officials bawling. Then I *knew* we were going to have problems."

It was all too much. Cousy would rather be at home, in his sweat suit, at his condo at the Bear Lakes Country Club, reading and meditating.

Or maybe he wanted to go to the Schayes event *a little*.

Schayes was a friend, and Boca Raton was only about forty minutes away. Schayes had been a relentless opponent on the court—he and Cousy were two of the NBA's most luminous stars during the fifties—and through the years a true friendship blossomed between them. Cooz and Missie, Dolph and Naomi had spent time together at functions for retired NBA players. During Missie's final years, Dolph had phoned a few times to ask how things were, knowing that Missie was sliding deeper into dementia. Cooz thought Schayes a good man.

He decided to go to the luncheon, for Dolph.

"But on my terms," he told organizers.

He would not speak at the event. He would only wave, upon introduction, from his seat. Neither would he sign autographs, or maybe just a few, for the kids, so he wouldn't look crotchety. He would need someone to serve as his shield and would stay for only an hour, maybe an hour-fifteen. He preferred to leave before lunch was served.

"And that's the extent of it," Cousy said. He intended to be home by four o'clock, in time to watch Cavuto.

The event was only six days away when one of the organizers, his voice catching, phoned to say that Schayes, in Syracuse, had died. Cousy was incredulous. He didn't know that Schayes had been diagnosed with terminal cancer months earlier; Dolph never mentioned it.

Told the luncheon would proceed as a tribute to Schayes, Cousy reassured the caller that he would be there, though still on his terms. (If forced to speak, he was willing now to tell Dolph's story from Bob Cousy Day, just as Dolph would have told it.) As his shield, he would bring Tony Stevens, his eighty-seven-year-old accountant friend, because he wasn't going to walk into this event alone.

What happened the moment he stepped into the festivities at the Polo Club was unexpected. The master of ceremonies, David Weissman, took up the microphone and made the introduction: "The Houdini of the Hardwood, Bob Cousy!"

The entire room—539 guests, to be precise—stood as one and erupted in cheers and applause. As Cousy, in sport coat and powder-blue shirt, slowly walked to his seat, leaning on his cane and with Stevens by his side, the cheers grew louder.

Weissman, a seventy-seven-year-old Boston native who grew up a Celtics fan and was known to sneak away from his family's Passover Seder to listen to Celtics playoff games on the radio, re-created Joe Dillon's call from the balcony, saying into the microphone, "We love you, Cooz!"

The cheering crowd picked up on it, chanting, in singsong fashion, "We love you, Cooz! We love you, Cooz!"

A powerful emotion surged deep within Cousy as he made his way to his seat. He saw a few familiar faces—a former Knicks broadcaster, a man who had attended Cousy's summer camp during childhood.

No kids showed up. Instead, old men rushed to his table, sharing stories sixty years old from the Catskills.

"You were my waiter at Tamarack, Cooz!"

"I played you in one-on-one at Kutsher's!"

More than merely remembering him, they were awed by him. They saw him score fifty points in four overtimes against Syracuse. They saw him dribbling behind his back, dribbling out the clock. They saw him run the Celtics' transition game. They saw him when he was young.

He autographed their programs, their slips of paper, their basketballs, anything, everything, and happily.

He thought, *Serenaded by five hundred old Jewish men singing, "We love you, Cooz!" And they're mostly Knicks fans!*

Once, as Houdini, he had heard the cheers. Now they came again. The old man stood straight and tall.

ACKNOWLEDGMENTS

For this book, I conducted fifty-three interviews with Bob Cousy. These interviews became like a two-and-a-half-year conversation during which Cousy catalogued his life, assigned meaning to people and moments, and attempted to close circles. Captivated throughout, I listened. For his candor, authenticity, and accessibility, I extend my gratitude to Cousy.

My original idea, broadly, was to write a narrative on the dynastic Boston Celtics as a companion to my most recent book, *Their Life's Work*, about pro football's great dynasty of the 1970s, the Pittsburgh Steelers. My aim would be to capture those Celtics, now in their late seventies and eighties, in their twilight years. As team captain, Cousy figured to be critical in the telling of this story, though not the narrative focus. I'd interviewed Cousy once before, by phone in 2003, as research for my book *WILT, 1962*, about Wilt Chamberlain's one-hundred-point game. In that forty-five-minute phone interview, Cousy had mentioned, almost in passing, his regrets about Russell. "I don't think I shared Russell's pain enough with him," he told me. "I should have." In my interview transcript, I highlighted that quote as a reminder that it required deeper probing.

ACKNOWLEDGMENTS

In summer 2015, I sent an email to Jeff Twiss requesting an interview with Cousy and several other former Celtics living in the Boston area (Heinsohn, Sanders, Havlicek). As the Celtics' publicist of nearly four decades, Twiss is a pro. He spoke to Cousy and then emailed back to say that Cooz wasn't doing interviews. His wife, Missie, had died, and Cousy had undergone a couple medical procedures, and so now, Twiss wrote, "his wish is to slow down." To write this book on the Celtics, I needed to interview the captain, so I wrote Twiss another email, more emphatic than the first. I explained that just as Cousy existed near the center of the dynasty, he would live near the center of my book. I cited my 2003 phone interview with Cousy and the way he had spoken with impressive candor and clarity about race, family, and his regrets. "I don't know if Mr. Cousy would be interested in talking about such meaning-of-life topics now," I wrote. Four days later, on my voice mail, I heard an energized voice with a slight speech impediment—it was unmistakably Cousy. He said he was available for an interview with me "on any day of the week that ends with a Y."

Soon after, I flew to Boston and drove to Worcester. On that day in August 2015, Cousy greeted me at his front door, cane in his left hand, his right hand extended. That's where our relationship began. The first interview, on his enclosed back patio, lasted nearly four hours. I probed and challenged. He engaged and was engaging. He answered questions directly, often with self-deprecating humor. Over the ensuing days we moved into his living room and conducted more interviews. Time had not diminished Cousy's impressive candor. His mind was sharp, his emotions close to the surface. Discussing the Celtics dynasty, he roared to life. Discussing Missie, tears came. He spoke with sadness about the distance in his relationship with Russell. I soon made an editorial decision: The story to tell was the captain's.

A few months later, I visited him at his condo in West Palm Beach for another series of interviews. Soon we began to conduct interviews by phone. We talked by phone every few weeks, typically for an hour or more. Occasionally he'd write me a note. A few times, in voice mail messages, I heard him say that he'd been thinking about our last interview and had more to say. We talked about the NBA and current events in American life.

He talked about books, his daughters. I watched an NBA game with him on his living room TV in West Palm Beach. I joined him at a Thursday night dinner at the Worcester Country Club.

I began to understand that Russell was, to Cousy, like a mirror: In looking to his old teammate, Cousy saw a reflection of himself, what he'd done, what he hadn't done. His enduring regret was palpable. I reached out to Russell for an interview and tried to gain entree through former teammates, old friends, journalists, the Celtics, and the NBA office, but without success.

Scott Moyers is the publisher of Penguin Press. He served as editor for this book. From the moment I stepped into Moyers's office at 375 Hudson Street in New York, I sensed his integrity and intellectual depth. Early on, in an email to me, he playfully tailored words often ascribed to MLK: "The arc of the moral universe is long, but it bends toward Boston Garden," Moyers wrote, and he said he hoped to help me in my narrative to "bend that curve a little more sharply." That he did. As I challenged Cousy, Moyers (on the phone and in my manuscript's margins) challenged me, and in the process made this a better book. His assistant, Mia Council, could not have been kinder or more efficient. David Black, my literary agent for the past thirty-two years, is a wise counselor and a very good man. He's old school: He takes friendship seriously. No surprise then that his team at the David Black Literary Agency—Gary Morris, Joy Tutela, Susan Raihofer, Sarah Smith, Jenny Herrera, and Matt Belford—has become like old friends. Throughout the writing process, I also leaned on the support and camaraderie of my colleagues at Stanford's Graduate Program in Journalism, in particular Jay Hamilton, Janine Zacharia, and Geri Migielicz, teammates in the truest sense.

To assess early drafts of my manuscript, I assembled a panel of readers who have studied or written about the NBA, race relations, sports journalism, and/or the city of Boston. I thank the following early readers: Jackie MacMullan, longtime NBA writer in Boston, now with ESPN, and coauthor of *When the Game Was Ours*, about the rivalry between Larry Bird and Magic Johnson; Ron Thomas, Morehouse College journalism professor and author of *They Cleared the Lane*, about the NBA's black pioneers; R. B. Brenner, my former teaching cohort at Stanford and now director of the School of Journalism at the University of Texas in Austin; Leigh Montville, former sports columnist for the *Boston Globe* and, more recently, author of fine books about Ted Williams and Muhammad Ali; Dave Kindred, decorated longtime sports columnist and author, and 2018 winner of the PEN/ESPN Lifetime Achievement Award for Literary Sports Writing; Aram Goudsouzian, University of Memphis historian and author of *King of the Court*, an incisive 2011 biography of Bill Russell; Howard Bryant of ESPN, author of *Shut Out: A Story of Race and Baseball in Boston*; and David J. Garrow, author of the Pulitzer Prize–winning *Bearing the Cross*, about Martin Luther King, Jr. and the Southern Christian Leadership Conference, and, more recently, *Rising Star*, a biography of Barack Obama. I'm indebted, too, to Lionel Aikin, Doug Kelly, and Glenn Pomerantz for their helpful suggestions on aspects of the manuscript.

I continue to be amazed by the devotion to craft exhibited by librarians and archivists across the land. They remain the unsung heroes of narrative nonfiction. I give thanks to Abbey Malangone at the John F. Kennedy Presidential Library and Museum in Boston; Wendy Essery at the Worcester Historical Museum; Laszlo Jakusovszky at Stanford University's Cecil H. Green Library; Aaron Schmidt at the Boston Public Library; Matt Zeysing at the Naismith Memorial Basketball Hall of Fame; and Jeremiah Manion at the *Boston Globe*. I also received assistance from sports media professionals, including the Celtics' Twiss; Raymond Ridder and Brett Winkler of the Golden State Warriors; Richard A. Johnson, curator of the Sports Museum in Boston; and Charles Bare at Holy Cross. James Mattone helped with research on the microfilm reader at the Boston Public Library, the *Boston Herald*'s Jim Mahoney with photos, and Swiss investigative journalist Titus Plattner with civil records in France.

I am forever indebted to two Cal-Berkeley historians, Leon Litwack and Larry Levine, whose love for history and keen attention to race relations in America inspired and exhilarated me as an undergraduate, and still do thirty-five years later.

ACKNOWLEDGMENTS

In book-writing mode, I become sort of the Red Auerbach of my own home: intense, single-minded, and grouchy. The kids—Ross, Win, and Leigh, our single-syllable pride-and-joys—live as adults in the real world now, Millennials on the make. That leaves Carrie alone at home to deal with her Auerbach. After thirty-three years of marriage and six books, I can say this about Carrie: She is a Hall of Famer.

NOTE ON SOURCES

LIST OF INTERVIEWS

The author conducted more than 150 interviews for this book between August 2015 and March 2018, including fifty-three with Bob Cousy. A number of the subjects listed here graciously agreed to multiple interviews. Earlier interviews by the author with Arnold "Red" Auerbach (2002), K.C. Jones (2003), Pete Newell (2002, 2004), Tom Gola (2002), and Leonard Koppett (2002) for the book WILT, 1962, *about Wilt Chamberlain's one-hundred-point game against the New York Knicks on March 2, 1962, proved instructive for this project and are also listed below.*

BOSTON CELTICS (1950-1969)

Arnold "Red" Auerbach (2002), Gene Conley, Bob Cousy, Mal Graham, Gene Guarilia, John Havlicek, Tom Heinsohn, K.C. Jones (2003), George Kaftan, Ed Leede, Willie Naulls, Togo Palazzi, Frank Ramsey, Tom "Satch" Sanders

NBA PLAYERS/COACHES/OPPONENTS

Dave Cowens, Tom Gola (2002), Richie Guerin, Steve Kerr, Tom Meschery, Pete Newell (2002, 2004), Cal Ramsey, Joe Ruklick, Dolph Schayes, Ray Scott, Gene Shue, Brad Stevens, Nate Thurmond, Lenny Wilkens

NOTE ON SOURCES

OTHERS

Steve Adelman, Dave Anderson, Randy Auerbach, Derek Barksdale, Taylor Branch, Bruce Brand, Howard Bryant, Tom Callahan, Bob Cohen, Nancy Auerbach Collins, P. Kevin Condron, Chuck Cooper III, Marie Cousy, Ticia Cousy, Frank Deford, Brian Dillon, Frank Dyer, Harry Edwards, Phil Elderkin, Charles Evers, Jocelyn Faubert, Julie Auerbach Flieger, Raymond Flynn, Peter Gammons, Daniel Gore, Pam Barksdale Gore, Brian Hanlon, Maura Healey, Diane Heinsohn, Paul Hornung, Cornelius (Con) Hurley Jr., Dan Imler, Richard Johnson, Mel King, Leonard Koppett (2002), Jane Leavy, Henry Lusardi, Jackie MacMullan, Rev. Earle Markey, Rollie Massimino, William (Bill) McSweeny, Leigh Montville, Jim Nelson, Dr. Tom O'Connor, Clyde Phillips, Charles Pierce, Andy Pradella, Bob Ryan, Bill Scheft, Max Shapiro, Jerry Sharman, Dan Shaughnessy, Tony Stevens, Bryan Stevenson, George Sullivan, Jeff Twiss, Tara VanDerveer, Brian Wallace, Patsy Ann (Pat) Ware, David Weissman

MAGAZINES AND JOURNALS CONSULTED

Basket Hebdo (Vannes, France), *Basketball–1950, Boston, Collier's, Cord Sports-Facts Pro Basketball Guide 1970, Ebony, Esquire, Holy Cross, Jet, Life, Look, Newsweek, New Yorker, Parade, Saturday Evening Post, Sport, Sporting News, Sports Illustrated, Time, Ventana Monthly*

NEWSPAPERS CONSULTED

Amsterdam News, Boston Evening American, Boston Globe, Boston Herald, Boston Herald Traveler, Boston Phoenix, Boston Post, Boston Record American, Boston Traveler, Chicago Tribune, Christian Science Monitor, Cincinnati Enquirer, Cleveland Plain Dealer, Daily News (New York), *Daily Record* (Boston), *Long Island Daily Press, Long Island Star-Journal, Los Angeles Herald Examiner, Los Angeles Times, Louisville Courier-Journal, Lowell* (MA) *Sun, National Observer, Newsday, New York Herald-Tribune, New York Post, New York Times, Philadelphia Evening Bulletin, Quincy* (MA) *Patriot Ledger, Real Paper* (Boston), *Seattle Post-Intelligencer, Seattle Times, Springfield* (MA) *Republican, Telegram & Gazette* (Worcester, MA), *Washington Post, Washington Star*

NOTE ON SOURCES

GOVERNMENT RECORDS AND LAWSUITS CONSULTED

Archive from the Region of Haut-Rhin, France. Civil Records 1793–1892. The Birth Register of Eteimbes, 1883–1892

New York Passenger Lists, 1820–1957, *Mauretania*, Cherbourg, France, to Ellis Island, New York, December 21–27, 1927

1900 United States Federal Census, 1930 United States Federal Census, U.S. 1940 United States Federal Census

U.S. Naturalization Records, 1882–1944 (Joseph Cousy)

U.S. World War II Draft Registration Cards, 1942 (Joseph Cousy)

In the Matter of William F. Russell, An Alleged Vulnerable Adult: Jacob Russell and Karen Russell, Petitioners, v Jeannine Fiorito, Respondent. King County (Washington) Superior Court. Case No. 15-2-15661-6 SEA.

CATALOGS, PROGRAMS, AND VIDEOS

Bob Cousy Day program, Boston Garden, March 17, 1963

Bob Cousy Day celebration video, March 17, 1963, NBA Entertainment archives, Secaucus, NJ

Boston Celtics Yearbook, 1962–63, edited by Bill Mokray

Boston College Basketball Facts Book, 1966–1967

College of the Holy Cross catalogues, course offerings, 1946–50

Marie A. (Missie) Cousy funeral Mass guest book, September 24, 2013

SportsCards Plus catalogue, Telephone/Internet Auction, Collections of Bob Cousy, Honus Wagner, Tony Lazzeri, November 20, 2003

Tribute to Mr. Basketball, testimonial program, Worcester Auditorium, Worcester, MA, April 27–28, 1963

World Series of Basketball 1950 National Tour, College All-Americans vs. Harlem Globetrotters official souvenir program

LIBRARIES AND ARCHIVES CONSULTED

Boston Public Library; Cecil H. Green Library, Stanford University, Stanford, CA; Doe Memorial Library, University of California, Berkeley, Berkeley, CA; John F. Kennedy Presidential Library and Museum, Boston, MA; Naismith Memorial Basketball Hall of Fame, Springfield, MA; NBA Entertainment, Secaucus, NJ; Worcester Historical Museum, Worcester, MA; Sterling Memorial Library, Manuscripts & Archives, Yale University, New Haven, CT

MISCELLANEOUS

Bob Cousy personal correspondence, scrapbooks, and photographs, Worcester, MA

BIBLIOGRAPHY

Araton, Harvey, and Filip Bondy. *The Selling of the Green: The Financial Rise and Moral Decline of the Boston Celtics*. New York: HarperCollins Publishers, 1992.

Auerbach, Arnold "Red." *Basketball for the Player, the Fan and the Coach*. New York: Pocket Books, Inc., 1953.

Auerbach, Arnold "Red," and Paul Sann. *Winning the Hard Way: Basketball's Greatest Coach Tells His Story*. Boston: Little, Brown and Company, 1966.

Auerbach, Red, with Joe Fitzgerald. *On & Off the Court*. New York: Macmillan Publishing Company, 1985.

Baldwin, James. *The Fire Next Time*. New York: Vintage International, 1993.

Bodanza, Mark C. *Ten Times a Champion: The Story of Basketball Legend Sam Jones*. Bloomington, IN: iUniverse, 2016.

Bradlee, Ben, Jr. *The Kid: The Immortal Life of Ted Williams*. New York: Little, Brown and Company, 2013.

Branch, Taylor. *Pillar of Fire: America in the King Years, 1963–65*. New York: Simon & Schuster, 1998.

Bryant, Howard. *Shut Out: A Story of Race and Baseball in Boston*. Boston: Beacon Press, 2002.

Carey, Mike, with Jamie Most. *High Above Courtside: The Lost Memoirs of Johnny Most*. Chicago: Sports Publishing, 2003.

Coates, Ta-Nehisi. *Between the World and Me.* New York: Spiegel & Grau, 2015.

Cousy, Bob, with John Devaney. *The Killer Instinct.* New York: Random House, 1975.

Cousy, Bob, as told to Al Hirshberg. *Basketball Is My Life.* Englewood Cliffs, NJ: Prentice-Hall, Inc., 1958.

Cousy, Bob, with Ed Linn. *The Last Loud Roar.* Englewood Cliffs, NJ: Prentice-Hall, Inc., 1964.

Cousy, Bob, and Bob Ryan. *Cousy on the Celtic Mystique.* New York: McGraw-Hill Publishing Company, 1988.

Cramer, Richard Ben. *Joe DiMaggio: The Hero's Life.* New York: Simon & Schuster, 2000.

Creamer, Robert W. *Babe: The Legend Comes to Life.* New York: Fireside, 1992.

Criblez, Adam J. *Tall Tales and Short Shorts: Dr. J, Pistol Pete, and the Birth of the Modern NBA.* Lanham, MD: Rowman & Littlefield Publishers, 2017.

Eig, Jonathan. *Luckiest Man: The Life and Death of Lou Gehrig.* New York: Simon & Schuster, 2005.

Feinstein, John, and Red Auerbach. *Let Me Tell You a Story: A Lifetime in the Game.* New York: Little, Brown and Company, 2004.

Frankel, Glenn. *High Noon: The Hollywood Blacklist and the Making of an American Classic.* New York: Bloomsbury USA, 2017.

Garrow, David J. *Bearing the Cross: Martin Luther King, Jr., and the Southern Christian Leadership Conference.* New York: William Morrow & Company, 1986.

George, Nelson. *Elevating the Game: Black Men and Basketball.* Lincoln: University of Nebraska Press, 1999.

Goudsouzian, Aram. *King of the Court: Bill Russell and the Basketball Revolution.* Berkeley: University of California Press, 2010.

Greenfield, Jeff. *The World's Greatest Team: A Portrait of the Boston Celtics, 1957–69.* New York: Random House, 1976.

Halberstam, David. *The Fifties.* New York: Villard Books, 1993.

Halberstam, David, ed. *The Best American Sports Writing of the Century.* Boston: Houghton Mifflin Company, 1999.

Heinsohn, Tommy, and Joe Fitzgerald. *Give 'Em the Hook.* New York: Random House, 1988.

Holtzman, Jerome. *No Cheering in the Press Box.* New York: Holt, Rinehart and Winston, 1973.

Isaacs, Neil D. *Vintage NBA: The Pioneer Era, 1946–56.* Indianapolis: Masters Press, 1996.

Johnson, Richard A. *A Century of Boston Sports.* Boston: Northeastern University Press, 2000.

Johnson, Richard A., and Robert Hamilton Johnson. *The Celtics: In Black and White.* Charleston, SC: Arcadia Publishing, 2006.

Kindred, Dave. *Basketball: The Dream Game in Kentucky.* Louisville: Data Courier, Inc., 1976.

BIBLIOGRAPHY

Koppett, Leonard. *24 Seconds to Shoot: The Birth and Improbable Rise of the NBA.* Kingston, NY: Total/Sports Illustrated, 1999.

Loscutoff, Lynn Leon. *Loscy and Me: The Artist & the Boston Celtics Legend, Jim Loscutoff, a Scrapbook Memoir.* CreateSpace Independent Publishing Platform, 2014.

Lukas, J. Anthony. *Common Ground: A Turbulent Decade in the Lives of Three American Families.* New York: Alfred A. Knopf, 1985.

Masur, Louis P. *The Soiling of Old Glory: The Story of a Photograph That Shocked America.* New York: Bloomsbury Press, 2008.

McPhee, John. *A Sense of Where You Are: Bill Bradley at Princeton.* New York: Farrar, Straus and Giroux, 1978.

Montville, Leigh. *Ted Williams: The Biography of an American Hero.* New York: Doubleday, 2004.

Ogden, David C., and Joel Nathan Rosen, eds, *Reconstructing Fame: Sport, Race, and Evolving Reputations.* Jackson: University Press of Mississippi, 2008.

Pluto, Terry. *Tall Tales: The Glory Years of the NBA, in the Words of the Men Who Played, Coached and Built Pro Basketball.* New York: Simon & Schuster, 1992.

Pomerantz, Gary M. *Where Peachtree Meets Sweet Auburn: A Saga of Race and Family.* New York: Penguin Books, 1997.

——————. *WILT, 1962: The Night of 100 Points and the Dawn of a New Era.* New York: Crown Publishing Group, 2005.

Povich, Shirley. *All Those Mornings . . . at the Post: The 20th Century in Sports from Famed Washington Post Columnist Shirley Povich.* New York: Public Affairs, 2005.

Rampersad, Arnold. *Jackie Robinson: A Biography.* New York: Alfred A. Knopf, 1997.

Reynolds, Bill. *Cousy: His Life, Career, and the Birth of Big-Time Basketball.* New York: Simon & Schuster, 2005.

Rhoden, William C. *Forty Million Dollar Slaves.* New York: Crown Publishing Group, 2006.

Robertson, Oscar. *The Big O: My Life, My Times, My Game.* Emmaus, PA: Rodale, 2003.

Russell, Bill, and Taylor Branch. *Second Wind: The Memoirs of an Opinionated Man.* New York: Random House, 1979.

Russell, Bill, as told to William McSweeny. *Go Up for Glory.* New York: Coward, McCann & Geoghegan, Inc., 1966.

Russell, Bill, with Alan Steinberg. *Red and Me: My Coach, My Lifelong Friend.* New York: HarperCollins, 2009.

Shaughnessy, Dan. *Seeing Red: The Red Auerbach Story.* New York: Crown Publishers, Inc., 1994.

Stevenson, Bryan. *Just Mercy: A Story of Justice and Redemption.* New York: Spiegel & Grau, 2014.

Sullivan, George. *The Boston Celtics: Fifty Years—A Championship Tradition.* Boston: Tehabi Books, 1996.

——————. *The Picture History of the Boston Celtics.* Indianapolis: The Bobbs-Merrill Company, Inc., 1981.

BIBLIOGRAPHY

Taylor, John. *The Rivalry: Bill Russell, Wilt Chamberlain, and the Golden Age of Basketball.* New York: Ballantine Books, 2006.

Thomas, Ron. *They Cleared the Lane: The NBA's Black Pioneers.* Lincoln: University of Nebraska Press, 1992.

West, Jerry, and Jonathan Coleman. *West by West: My Charmed, Tormented Life.* New York: Little, Brown and Company, 2011.

NOTES

PREFACE

xvi **He shot forty-five covers:** *Newsday* (February 1, 2003).

xvi **"a big batch of smoldering Black Panther . . .":** Bill Russell and Taylor Branch, *Second Wind: The Memoirs of an Opinionated Man* (New York: Random House, 1979), 227.

xvi **left reassured by the sight of Cousy:** Bill McSweeny interview.

xvii **"Hey, if you guys are worrying . . .":** *Boston Herald* (December 31, 1984).

xviii **Don Barksdale once marveled at a Cousy maneuver:** Togo Palazzi interview.

xix **"I've never heard of a fatality":** Paul Gardner, "He Sinks 'Em Blindfolded," *Parade* (November 20, 1955): 30.

xxi **all-time NBA team of five great players with a social:** Richard Lapchick, "My NBA All-Star Team of Social Conscience" (July 1, 2015), http://today.ucf .edu/my-nba-all-star-team-of-socially-conscience-players.

CHAPTER 1

5 **Joe Cousy's place of birth as Welschensteinbach:** Archive from the Region of Haut-Rhin, France, Civil Records 1793–1892, The Birth Register of Eteimbes, Eteimbes 5E. NMD 1883–1892, entry 5, p. 39.

5 **There his family struggled to raise apples:** Herbert Warren Wind, "Bob Cousy: The Man and the Game," *Sports Illustrated* (January 16, 1956): 30.

6 Joe boarded the ocean liner *Mauretania*: U.S. Naturalization Records, 1882–1944, Joseph Cousy, New York, NY, July 5, 1928. Microfilm roll 0953-0986–Petition Nos. 247501–247848. No. 21490. Supreme Court, Queens County, NY.

6 **taught language to children of affluent French families**: Wind, *Sports Illustrated* (January 16, 1956): 30.

6 **neighborhood knew her as** *the crazy French woman*: Marie Cousy interview. She was told this story by her mother, Missie Cousy.

7 **she found him once sitting on the third-story ledge**: Bob Cousy as told to Al Hirshberg, *Basketball Is My Life* (Englewood Cliffs, NJ: Prentice-Hall, Inc., 1958), 178.

7 **"Hey, Frenchy, the handkerchief is out!"**: Ibid., 8.

8 **"Alound the lugged lock . . ."**: Ibid.

8 **Joe told a sportswriter that he had raced**: Wind, *Sports Illustrated* (January 16, 1956): 30.

8 **he fixed cars and rented one of his own**: Ibid.

CHAPTER 2

10 **Arkin taught basketball mechanics**: Cousy as told to Hirshberg, *Basketball Is My Life*, 25.

11 **Cousy failed to catch Grummond's eye**: Ibid., 31.

11 **"Don't ever be predictable"**: Ibid., 34.

11 **"My boys tell me that you have a Chinese boy . . ."**: Lew Grummond, "The Bob Cousy I Know," *Tribute to Mr. Basketball,* testimonial program, Worcester Auditorium, Worcester, MA, April 27–28, 1963, 9.

12 **"The kid's reputation in the church league . . ."**: *Boston Globe* (March 8, 1963), and Bill Roeder, "'We Love Ya, Cooz,'" *Newsweek* (April 1, 1963): 50.

13 **"the ebon forward"**: *Long Island Star-Journal* (January 15, 1946).

13 *"Bob Cousy, who plays a mighty fine game"*: Grummond, "The Bob Cousy I Know," 10.

CHAPTER 3

15 **He cofounded the Ice Capades**: Walter Brown's biography is detailed in the coverage of his death: *Boston Record American, Boston Globe, Boston Herald, Boston Traveler*, September 8, 1964.

15 **Across New England he delivered talks**: George Sullivan, *The Boston Celtics: Fifty Years—A Championship Tradition* (Boston: Tehabi Books, 1996), 152–53.

16 **"He went from worst shot in the East . . ."**: Tom Heinsohn interview.

16 **It took an hour of mad scrambling to find**: Sullivan, *The Boston Celtics*, 153.

17 **His teammate Swede Carlson loved to hear the sound**: Ron Fimrite, "Big George," *Sports Illustrated* (November 6, 1989): 133.

17 GEO MIKAN VS KNICKS: Ibid.

17 **To Auerbach, the best ball handlers came from New York**: *Washington Star*, February 7, 1971.

17 "He looked like some fat broad in slacks": Ibid.

18 "The Knicks thought that they could just get . . .": Red Auerbach interview.

18 he landed a $13,000 salary: Jack Cavanaugh, "The Celtics' Music Man," *Sports Illustrated* (March 23, 1992): 88–89.

18 He played "Granada" and "Lady of Spain": *New York Times* (January 13, 1998).

19 Future president John Adams spent several years: *Telegram & Gazette* (June 30, 1985).

19 And on July 14, 1776, Isaiah Thomas, editor: *Telegram & Gazette* (January 22, 1899).

19 "He arrived with a reputation . . .": George Kaftan interview.

19 "I saw the greatest basketball player . . .": Dave Anderson interview.

19 "One night he asked me if I would write . . .": Bill Reynolds, *Cousy: His Life, Career, and the Birth of Big-Time Basketball* (New York: Simon & Schuster, 2005), 75.

20 "Cousy is not a man to make friends easily . . .": Al Hirshberg, "Cousy Shoots Like Crazy," *Sport* (March 1953): 83.

20 "Our new coach is a very good man . . .": Bob Cousy to Missie Ritterbusch, Worcester, MA, September 1948. Bob Cousy personal papers.

20 Cousy took classes entitled Logic, The Sacraments: *The College of the Holy Cross Catalogue*, February 1947 (Volume XXXXIV) and April 1950 (Volume XXXXVI).

21 "It made me feel like I was fourteen again . . .": Missie Ritterbusch to Bob Cousy, St. Albans, NY, September 1947. Bob Cousy personal papers.

21 Honest to goodness Miss . . .: Bob Cousy to Missie Ritterbusch, Worcester, MA, September 30, 1947. Bob Cousy personal papers.

21 "It's funny every time I have anything . . .": Bob Cousy to Missie Ritterbusch, Worcester, MA, October 18, 1948. Bob Cousy personal papers.

22 "I suppose it's good in a way . . .": Bob Cousy to Missie Ritterbusch, Worcester, MA, September 1948. Bob Cousy personal papers.

22 "To Holy Cross games in Boston . . .": *Boston Post* (January 25, 1950).

23 "They're overplaying your right side . . .": Dave Anderson, "Hands Behind His Back," *Sports Illustrated* (February 13, 1961): E-7.

23 They stalled, shuttling the ball out near midcourt: *Daily Record, Boston Herald, Boston Globe* (January 12, 1949).

24 "The atomic, chain-reaction explosion . . .": *Boston Herald* (January 12, 1949).

24 "He's done something like it in practice . . .": Anderson, *Sports Illustrated* (February 13, 1961): E-8.

24 "I was on my way out to strangle him": Ibid.

24 Adolph Rupp, the noted Kentucky coach, wrote back: *Boston Globe* (January 13, 1949).

25 "This boy was made for basketball . . .": Lester Sheary, "The Bob Cousy I Know," *Tribute to Mr. Basketball*, testimonial program, Worcester Auditorium, Worcester, MA, April 27–28, 1963, 1, 13.

25 "You want to learn fast?": Rev. Earle Markey interview.

26 "You had to be careful what you said . . .": George Kaftan interview.

27 "How'd you like that, young white boy?": Gary M. Pomerantz, *WILT, 1962* (New York: Crown Publishers, 2005), 44–45.

27 "Approximately one month from tonight . . .": *World Series of Basketball 1950 National Tour, College All-Americans vs. Harlem Globetrotters*, official souvenir program, 14.

CHAPTER 4

30 occasionally even loaned them money: Phil Elderkin interview.

30 "You guys are my friends . . .": *Boston Herald* (March 23, 1980).

31 "Boston is my town . . .": Cousy as told to Hirshberg, *Basketball Is My Life*, 130.

31 Cohen sized him up quickly: *Boston Herald* (October 8, 1980).

31 "Is Walter Brown public enemy . . .": *Boston Globe* (April 28, 1950).

32 "I took care of this. I put you here": Red Auerbach interview.

32 "typical, wise-ass Brooklyn character" from *Thoity-thoid:* Red Auerbach with Joe Fitzgerald, *On & Off the Court* (New York: Macmillan Publishing Company, 1985), 9.

33 How to make a fist: Randy Auerbach interview.

33 "You can't shit an old shitter . . .": Togo Palazzi interview.

33 "When a man has the ball watch his hips . . .": Gilbert Rogin, "They All Boo When Red Sits Down," *Sports Illustrated* (October 5, 1965): 112.

33 "Meet Red Auerbach . . .": *Boston Traveler* (April 27, 1950).

33 "I don't give a darn for sentiment . . .": *Boston Globe* (April 28, 1950).

33 "I'd love to have Cousy . . .": *Boston Globe* (April 28, 1950).

33 "If there was an open draft in the professional league . . .": Ibid.

34 "He still has to learn what to do . . .": Ibid.

34 "Owning a player who won't sign . . .": *Boston Traveler* (April 27, 1950).

35 "Whoever you draw . . .": Bob Cousy with Ed Linn, *The Last Loud Roar* (Englewood Cliffs, NJ: Prentice-Hall, Inc., 1964), 132.

35 "I figured I'd got the dirty end . . .": Ed Linn, "The Wonderful Wizard of Boston," *Sport* (January 1960): 59.

35 "monkey business," he called them: Arnold (Red) Auerbach as told to Al Hirshberg, "How I Handle the Boston Celtics," *Saturday Evening Post* (December 16, 1961): 92–95.

35 "He's going to be one of the great ones": Howie McHugh, "The Hand Is Quicker Than the Eye," Bob Cousy Day program, Boston Garden (March 17, 1963), 7.

37 She wore black to the wedding: Marie Cousy interview.

37 *Oh my God, his mother is the crazy French woman!*: Ibid.

37 Brown had given Cousy twenty-five tickets: Cousy as told to Hirshberg, *Basketball Is My Life*, 117.

38 "Garbo dating George Schlee . . . Ex-Holy Cross . . .": Ed Sullivan, *Daily News* (New York), undated, Bob Cousy personal scrapbook.

NOTES

CHAPTER 5

39 "Every time a pass is dropped . . .": Auerbach as told to Hirshberg, *Saturday Evening Post* (December 16, 1961), 92–95.

39 "His receivers are highly-coordinated . . .": Linn, *Sport* (January 1960): 60.

39 "After a man has played with me . . .": Ibid.

40 The Pistons took just thirteen shots: Pomerantz, *WILT, 1962*, 32.

40 Fans threw pennies, oranges, and a shoe: Ibid.

40 "like atomic energy that hasn't been controlled": Linn, *Sport* (January 1960): 60.

41 As Beard reached for the ball, Cousy took it: Dave Anderson interview.

41 "The only kick I have with Cousy . . .": Wind, *Sports Illustrated* (January 16, 1956): 57.

41 "Do you realize that Cooper is a Negro?": *Daily Record* (April 28, 1950).

42 "Thus another invisible barrier crumbled . . .": Ibid.

42 threatened that his Globetrotters wouldn't play: Ron Thomas, *They Cleared the Lane: The NBA's Black Pioneers* (Lincoln: University of Nebraska Press, 1992), 27.

42 "Go back to Africa!": *New York Times* (February 27, 2015).

42 "He's a different kind of person . . .": Patsy Ann (Pat) Ware interview. Ware was Cooper's first wife.

42 Jackie Robinson once thanked a white teammate: *New York Times* (May 29, 2016).

43 "You know he looks one way, feints . . .": Dave Anderson, "Final Whistle," *Saturday Evening Post* (March 16, 1963): 34.

43 "Cousy made it work with a speed and fluency": Herbert Warren Wind, "The Sporting Scene: Farewell to Cousy," *New Yorker* (March 23, 1963): 150.

44 a Hawks player called Cooper a "black bastard": George Sullivan, *The Picture History of the Boston Celtics* (Indianapolis: The Bobbs-Merrill Company, Inc., 1981), 161. Also: *Globe* (February 18, 1952).

45 It wasn't until Cooper saw the photos: Sullivan, *The Picture History of the Boston Celtics*, 161–62.

46 "Hitler persecuted the Jews . . .": Cousy as told to Hirshberg, *Basketball Is My Life*, 189.

46 "I had great respect for his attitudes . . .": Sullivan, *The Picture History of the Boston Celtics*, 161–62.

46 "the highest kind of individual . . .": Ibid.

48 "You can't do that . . .": *Boston Globe* (December 14, 1959).

48 They asked him to come to the DA's office: Cousy with Linn, *The Last Loud Roar*, 100–105.

49 "Will you go to Cousy and ask him . . .": *Boston Globe* (September 13, 1967).

49 Players called him Poison Pen: Frank Deford, "Lots of Fun with a Poison Pen," *Sports Illustrated* (October 3, 1966): 57.

49 "Are you involved in any way?": *Boston Globe* (September 13, 1967).

49 "Mr. Brown, I've never in my life . . .": Cousy with Linn, *The Last Loud Roar*, 98–99. Also: Hirshberg, "Cousy Shoots Like Crazy," 30.

49 He told investigators that he took a total of $1,300: Dave Kindred, *Basketball: The Dream Game in Kentucky* (Louisville: Data Courier, Inc., 1976), 108.

50 "If I so much as touched a basketball . . .": Ibid., 109.

50 Even as Cousy insisted he didn't know the bookie: Cousy with Linn, *The Last Loud Roar*, 100–105.

50 Soon, Beard was in Louisville, bouncing from job: Kindred, *Basketball*, 111.

CHAPTER 6

52 "Now Cousy is Target for Tonight every night . . .": *Boston Globe* (February 12, 1953).

53 "the greatest one-man show . . .": *Boston Globe* (March 22, 1953).

53 publicity man, McHugh, overcome by headaches: Ibid.

53 "he could have done anything": Ibid.

54 "The Celtics have won their way to a high place . . .": *Daily Record* (March 21, 1953).

54 "He'd call up at ten o'clock in the morning . . .": Bill McSweeny interview.

54 "Wouldn't you like to be able to write . . .": Ibid.

54 "They tore the rafters from the Garden roof . . .": *Daily Record* (March 22, 1953).

55 "Get out or I'll call the cops": *Boston Globe* (December 8, 1953).

55 "There goes Auerbach out of the place!": Ibid.

56 "There may be some spilled": *Boston Globe* (December 12, 1953).

56 "You did it, you sonovabitch": Auerbach and Sann, *Winning the Hard Way*, 146–47.

57 But as he wound up, Cousy let the ball roll: Herbert Warren Wind, "Bob Cousy: Basketball's Creative Genius," *Sports Illustrated* (January 9, 1956): 43–44.

58 "but they were overpaid for what it brought in . . .": Linn, *Sport* (January 1960): 54.

59 "We've got to stabilize so we can command respect . . .": Hirshberg, *Sport* (March 1963): 21.

60 "Why do you think?": Cousy as told to Hirshberg, *Basketball Is My Life*, 160.

60 In January 1955, he delivered five demands: Ibid., 163–64.

60 He told Gottlieb he was ten dollars short: Gene Shue interview.

60 Hurley was a former minor league baseball player: Cornelius (Con) Hurley Jr. interview.

61 "more soap in the shower room . . .": Gene Conley interview.

61 "I don't think I've ever received a greater thrill . . .": Cousy as told to Hirshberg, *Basketball Is My Life*, 173–74.

CHAPTER 7

62 "A boo is a boo": Gilbert Rogin, "They All Boo When Red Sits Down," *Sports Illustrated* (April 5, 1965): 102.

63 **silver box on which they engraved "Houdini, 1954":** SportsCards Plus catalogue, Telephone/Internet Auction, Collections of Bob Cousy, Honus Wagner, Tony Lazzeri, November 20, 2003, 11. This sterling silver box is shown as an auction item.

63 **suggested he write about Brannum instead:** Bill Scheft interview. Scheft's uncle, writer Herbert Warren Wind, related this anecdote to him.

64 **"People had a tendency to rate us as ruffians . . .":** *Boston Globe* (October 19, 1965).

64 **"Grabbing or pulling the pants or shirt . . .":** Arnold "Red" Auerbach, *Basketball for the Player, the Fan and the Coach* (New York: Pocket Books, Inc., 1953): 187.

65 **"This kid is as smart as hell . . .":** Red Auerbach interview, 2002.

65 **Newell said Russell moved laterally in a wide arc:** Pete Newell interviews, 2002 and 2004. Also: Pomerantz, *WILT, 1962*, 126.

65 **"This kid can't shoot to save his ass":** Auerbach and Sann, *Winning the Hard Way*, 88.

65 **heard Auerbach making phone calls to the West:** *Boston Herald* (October 8, 1980).

66 **"the greatest array of U.S. sports stars ever . . .":** "The Wonderful World of Sport," *Sports Illustrated* (July 25, 1955): 27.

66 **"You all look bigger on television . . .":** Goudsouzian, *King of the Court*, 55.

67 **"He's full of shit":** *Boston Herald* (October 8, 1980).

CHAPTER 8

72 **"I'll write you a basketball column . . .":** Red Auerbach interview.

73 **Yankees reportedly put up more than $400,000:** Robert Creamer, *Babe: The Legend Comes to Life* (New York: Fireside, 1992): 207–10.

73 **"Those are the only friends that son of a bitch has":** Ibid., 212.

74 **"a well-spoken young man of twenty-one . . .":** *New York Times* (December 22, 1953).

75 **Russell was said to be seeking $25,000:** Goudsouzian, *King of the Court*, 63–65.

76 **Auerbach and Brown secretly met at Boston Garden:** *Boston Globe* (April 30, 1956).

76 **"A shrewd maneuver":** Ibid.

76 **"shocking the basketball world":** *Boston Evening American* (May 1, 1956).

76 *I'm a dead pigeon:* George Plimpton, "Sportsman of the Year: Bill Russell," *Sports Illustrated* (December 23, 1968): 43.

76 **"I am much better than that":** Bill Russell with Alan Steinberg, *Red and Me: My Coach, My Lifelong Friend* (New York: HarperCollins, 2009), 33.

77 **At the San Francisco airport, reporters saw him kiss:** Goudsouzian, *King of the Court*, 63.

77 **"How do you do, Mr. Cousy?":** Ibid., 74.

77 **Sharman was impressed:** *Boston Traveler* (December 21, 1956).

77 **"The Photo Boston Waited to See":** *Boston Traveler* (December 23, 1956).

77 "Sensational! Gigantic! Can't Miss!": *Boston Evening American* (December 21, 1956).

77 "The Celtics have acquired their dream . . .": *Boston Evening American* (December 22, 1956).

77 "has had the biggest buildup since one stone . . .": *Boston Herald* (December 22, 1956).

77 "You don't know what they'll do": Bill Russell interview with Taylor Branch, Civil Rights History Project, Southern Oral History Program, Smithsonian Institution's National Museum of African-American History & Culture, Library of Congress, May 13, 2013, transcript p. 8, https://www.loc.gov /item/afc2010039_crhp0088/.

78 "A man has to draw a line inside himself . . .": Russell with Steinberg, *Red and Me*, 6.

78 "Some people call it instinct . . .": Ibid., 19.

78 "I found out that in order . . .": Russell interview with Branch, transcript p. 19.

79 "You don't think I'd give anybody as much . . .": *Boston Globe* (December 20, 1956).

79 He had been a newsboy, hawking newspapers: Bill McSweeny interview.

79 Now, over lunch, Russell ordered a martini: Ibid.

80 "He must learn to fit in with the fast breaking . . .": *Daily Record* (December 22, 1956).

80 *They dumped Ed Macauley to get:* Cornelius (Con) Hurley Jr. interview.

80 "Ed, be careful!": Linn, *Sport* (January 1960): 56.

80 "A one-in-a-thousand pass": *Boston Globe* (December 24, 1956).

81 "two plays you couldn't condone if a rookie . . .": Ibid.

81 "Never saw the Boston fans so steamed up": *Boston Herald* (December 23, 1956).

CHAPTER 9

82 "Sharman would've cold-cocked him . . .": Tom Heinsohn interview.

82 Auerbach usually fell asleep ten minutes: Ibid.

83 "bribe some high school kids to drive us": Heinsohn and Fitzgerald, *Give 'Em the Hook*, 56–57.

83 "Who the hell let the broads in here?": Diane Heinsohn interview.

84 "One of *your* friends?": Ibid.

84 She wrote to Harold Stassen, director: Cousy as told to Hirshberg, *Basketball Is My Life*, 202.

84 Cousy challenged Heinsohn in Labyrinth: Tom Heinsohn interview.

85 He bolted outside into the darkness: Cousy as told to Hirshberg, *Basketball Is My Life*, 179–81.

85 "See that, rookie?": *Boston American* (March 11, 1963).

86 "They took so much out of themselves": Tom Heinsohn interview.

86 *They'd kill their mothers:* Ibid.

86 "After they take a shot and you rebound . . .": Russell with Steinberg, *Red and Me*, 129–30.

86 Russell later estimated that about one third: Ibid.

87 "Don't talk too soon": Willie Naulls interview.

87 "He didn't seem to want to hit anyone . . .": Plimpton, *Sports Illustrated* (December 23, 1968): 43.

87 "I'm not afraid of any man in this league . . .": *Boston Globe* (January 21, 1957).

87 "He destroyed him . . .": Plimpton, *Sports Illustrated* (December 23, 1968): 43.

87 "It's come to a point where you sit . . .": *Boston Globe* (January 21, 1957).

87 "Take that finger off me or I'll tear it off . . .": Auerbach and Sann, *Winning the Hard Way*, 203.

87 "The writers began forming their own fan clubs . . .": Auerbach with Fitzgerald, *On & Off the Court*, 154–55.

88 "It hurt Bill Russell": Auerbach and Sann, *Winning the Hard Way*, 205.

88 noticed immediately how much it had improved: Frank Ramsey interview.

88 "I naturally had been reading about him . . .": *Boston Globe* (March 26, 1957).

89 called Auerbach a "bush-leaguer": *Boston Globe* (April 7, 1957).

89 "You can coach that team of yours . . .": *Boston Herald* (January 2, 1985).

90 "Russell went by me like I was standing still": Tom Heinsohn interview.

90 "I don't know how he could've stopped it": *Boston Globe* (March 26, 1957).

90 "Did that just happen?": Bill McSweeny interview.

90 "Who has got a razor?": *Boston Globe* (April 14, 1957).

91 "Want to be my agent?": Ibid.

91 this was the moment that basketball was made . . .": Bill McSweeny interview.

92 "You ought to give me half of that": Tom Heinsohn interview.

92 CELTS CINCH TO REPEAT: *Daily Record* (April 16, 1957).

CHAPTER 10

93 Several times Warriors coach George Senesky benched: *Boston Globe* (March 24, 1958).

94 Russell blocked a shot by Pettit, landed on Pettit's foot: *Boston Globe* (April 3, 1958). Also: Bill Russell as told to William McSweeny, *Go Up for Glory* (New York: Coward, McCann & Geoghegan, Inc., 1966), 133–34.

94 He spent the next three days on crutches: Goudsouzian, *King of the Court*, 92.

94 Auerbach ordered Cousy to slow down the fast break: *Boston Globe* (April 6, 1958).

94 "There will be other seasons, Russ": Russell, as told to McSweeny, *Go Up for Glory*: 133–34.

94 said that this title validated his decision to trade Russell: *Boston Globe* (April 14, 1958). Also: Goudsouzian, *King of the Court*, 93.

94 Cousy lost his stoic façade: Robert Rice, "Profiles: A Victim of Noblesse Oblige," *New Yorker* (February 4, 1961): 42–44.

95 he didn't feel the inner rage that had always driven him: Ibid.

95 He brought the ball upcourt and called a nonexistent: Russell and Branch, *Second Wind*, 150.

98 In March 1957, all 244 public high: *Boston Globe* (March 24, 1957).

98 "The player boys most wanted to emulate . . .": *Boston Globe* (March 10, 1957).

98 the Knicks' Richie Guerin as a Pinkerton detective: Richie Guerin interview.

98 *May through July (State Department trip*: *Daily Record* (February 3, 1957).

99 "Cousy has a hard time generating a feud . . .": Al Hirshberg, "A Visit with Bob Cousy," *Saturday Evening Post* (December 12, 1959): 92.

100 He studied a dictionary and tried to learn five new: Rice, *New Yorker* (February 4, 1961): 44.

100 Cooz meeting in the locker room with a blind teen: *Boston Globe* (March 14, 1955).

100 "Mrs. Cousy Talks of Her Bob": *Boston Globe* (March 2, 1958).

100 "He isn't an overly talkative person . . .": Ibid.

100 "as beautiful as any ballet movement": *Boston Globe* (September 9, 1962).

101 stories of Russian coaches asking to see movies: Linn, *Sport* (January 1960): 55.

101 "greater now than he ever was": *Sporting News* (February 25, 1959).

101 "Cousy is having his finest year in pro ball . . .": *Boston Globe* (February 17, 1959).

102 "The worst fans in the league": *Boston Globe* (January 21, 1959).

102 "I hope Boston fans give them a taste": *Boston Globe* (January 29, 1959).

102 "Red, you are driving too fast!": Gene Conley interview.

103 "Covering Cousy's dribble for nine years . . .": *Sporting News* (February 25, 1959).

103 "the greatest team ever assembled": Jeremiah Tax, "Short, Sweet Series for Slick Celtics," *Sports Illustrated* (April 20, 1959): 66.

103 "They could lose Mickey Mantle . . .": *Boston Globe* (January 6, 1959).

103 "professional basketball in Boston was on trial": *Boston Record American* (March 12, 1963).

103 "Cousy on his knees . . . the Garden in tumult . . .": *Boston Record American* (March 11, 1963).

104 There he was playing with almost blind eyes: William McSweeny, "Bob's Biggest Moment," Bob Cousy Day program, Boston Garden, March 17, 1963: 3, 32.

104 Cousy looked forward to a brief beach vacation: Tax, *Sports Illustrated* (April 20, 1959): 66.

CHAPTER 11

106 To Sunday afternoon games, she sometimes brought: Marie Cousy interview.

107 "We were appendages of the players": Lynn Leon Loscutoff, *Loscy & Me: The Artist & the Boston Celtics Legend, Jim Loscutoff, a Scrapbook Memoir* (CreateSpace Independent Publishing Platform, 2014): 43.

107 "Jesus Christ, is that a new hat . . .": Diane Heinsohn interview.

107 "Listen, Red, if you planned your schedule . . .": Ibid.

107 If Red flicks cigar ashes on your jacket: Dan Shaughnessy, *Seeing Red: The Red Auerbach Story* (New York: Crown Publishers, Inc., 1994), 15.

108 "Bill Russell refused to let Rose . . .": Diane Heinsohn interview.

108 a small steak, small salad, and baked potato: Jerry Sharman interview.

108 "These are all Jean's!": Diane Heinsohn interview.

108 Missie accidently burned the man sitting in front: Ibid.

109 He called young Jerry Sharman "Bullseye Junior": Jerry Sharman interview.

109 "Hey, lil' Cooz!": Marie Cousy interview.

CHAPTER 12

110 Cousy was among his honorary pallbearers: Leigh Montville, *Ted Williams: The Biography of an American Hero* (New York: Doubleday, 2004), 215.

111 a "hero worshipper, a romanticist": Jerome Holtzman, *No Cheering in the Press Box* (New York: Holt, Rinehart and Winston, 1973), 125.

111 "Basketball is for the birds . . .": Shirley Povich, "Basketball Is for the Birds?," *Sports Illustrated* (December 8, 1958): 24.

111 "If Mr. Povich ever elects to attend a game . . .": Bill Mokray, "Letters to the Editor: A Game for the Birds?," *Sports Illustrated* (December 22, 1958), 115.

111 "That's not a gripe . . .": *Boston Globe* (December 23, 1958).

112 "It isn't the game itself so much . . .": Hirshberg, *Saturday Evening Post* (December 12, 1959), 30.

112 by his measure the third-tier basketball assignment: Leonard Koppett interview, 2002.

112 "Think this sport will ever be big league?": Leonard Koppett, "Does Pro Basketball Have a Future?," *Saturday Evening Post* (December 6, 1958), 36.

112 1. Refereeing; 2. Scheduling; and 3. Packaging: Ibid., 81.

113 "The owners claim they have 'a million dollars' worth . . .": Ibid., 82.

113 competed against black players who threw no-look passes: Lenny Wilkens interview.

114 "What are you trembling for?": Goudsouzian, *King of the Court*, 102.

CHAPTER 13

115 "Chamberlain will score about a hundred thirty . . .": Jimmy Breslin, "Can Basketball Survive Chamberlain?," *Saturday Evening Post* (December 1, 1956): 106.

115 "the most perfect instrument ever made by God . . .": Pomerantz, *WILT, 1962*, xviii.

116 "a first sight of the New York skyline": Ibid.

116 "dominated the game as he has so often done . . .": Jeremiah Tax, "The Tall Ones in Boston," *Sports Illustrated* (November 16, 1959), 28.

116 "What the duel proved, chiefly . . .": Ibid.

117 "The Celtics are unique, awe-inspiring . . .": *New York Post* (January 4, 1960).

117 "[They] put out just what they've got . . .": Ibid.

117 "He sees things before anybody else ever sees them . . .": *New York Post* (February 5, 1960).

117 "I can still hear that damn noise": Joe Ruklick interview.

118 "Wilt, bring your fuckin' lunch!": Tom Heinsohn interview.

118 "I'm completely exhausted": *Boston Globe* (April 5, 1960).

118 "Heck, I died a thousand times a game . . .": *Boston Globe* (April 6, 1960).

118 "Will you all look at Russell's little pinky?": Goudsouzian, *King of the Court*, 109.

119 "I've won all these titles . . .": Ibid., 110.

119 "it would reflect on me and then indirectly . . .": *New York Times* (March 28, 1960).

119 "In my ten years in the NBA, I never saw . . .": *New York Times* (March 27, 1960).

119 "Maybe if Bill Russell said it . . .": *Philadelphia Evening Bulletin* (March 29, 1960).

119 "the loneliest town in the world": Russell, as told to McSweeny, *Go Up for Glory*, 121.

119 "BABOON! BLACK GORILLA! NIGGER!": Ibid., 122.

120 "a big lean copper spring . . . his nostrils like . . .": David Halberstam, ed., *The Best American Sports Writing of the Century* (Boston: Houghton Mifflin Company, 1999), 138–39. Bob Considine wrote this column for the International News Service on June 22, 1938.

120 "the more they questioned, the more I dug . . .": Bill Russell interview with Taylor Branch, May 13, 2013, transcript p. 41.

120 Russell believed they didn't come to him because he was black: *Boston Herald* (March 6, 1977).

120 He drove Green around Boston, showing him: Howard Bryant, *Shut Out: A Story of Race and Baseball in Boston* (Boston: Beacon Press, 2002), 54–55.

121 "To sit there and hear Russ expound . . .": Nate Thurmond interview.

121 he eyed women in the interracial crowd and gauged: Pomerantz, *WILT, 1962*, 16–17.

121 A year later, he bought a rubber plantation: *Boston Globe* (November 20, 1960).

121 "I'm a Negro, but I'm no causist . . .": Ibid.

122 "He had his agenda and I had mine": Tom Gola interview, 2002.

122 "Practicing our offense—throw the ball to Wilt . . .": Ibid.

122 "Okay, Momma. See you soon . . .": Russell as told to McSweeny, *Go Up for Glory*, 56–57.

123 "the queen of streetwise . . . black, with light copper skin . . .": Russell and Branch, *Second Wind*, 249.

123 Angry that Russell had been eyeing another woman: Ibid., 252–53.

123 A doctor treated his wound and agreed to tell: Ibid., 255–56.

123 "a tall, stately brunette, with green eyes . . .": Ibid., 258.

124 "They can't *see* it . . .": Tom Heinsohn interview.

124 "It was always Cousy made . . .": Bill McSweeny interview.

125 took a subway to Columbia University to hear a lecture: Ibid.

125 "seventy-thirty: seventy [percent] acceptable . . .": Ibid.

126 "like a hyena in full throat . . .": *Boston Herald* (June 17, 1973).

126 "You know, they think that every time a colored . . .": Jeremiah Tax, "The Man Who Must Be Different," *Sports Illustrated* (February 3, 1958): 29.

126 "distant, cold and oppressive": Russell and Branch, *Second Wind*, 263.

126 "at least some whites got the blues, were irreverent . . .": Ibid.

126 originally he smoked Robert Burns: Shaughnessy, *Seeing Red*, 132.

126 "Why run [onto the court] when you're going to run . . .": *Boston Globe* (February 2, 1965).

127 "I'm a Jew": Russell with Steinberg, *Red and Me*, 71.

127 From out of the smoky darkness he heard: Cousy and Linn, *The Last Loud Roar*, 187.

128 "For Christ's sake, it takes you ten seconds . . .": Tom Heinsohn interview.

128 "This was about him as an individual": Ibid.

128 "that his color didn't mean a damn thing . . .": Auerbach with Fitzgerald, *On & Off the Court*, 213.

128 "I want to scream bloody murder . . .": Russell with Steinberg, *Red and Me*, 142.

128 "The real Russell is a very difficult man . . .": *Boston Herald* (June 17, 1973).

128 "You know why he's the greatest?": Tax, *Sports Illustrated* (February 3, 1958): 31.

129 "What has Russell meant to us?": Linn, *Sport* (January 1960): 57.

129 "There is no doubt that Cousy saved basketball in Boston": Ibid., 55.

130 then Keane shoved him: Bill McSweeny interview.

130 "I've got to see this guy play": Ibid.

130 "other than myself . . .": Ibid.

CHAPTER 14

132 "You could step into that room . . .": Bill McSweeny interview.

133 earned him the neighborhood nickname "Satch": Tom (Satch) Sanders interview.

133 "Not so rough, Satch": Ibid.

133 "Hey, kid. Don't worry": Ibid.

134 "He cursed me out in French": Ibid.

134 They found that Cousy's adrenal glands produced: Rice, *New Yorker* (February 4, 1961): 40–42.

134 "Because we are talking about visual cues . . .": Jocelyn Faubert interview.

135 "No. Hell, no! Certainly not!": Plimpton, *Sports Illustrated* (December 23, 1968): 43.

135 "Satch, you like Frank, doncha?": Tom (Satch) Sanders interview.

135 "Whatever you do, don't open Frank's trunk . . .": Ibid.

136 "Why don't you come down and spend a week . . .": Bill Russell interview with Taylor Branch, May 13, 2013, transcript p. 26.

136 *He's just a man of many ideas*: Gene Conley interview.

136 "What'd I do wrong this time, Red?": Tom Heinsohn interview.

136 "Red! He's late!!!": Tom (Satch) Sanders interview.

136 "A pain in the ass": Ibid.

137 Russell likened Auerbach to the leeches: Russell and Branch, *Second Wind*, 157.

137 K.C. Jones habitually broke into song: Gene Guarilia interview.

137 actresses Sophia Loren and Angie Dickinson: Ibid.

137 Missie Cousy got her a choice seat: Tom (Satch) Sanders interview.

138 "That Ramsey has an angelic look . . .": *Boston Celtics Yearbook, 1962–63*, edited by Bill Mokray.

138 "On another team who would be pissed off?": K.C. Jones interview, 2003.

139 He had been taught years before to aim for a rivet: *Boston Celtics Yearbook, 1962–63*, edited by Bill Mokray.

139 stunned forward Cal Ramsey by throwing a bounce pass: Cal Ramsey interview.

139 "How can you make a call like that?": Lenny Wilkens interview.

139 "Officials deserved combat pay for working": Terry Pluto, *Tall Tales: The Glory Years of the NBA, in the Words of the Men Who Played, Coached and Built Pro Basketball* (New York: Simon & Schuster, 1992), 36.

140 "There's my boy . . .": *Boston Globe* (April 12, 1961).

140 "He beat us tonight . . .": Ibid.

140 "The N.B.A. publicity has been stupid . . .": *Boston Globe* (March 12, 1961).

140 "Statistics. What do they prove?": Ibid.

CHAPTER 15

141 "Who is going to finish second?": Ray Scott interview.

142 he must carry himself as a gentleman at all times: Ibid.

142 "What Russell talked about primarily was respect": Ibid.

142 in Marion, Indiana, a restaurant had refused service: *Boston Record American* (October 18, 1961).

142 the two Celtics were told they would not be served: *Boston Traveler* (October 18, 1961).

142 "Let's think about it awhile . . .": *Boston Herald* (October 18, 1961).

143 "Why not go out there": Auerbach and Sann, *Winning the Hard Way*, 122.

143 Auerbach insisted the Celtics had a contract: *Boston Globe* (October 18, 1961).

143 "I wouldn't have played it": Ibid., 123.

143 "I don't blame them a bit [for leaving]": *Boston Record American* (October 18, 1961).

143 "I was one hundred percent behind Bill Russell . . .": *Boston Globe* (October 18, 1961).

143 "All Sam and Tom wanted to do . . .": *Boston Herald* (October 18, 1961).

144 "If they don't think about themselves . . .": Cousy and Linn, *The Last Loud Roar*, 98–99.

144 "The Big Fella finally did it": Pomerantz, *WILT, 1962*, 189.

144 "The Celtics are the aristocrats of basketball . . .": *Los Angeles Times* (February 5, 1962).

144 Dressed in a white T-shirt and underwear: *Daily Record* (February 8, 1962).

144 WHAT A WAY TO WAKE UP: Ibid.

145 NBA games had slipped to 4.8 (roughly nine million viewers): William Leggett, "Growing to Greatness," *Sports Illustrated* (October 29, 1962): 41.

145 "It's not like a Russell would be leaving": *New York Post* (February 13, 1962).

145 "I guess you'll be seeing me running up and down . . .": *Boston Globe* (March 22, 1962).

146 "Bill looked like a big bird, arms in the air . . .": Tom Meschery interview.

146 "You should go kiss Red Auerbach's ass . . .": John Havlicek interview.

146 Guy Rodgers threw a punch: Pomerantz, *WILT, 1962*, 201.

146 *What have I gotten myself into?*: John Havlicek interview.

147 "No, they will go to Sam Jones . . .": Tom Meschery interview.

147 "See if you can step in front of him . . .": Gene Guarilia interview.

148 "like descending into the catacombs of hell": Jerry West and Jonathan Coleman, *West by West: My Charmed, Tormented Life* (New York: Little, Brown and Company, 2011), 100.

148 "That's okay, boys, we'll get 'em on Tuesday!": Ibid.

148 In Hollywood across the decades he had shot Gable, Garbo: Nancy D. Lackey Shaffer, "Frame of Reference," *Ventana Monthly Magazine*, January 2016, www.ventanamonthly.com.

149 he was part of the first generation of Russells born free: Frank Deford, "The Ring Leader: Bill Russell Helped the Celtics Rule Their Sport Like No Team Ever Has," *Sports Illustrated* (May 10, 1999): 107.

149 Jake Russell had raised money among impoverished blacks: Ibid.

150 "I never thought I'd see anything like that": Ibid.

150 "I MUST HAVE MY MANHOOD": Russell as told to McSweeny, *Go Up for Glory*, 136–37.

150 "Daddy, can't we stop?": Ibid.

CHAPTER 16

154 He struck a deal with the Gillette Razor Company: Wind, *New Yorker* (March 23, 1963): 160.

154 someone accidentally brushed against little Ticia: Ticia Cousy interview.

154 Missie filled two plastic jugs with holy water: Marie Cousy interview.

155 "but it will take me two or three days to find . . .": Pascal Legendre, "The Frenchman from the Celtics," *Basket Hebdo*, No. 99, July 23, 2015. Legendre cites a story by journalist Louis Laeyre in *L'Équipe* on May 2, 1962.

155 "I think they are a little delayed in their physical . . .": Ibid.

155 Ticia pretended to be a little girl from a French family: Ticia Cousy interview.

156 when they saw a hole in the floor: Ticia Cousy and Marie Cousy interviews.

CHAPTER 17

157 "Who'd you punch?": John Havlicek interview.

158 "Sauerback crybaby!" and kicked the Celtics: *Boston Globe* (December 3, 1962).

158 aggrieved fan holding a handkerchief: Auerbach and Sann, *Winning the Hard Way*, 176–77.

158 Auerbach would pay $250: Ibid.

158 A nerve was jumping beneath: Cousy with Linn, *The Last Loud Roar*, 54.

159 pressure from an FBI man who quietly pulled him: *Boston Globe* (September 9, 1967).

159 He considered himself a high-strung man: *Boston Record American* (March 11, 1963).

159 "For thirteen years, I've seen Cousy drive . . .": *Boston Globe* (February 7, 1963).

160 "He was uncanny in that way": John Havlicek interview.

160 on a phonograph played songs from Broadway: Ticia Cousy and Marie Cousy interviews.

160 she tried to keep him vibrant and present: Ibid.

160 Cousy felt like a soldier in combat: *Boston Record American* (March 11, 1963).

161 an Allen Drury novel; Theodore H. White's *The Making*: Wind, *New Yorker* (March 23, 1963): 164. Also: Cousy with Linn, *The Last Loud Roar*, 68.

161 Cousy would run a hot bath in his hotel: Cousy with Linn, *The Last Loud Roar*, 56–58.

161 Once they created a list of fifty jobs: Bill Sharman as told to Phil Elderkin, "It Wasn't Going to Happen to Us!" Bob Cousy Day program, Boston Garden (March 17, 1963): 37–38.

162 would make only $12,000 as a college coach: *Boston Globe* (February 3, 1966).

162 he even offered to return his endorsement money: Cousy and Linn, *The Last Loud Roar*, 154–55.

163 "It was a good thing this trip . . .": Wind, *New Yorker* (March 23, 1963): 161.

164 "My partner wants to call it 'Bob Cousy's Abner . . .": Ibid., 165–66.

164 "He has made his farewell season a suitably": Ibid.

164 "great basketball dynasty is abuilding": William Leggett, "Growing to Greatness," *Sports Illustrated* (October 29, 1962): 36.

164 "The Lakers aren't the champions of anything": William Leggett, "Basketball at Its Toughest," *Sports Illustrated* (February 25, 1963): 15.

164 "I respect Auerbach as a coach": Ibid.

165 "Oh, great and noble, bearded one . . .": Ibid., 14.

165 "This is the kind of victory I could savor . . .": Ibid.

CHAPTER 18

166 "We think that the president is a fine man . . .": Arnold Rampersad, *Jackie Robinson: A Biography* (New York: Alfred A. Knopf, 1997): 362–63.

166 "The details and symbols of your life . . .": James Baldwin, *The Fire Next Time* (New York: Vintage International, 1993), 8.

167 **Russell, with a DO NOT DISTURB request:** Tom Heinsohn interview.

167 **spotted First Lady Jacqueline Kennedy:** Frank Ramsey interview.

168 **"If it ever gets in the newspaper . . .":** Francis X. Dooley Oral History Interview—JFK #1, interviewed by William J. Hartigan, March 9, 1976. transcript: 85–86. John F. Kennedy Presidential Library and Museum, Boston. Dooley was a member of the Office of Emergency Planning.

168 **the players studying the nameplates as they sat:** Frank Ramsey and Tom Heinsohn interviews.

168 **"the only match dropper in the world . . .":** Leggett, *Sports Illustrated* (February 25, 1963): 16.

169 **"for a sober assessment of our failures":** *New York Times* (March 1, 1963).

169 **"The happiness that I had . . .":** Tom (Satch) Sanders interview.

169 **For that they called him "Posture":** Cal Ramsey interview. Ramsey was Sanders's teammate at NYU.

169 **"What time did your wife get home last night?":** Tom (Satch) Sanders interview.

169 **That response shut up several audiences:** Ibid.

170 **Boston's black population had nearly tripled since 1940:** *Boston Globe* (June 2, 1963).

170 **its system suffered from "***de facto*** segregation":** *Boston Globe* (June 18, 1963). Also: J. Anthony Lukas, *Common Ground: A Turbulent Decade in the Lives of Three American Families* (New York: Alfred A. Knopf, 1985), 126.

170 **stage a one-day "Stay Out for Freedom Day" boycott:** *Boston Globe* (June 19, 1963).

170 **"wear your color as a badge":** Ibid.

170 **"You don't have to go to Alabama to find segregation . . .":** *Boston Herald* (May 13, 1963).

171 **"I played for the Celtics, period":** *New York Times* (June 14, 1987).

171 **Russell flew to Jackson where, protected by armed guards:** Charles Evers interview. Also: *Boston Globe* (July 10, 1964, July 13, 1964, July 14, 1964).

171 **He stayed at the same hotel as MLK:** Russell interview with Branch, May 13, 2013, transcript p. 39.

171 **To one civil rights leader, Hicks was "the Bull Connor of Boston":** *Los Angeles Times* (October 23, 2003).

171 **Hicks wore flowered hats, white gloves:** *Boston Globe* (October 22, 1963).

172 **"The Only Mother on the Ballot":** *Boston Globe* (October 27, 2003).

172 **"the greatest fellow that ever walked this earth . . .":** *Boston Globe* (August 6, 1967).

172 **Judge Day raised his family in a handsome three-story:** Lukas, *Common Ground,* 116–17.

172 **"Take care of my people":** Ibid.,118.

172 **"A large part of my vote probably does come from bigoted":** *Boston Globe* (October 22, 2003).

172 "Segregation means to separate or set apart": *Boston Globe* (June 18, 1963).

173 "a magnificent expression of confidence in my candidacy": *Boston Globe* (September 25, 1963).

CHAPTER 19

174 *"If I had to do it all over again . . . "*: *Boston Globe* (March 18, 1963).

174 *"I just would like to say that it has always been . . ."*: Ibid.

175 Yankees owner Ed Barrow decorated the moment: Jonathan Eig, *Luckiest Man: The Life and Death of Lou Gehrig* (New York: Simon & Schuster, 2005), 312.

175 "My God, man, you were never that": Ibid., 315.

176 "For the past two weeks, you've been reading . . .": Ibid., 317.

176 when Cooper visited U.S. naval bases on a South Pacific tour: Glenn Frankel, *High Noon: The Hollywood Blacklist and the Making of an American Classic* (New York: Bloomsbury USA, 2017), 44.

176 "In spite of all the terrible things that have been said . . .": John Updike, "Hub Fans Bid Kid Adieu," *New Yorker* (October 22, 1960): 124.

177 "But immortality is nontransferable . . .": Ibid.

177 "This is going to be a wingding . . .": *Boston Globe* (February 27, 1963).

178 "Now, if we had to go back and pick from that hat . . .": *Boston Record American* (March 15, 1963).

178 "Love from all the Girls on the Row": *Boston Globe* (March 18, 1963).

178 "Actually, it's very important to me . . .": *Christian Science Monitor* (February 13, 1963).

179 "Getting to know Bob Cousy is a rich, rewarding . . .": Ibid.

179 "You don't predicate a thing like this on money": *Boston Record American* (March 11, 1963).

179 "In twenty years of sitting in that place . . .": *Boston Record American* (March 15, 1963).

CHAPTER 20

180 He ate a small breakfast, greeted people: *Boston Record American* (March 18, 1963).

180 "This is going to be a great place to spend Cousy Day . . .": Bill Roeder, "'We Love Ya, Cooz,'" *Newsweek* (April 1, 1963): 50.

181 "Locked in the catacombs": Ibid.

181 "Do you think planes will fly?": *Boston Record American* (March 18, 1963).

181 "What a coach, this Cousy . . .": Ibid.

182 "I hope my nerves don't go": Ibid.

182 blue collar, loyal to his family, a neighborhood guy: Raymond Flynn, Brian Wallace, Brian Dillon interviews. Also: *Boston Globe* (March 20, 1963).

183 "Ladies and gentlemen, Bobby baby": *Boston Globe* (March 18, 1963).

184 "There has only been one Bob Cousy . . .": Bob Cousy Day Celebration video, March 17, 1963, NBA Entertainment archives, Secaucus, NJ.

184 "I know you people here are here to honor Bob . . .": Ibid.

184 "Dear Bob, Your record is an eloquent testimonial . . .": John F. Kennedy letter to Bob Cousy, March 4, 1963, reprinted in Bob Cousy Day program, Boston Garden (March 17, 1963): 19.

185 A few opposing players told Cousy they had nightmares: Cousy and Linn, *The Last Loud Roar*, 95.

185 He sensed that Russell was suspicious of the old breed: Bill McSweeny interview.

186 *I'm supposed to miss those folks?*: Russell with Steinberg, *Red and Me*, 167.

186 "Hey, Red, can I wear number fourteen next year?": *Boston Globe* (March 18, 1963).

186 "I'm the guy that didn't want Bob Cousy": Bob Cousy Day Celebration video, March 17, 1963.

186 "His Celtics are living exponents of the theory . . .": Goudsouzian, *King of the Court*, 164.

186 Brown's widow, Marjorie, would loan Auerbach the good-luck: *Boston Globe* (April 27, 1965).

187 "Bob never said a word . . .": Bob Cousy Day Celebration video, March 17, 1963.

187 "If you'll see my wife, she'll tell you": Tom O'Connor interview.

188 "He didn't say a word": Ticia Cousy interview.

188 suddenly dropped his head on the sportswriter's shoulder: Tom Callahan interview.

189 "Mama, I will be a big man someday": *Boston Globe* (March 18, 1963).

189 "attended by her quiet and dignified husband . . .": *Boston Herald* (March 18, 1963).

189 "It seems difficult to find mere words . . .": Bob Cousy Day Celebration video, March 17, 1963.

191 "An affair like this takes only a few minutes . . .": Ibid.

191 standing ovation that lasted three minutes, twenty seconds: *Boston Globe* (March 18, 1963).

192 "Okay, Cousy, turn in your uniform!": *Boston Herald* (March 18, 1963).

192 HUB'S TEARS STIR COUSY . . .: *Boston Globe* (March 18, 1963).

192 "A tear bath": Ibid.

192 "He acted like a very big man": *Boston Herald (*March 18, 1963).

192 "He now ends his career on the court . . .": *Boston Globe* (March 18, 1963).

192 "exemplar of American youth": *Boston Globe* (March 26, 1963).

193 "The retirement of Cousy and the emotions it evoked . . .": *Boston Globe* (March 19, 1963).

CHAPTER 21

194 They drove fifty miles: *Boston Globe* (March 29, 1964).

195 Suddenly, he pushed McSweeny and started to throw a punch: Bill McSweeny interview.

195 "They just banned Hornung": George Sullivan interview.

195 an act of friendship Hornung would not forget: Paul Hornung interview.

196 He took room-service meals, blocked all calls: Cousy and Linn, *The Last Loud Roar*, 52.

196 "We're a team that has to run . . .": Ibid., 115.

197 "I think I can go": Ibid., 242.

197 "You were a tiger tonight, baby": *Boston Globe* (April 25, 1963).

197 "It must have been old age creeping up . . .": Video of television interview with Bob Cousy and Red Auerbach after Game 6 of the 1963 NBA Finals, Los Angeles Sports Arena, April 24, 1963, https://www.youtube.com/watch?v=VWPCi1YCCZw; sportscaster Bob Wolff conducted the joint interview.

198 "God, it was wonderful!": Ibid.

198 "And as the basketball capital of the world sinks . . .": Cousy and Linn, *The Last Loud Roar*, 267–68.

198 "But Red said you should stay here": Diane Heinsohn interview.

199 "If Bob Cousy were this much less a man . . .": *Boston Globe* (April 27, 1963).

199 "I didn't want to come tonight . . .": Ibid.

200 "I've got to get something special for Cooz . . .": Bill McSweeny interview.

200 They stepped into Shreve, Crump & Low: Ibid.

200 "You better hustle now that you don't have Cousy . . .": *Boston Globe* (November 14, 1963).

201 "He's not here. He's not going to be . . .": Ibid.

CHAPTER 22

206 "I don't regard it as a particularly pretentious house": *Christian Science Monitor* (January 31, 1964).

206 asking the sportswriter to leave them under: Phil Elderkin interview.

208 "I'll do the West Coast funerals . . .": Randy Auerbach interview.

212 Daughter Ticia describes her: Ticia Cousy interview.

214 "Russ says to me, '*You are one of the few* . . .'": Tom Heinsohn interview.

214 *Frank, There are no chasms of time or distance* . . .: Frank Ramsey interview.

CHAPTER 23

217 "You can start only one black player at home . . .": Pomerantz, *WILT, 1962*, 9.

217 "Hey, Barry! Barry!!!!": George Sullivan interview.

218 "Listen, we should all be so lucky to play . . .": Tom Heinsohn interview.

218 "Who needs LSD?": *Boston Globe* (April 29, 1966).

218 "My wife," he said, "and Russell's laugh": Rogin, *Sports Illustrated* (November 18, 1963): 77.

218 "Red, I can't coach this team . . .": Tom Heinsohn interview.

218 "I have fought a problem the only way I know how . . .": Russell, as told to McSweeny, *Go Up for Glory*, 167.

219 "There should, one would think, be one team . . .": *New York Post* (January 22, 1964).

219 "You owe the public the same thing it owes you . . .": Edward Linn, "I Owe the Public Nothing," *Saturday Evening Post* (January 18, 1964): 61.

219 "It's like the story of the old man . . .": Ibid., 62.

219 "an articulate grown man who happens . . .": *New York Post* (January 29, 1964).

220 "charged Boston with de facto segregation": David J. Garrow, *Bearing the Cross: Martin Luther King, Jr., and the Southern Christian Leadership Conference* (New York: William Morrow & Company, 1986), 377.

220 replaced by terms such as "racial agitators," "un-American": *Boston Globe* (April 16, 1965).

220 A Brandeis professor compared Hicks to Adolf Hitler: Ibid.

220 "No [NBA] owner was going to have on his team . . .": Oscar Robertson, *The Big O: My Life, My Times, My Game* (Emmaus, PA: Rodale, 2003), 147.

220 a black minister had leaped onto the stage: *Boston Herald* (June 23, 1966).

221 "Since you're committed, go and do it . . .": *Boston Globe* (June 23, 1966).

221 "There's a fire here in Roxbury . . .": Ibid.

221 "Boston is the most prejudiced city . . .": George Sullivan interview.

222 "I can't find it . . .": Ibid.

223 "In all the slow processes of history . . .": *Los Angeles Times* (January 17, 1965).

223 "Russ, how many parts do you think . . .": Auerbach with Fitzgerald, *On & Off the Court*, 233.

223 "the greatest generation the world has ever known . . .": *Boston Globe* (May 17, 1969).

223 "I want you to be a pallbearer at Jackie's funeral . . .": Russell interview with Branch, May 13, 2013, transcript p. 53.

223 "You were Jackie's favorite athlete": Ibid.

224 He held an informal ceremony before a game: *Boston Herald, Boston Globe* (March 12, 1972).

224 "a very traumatic experience": *Boston Herald* (June 6, 1973).

224 "Hey, I had that scoop years ago!": George Sullivan interview.

224 "I felt they had a code of conduct . . .": *Boston Globe* (June 6, 1973).

224 "I tried to do things to change it . . .": *Boston Globe* (November 15, 1973).

224 "He was the most surly, selfish, boorish . . .": *Boston Herald* (June 7, 1973).

224 "[Russell] built a cover of aloofness and called it 'dignity'": *Boston Globe* (June 7, 1973).

225 "just wishes the whole matter would go away": *Boston Globe* (May 4, 1975).

225 "Excuse me, sir, but did something . . .": *Boston Herald* (October 23, 1984).

226 "A black bigot is still a bigot . . .": *Boston Herald* (August 9, 1979).

226 thieves wrote racist graffiti ("NIGGA") on the walls: *New York Times* (June 14, 1987).

226 Two whites pinned back Landsmark's arms: *Boston Herald, Boston Globe* (April 6, 1976).

226 The white hooligans broke Landsmark's nose: Ibid.

226 "The chickens have come home to roost . . .": *Boston Globe* (April 7, 1976).

227 "a graveyard where black players went to die": West and Coleman, *West by West,* 134.

227 "flea market of racism": Russell and Branch, *Second Wind,* 207.

227 "If Paul Revere were riding today . . .": Ibid., 208.

227 "Cousy was captain of the 1957 team . . .": Russell as told to McSweeny, *Go Up for Glory,* 122.

228 I have always believed . . . that there are limitations: Russell and Branch, *Second Wind,* 159.

CHAPTER 24

231 "They are all Republicans . . .": Henry (Hank) Lusardi interview.

231 "If somebody said it's raining out . . .": Tony Stevens interview.

232 "We don't do that!": Jim Nelson interview. Nelson played for Cousy at Boston College.

232 his intensity off the charts: Steve Adelman interview. Adelman played for Cousy at Boston College.

232 *Life* identified a friend of Cousy's, Andrew Pradella: Sandy Smith, "The Mob, Part 2," *Life* (September 8, 1967): 92.

233 "I don't see why I should stop seeing my friends . . .": Ibid.

233 "Dragging Cousy into this was cruel . . .": *Boston Globe* (September 12, 1967).

233 "For those of us who've known him . . .": *Boston Globe* (September 8, 1967).

233 "Cousy, by his own choice, has not fulfilled . . .": *Boston Globe* (September 9, 1967).

234 "This was a golf course started by old Yankees . . .": Henry (Hank) Lusardi interview.

234 "Bob would bring blacks to Worcester Country . . .": Tony Stevens interview.

234 Cousy cosponsored the club's first African-American: Milan Brown interview.

CHAPTER 25

237 There came no congratulatory telephone calls, no well-wishers: Bill McSweeny interview.

237 McSweeny was struck by the loneliness of it: Ibid.

238 like Vince Lombardi in the NFL, he missed the pro game: *Boston Herald, Boston Globe* (May 9–10, 1969).

238 "walked onto the court in such an arrogant way . . .": Adam J. Criblez, *Tall Tales and Short Shorts: Dr. J, Pistol Pete, and the Birth of the Modern NBA* (Lanham, MD: Rowman & Littlefield Publishers, 2017), 9.

238 "One month into the season, Bob Cousy . . .": Robertson, *The Big O,* 227.

239 sensed that Cousy became frustrated because: Tom Callahan interview.

239 The Big O tired of hearing Cousy call everyone *Babe*: Robertson, *The Big O,* 226.

239 *"If he would just touch me . . .":* Tom Callahan interview.

239 "As a man with deep liberal convictions . . .": Bob Cousy, "Black Is Beautiful," *Cord SportsFacts Pro Basketball Guide 1970,* 17.

240 "Negroes stand as equal to white men . . .": Ibid., 20.

240 "he's calling for *me*": Marie Cousy interview.

240 "Boy . . . if I had known you was colored . . .": *Chicago Tribune* (March 1, 2009).

240 "Why is Norm's car in our driveway?": Marie Cousy interview.

241 "I'd be proud to have you as a son-in-law": *Chicago Tribune* (March 1, 2009).

241 "Thank you very much, have a good year": *Telegram & Gazette* (October 10, 2008).

241 She recognized it because she was wearing a similar: Randy Auerbach interview.

242 *I know who you are*: Ibid.

242 They talked about their fathers, and their medallions: Marie Cousy and Randy Auerbach interviews.

243 "Probably the best fighter I ever had": Red Auerbach interview, 2002.

243 "Well, she's OK, but she'll need a nose job": *Boston Herald* (January 3, 1985).

243 a doting grandfather known to her as *Goomp*: Julie Auerbach Flieger interview.

243 regular gin rummy game at Woodmont Country Club: John Feinstein and Red Auerbach, *Let Me Tell You a Story: A Lifetime in the Game* (New York: Little, Brown and Company, 2004), 9.

244 "I'd go to Washington to see my dad . . .": Randy Auerbach interview.

244 Auerbach brought home live lobsters from Boston: Julie Auerbach Flieger interview.

244 "Dad, you don't need *ten pounds* of steak!": Nancy Collins interview.

244 "Tip this guy a T-shirt": Randy Auerbach interview.

245 "Well, the corned beef is kind of fatty": Ibid.

245 "This is my wedding . . .": Julie Auerbach Flieger interview.

245 "It wasn't an act . . .": Nancy Collins interview.

246 "They practically had to drag him off": Ibid.

246 Nancy phoned only two to personally break the news: Nancy Collins interview.

CHAPTER 26

248 "It was a very deep collection in terms of content . . .": Dan Imler interview.

248 "Bob Cousy, Picked this off table Sunday . . .": SportsCards Plus catalogue, Telephone/Internet Auction, Collections of Bob Cousy, Honus Wagner, Tony Lazzeri, November 20, 2003: 24.

248 Cousy's memorabilia raised more than $450,000: The sale prices of items from the Cousy auction were detailed on the Professional Sports Authenticators (PSA) website, December 3, 2003: https://www.psacard .com/articles/articleview/4018/estate-fresh-items-from-cousy-lazzeri-wagner-soar-sportscards-pluss-record-setting-november-auction.

249 Ramsey never recovered the same Oval Office photo: Frank Ramsey interview.

249 "At our age, that puts you on notice": Tony Stevens interview.

249 "Ask your friends if you do . . .": Ticia Cousy interview.

250 "Clyde, if anybody is looking at you strange . . .": Clyde Phillips interview.

250 "This is my son": Ibid.

251 He created a home atmosphere that played into Missie's denial: Worcester *Telegram & Gazette* (September 29, 2013). Dianne Williamson wrote a poignant column about Cousy's relationship with Missie during her years with dementia.

252 Missie, with panic in her eyes, didn't know who: Bruce Brand interview.

252 "I tried to change the subject": Diane Heinsohn interview.

253 "We saw a very tender side of Dad . . .": Marie Cousy interview.

253 "I'm growing in my old age . . .": *Telegram & Gazette* (September 7, 2012).

254 She updated other wives from the Celtics dynasty: Marie Cousy interview.

254 So were John and Beth Havlicek, Tom and Diane Heinsohn: Marie A. (Missie) Cousy funeral Mass guest book, September 24, 2013, Bob Cousy personal papers.

254 Clyde Phillips drove twenty-two hours from Florida: Clyde Phillips interview.

254 "I think everyone knew that I was . . .": Ticia Cousy interview.

CHAPTER 27

256 "I guess I was gritty": Richie Guerin interview.

257 His Knicks teammate Donnie Butcher: Pomerantz, *WILT, 1962*, 104.

257 Guerin played golf with the Yankees' Whitey Ford: Richie Guerin interview.

257 *Cousy never saw the day he had moves like Pete*: *New York Times* (October 11, 1970).

257 "an American phenomenon, a stepchild of the human imagination": Curry Kirkpatrick, "No One Can Cap the Pistol: Twilight for Pete Maravich, Hoops' Most Talented Loser," *Sports Illustrated* (December 4, 1978): 96.

257 "He was an entertainer . . .": Richie Guerin interview.

259 created an unforgettable, feel-good scene: Marie Cousy interview.

260 "People can wax poetic about those years . . .": Tom (Satch) Sanders interview.

261 "The same team, over and over?": West and Coleman, *West by West*, 84.

261 "I dislike the color green": Ibid., 114.

261 "You are one of those people . . .": John Havlicek interview.

262 "A few of us got together for the Havlicek Stole . . .": Tom (Satch) Sanders interview.

262 "They talk about the Spurs . . .": Tom Heinsohn interview.

263 "I think the Celtics were *light-years* . . .": Steve Kerr interview.

263 "I think he'd be great": Ibid.

264 "why he's known as the flashiest basketball player . . .": "Collier's Color Camera: Flashy Bob Cousy," *Collier's* (January 10, 1953): 62–63.

264 Wind pantomimed Cousy's passing style: Bill Scheft interview.

264 vodka splashed the face of his young nephew: Ibid.

264 "The vet-lan tulned to the lookie . . .": Ibid.

264 "the commanding figure: a bravura individual star . . .": Wind, *New Yorker* (March 23, 1963): 148–49.

264 "You may be looking up in Rome . . .": https://www.youtube.com/watch?v= m0uhJfZdQjc.

265 "Cousy had no muscle on his body . . .": Brian Hanlon interview.

266 "was like my Valium": Bob Cohen interview.

266 "Hey, how many did Havlicek get last night?": Brian Wallace interview.

266 Dillon died from a coronary attack in 1997: Brian Dillon interview.

267 His funeral drew a sizable crowd in Southie: Raymond Flynn, Brian Dillon, and Brian Wallace interviews.

267 "Because people liked them . . .": Raymond Flynn interview.

268 he wants the Cousy photograph on display: Ibid.

269 "that little jitterbug move Cousy used to do . . .": Rollie Massimino interview.

269 Supreme Court justice was known to friends by his hero's: *Baltimore Sun* (July 3, 1991).

269 "a very clever passer, a leader . . .": Tara VanDerveer interview.

269 "growing up, the girls used to swoon . . .": Maura Healey interview.

270 "one of the most influential guards ever": CBS Sports website, February 17, 2017; https://www.cbssports.com/nba/news/cbs-sports-50–greatest-nba -players-of-all-time-where-do-lebron-curry-rank.

270 "Let me improvise": Bob Cousy letter to the author, May 3, 2017.

271 "In making a case for '*Moi*'": Ibid.

CHAPTER 28

274 "Both have pride; both love to win . . .": *Boston Record American* (February 16, 1965).

274 "Winning helps. It's the glue . . .": Tom (Satch) Sanders interview.

275 "No, I'd like to be your friend . . .": Frank Deford, "The Ring Leader," *Sports Illustrated* (May 10, 1999): 90.

275 "I'd rather be in jail in Sacramento . . .": "People Are Talking About . . . ," *Jet* (December 21, 1987): 64.

275 "Russell Redux is, in essence, a product relaunch . . .": *New York Times* (June 16, 2000).

276 "a forgiveness episode": Dolph Schayes interview.

276 Russell landed a $400,000 deal: *New York Times* (June 16, 2000).

276 He was seen in a new context: David C. Ogden and Joel Nathan Rosen, eds., *Reconstructing Fame: Sport, Race, and Evolving Reputations* (Jackson:

University Press of Mississippi, 2008), 87–101. In this book of essays, Murry Nelson, professor emeritus of education and American studies at Penn State University, writes compellingly of how the public assessment of Russell has shifted over time in "Bill Russell: From Revulsion to Resurrection."

277 "Bob Cousy's last team": Deford, *Sports Illustrated* (May 10, 1999): 98.

277 "We could've done more to ease his pain . . .": ESPN *SportsCentury* documentary on Bill Russell, July 2, 2001; https://www.youtube.com/watch?v=8lob_Tvg7LY.

277 He broke down weeping, his hands covering his face: Ibid.

280 Russell sat with other honorees, including former president: *Washington Post*, and ESPN.com (February 15, 2011).

280 "I'm very proud of you as my son . . .": Russell interview with Branch, May 13, 2013, transcript p. 41.

280 "He marched with King; he stood by Ali": The White House, Office of the Press Secretary, Remarks by the President Honoring the Recipients of the 2010 Medal of Freedom (February 15, 2011), https://obamawhitehouse.archives.gov/the-press-office/2011/02/15/remarks-president-honoring-recipients-2010-medal-freedom.

280 "From when people are breaking into your home . . .": Randy Auerbach interview.

280 "To us, who have lived with him . . .": Tom (Satch) Sanders interview.

281 "Was he the greatest human being?": Tom Heinsohn interview.

281 Behind the scenes, a movement had taken flight: P. Kevin Condron interview.

CHAPTER 29

283 they talked basketball and politics: Maura Healey interview.

283 "I've never smoked a cigar in my life . . .": Brad Stevens interview.

283 "know how many banners are on the wall . . .": Ibid.

284 "'walk the walk' as well as fight the 'good fight'": Bob Cousy letter to Bryan Stevenson, founder of the Equal Justice Initiative, March 16, 2016, West Palm Beach, FL, Bryan Stevenson personal correspondence.

284 "I'm hoping that this 'conversation' the country is having . . .": Ibid.

285 "Even if it wasn't Bob Cousy I would've still remembered . . .": Bryan Stevenson interview.

285 "Go back to Roxbury, nigger . . .": Ibid.

285 "My big critique of the American psyche . . .": Ibid.

CHAPTER 30

288 There is nothing uniquely evil in these destroyers: Ta-Nehisi Coates, *Between the World and Me* (New York: Spiegel & Grau, 2015), 10.

290 "[Cousy] could've bragged on him . . .": Gene Conley interview.

290 "Whatever Cousy said would've gone": Tom Heinsohn interview.

290 "Cousy would just be seen as a nice man . . .": Tom (Satch) Sanders interview.

290 "Of course it would have made a difference . . .": Mel King interview.

290 "I couldn't say that Cousy could have done . . .": Raymond Flynn interview.

292 "It's almost scary to meet him": Steve Kerr interview.

293 Barksdale, who once played a full quarter: Pluto, *Tall Tales*, 76.

293 "a gentleman from the word go . . .": Sportscaster Roy Firestone on ESPN's *SportsLook*, in a tribute to Don Barksdale upon his death on March 8, 1993, aired portions of an earlier interview he had conducted with Barksdale; https://www.youtube.com/watch?v=NkehQ7sk8Ls.

293 Cousy presented their father at his posthumous induction: Derek Barksdale interview.

294 "The baseball hero must always act . . .": Gay Talese, "The Silent Season of a Hero," *Esquire* (July 1966): 114.

295 "Cousy probably saw more than some . . .": Harry Edwards interview.

296 "On Thanksgiving, I make it a habit . . .": Frank Deford interview.

296 "I couldn't have done anything wrong . . .": Ibid.

296 "Old age is factored into this as well . . .": Ibid.

CHAPTER 31

297 initially left him with facial drooping: *In re the Matter of: William F. Russell, a Vulnerable Adult (Person to be Protected), Jeannine Fiorito, Respondent (Person to be Restrained). King County (Washington) Superior Court*, Case No. 15-2-15661-6 SEA, Petition for Vulnerable Adult Order for Protection, June 26, 2015: 3.

297 They stopped by his home, dropped off food: *In the Consolidated Matter of William F. Russell, An Alleged Vulnerable Adult: Jacob Russell and Karen Russell, Petitioners, v Jeannine Fiorito, Respondent; William F. Russell, Petitioner, v Anita Dias, Respondent, King County (Washington) Superior Court*, Case No. 15-2-15661-6 SEA, Report of Guardian Ad Litem, December 4, 2015: 10.

298 She ran a bedbug detection business: Ibid., 5.

298 Russell had been paying some of Fiorito's expenses: Ibid., 7.

298 "shrugging his shoulders and just wanting everyone to stop yelling": Ibid., Report of Guardian Ad Litem pursuant to August 26, 2016 CR2A, filed October 13, 2016: 4.

299 "a good job of providing Mr. Russell's care . . .": Ibid., Report of Guardian Ad Litem, December 4, 2015. Exhibit B: Report of Geriatric Care Manager Lisa Mayfield: 8, 10.

299 "cognitive decline, memory loss, and altered mental status": Ibid., Recommendations of Guardian Ad Litem for Arbitration Hearing on June 2, 2016: 5.

299 "variable memory and cognitive issues": Ibid., 25

299 "Despite sixteen months, multiple court hearings . . .": Ibid., Report of Guardian Ad Litem pursuant to August 26, 2016 CR2A, filed October 13, 2016: 5.

300 "[He] is adamant he wants to be left alone . . .": Ibid., 25.

300 "is generally considered inadvisable and a blurring . . .": Ibid., 26.

300 "commit to providing as calm and positive an atmosphere . . .": Ibid.

CHAPTER 32

303 was known to sneak away from his family's Passover Seder: David Weissman interview.

303 "We love you, Cooz! We love you, Cooz!": Tony Stevens, David Weissman interviews.

PHOTOGRAPHY CREDITS

INDEX

Page numbers in italics refer to illustrations.

INDEX

INDEX

INDEX